Garfield
food for thought

BY JIM DAVIS

Ballantine Books • **New York**

2006 Ballantine Books Trade Paperback Edition

Copyright © 1987, 2006 by PAWS, Inc. All rights reserved.
"GARFIELD" and the GARFIELD characters are registered and unregistered trademarks of PAWS, Inc.

Published in the United States by Ballantine Books, an imprint of The Random House Publishing Group,
a division of Random House, Inc., New York.

BALLANTINE and colophon are registered trademarks of Random House, Inc.

Originally published in slightly different form in the United States by Ballantine Books, an imprint of
The Random House Publishing Group, a division of Random House, Inc., in 1987.

ISBN 0-345-47563-1

Printed in the United States of America

www.ballantinebooks.com

9 8 7 6 5 4 3 2 1

First Colorized Edition

THE ZODIAC ACCORDING TO garfield

AQUARIUS

JANUARY 20 – FEBRUARY 18

THIS ONE IS A REVOLUTIONARY. THE AQUARIAN IS INVENTIVE, ORIGINAL, AND VERY UNCONVENTIONAL. DON'T LET THIS PERSON BORROW MONEY.

PISCES

FEBRUARY 19 – MARCH 20

AN INTROVERT, FULL OF DEEP EMOTIONS, AND SEEMS TO BE VERY INTUITIVE. A FISHY CHARACTER WHO PROBABLY WORKS FOR SCALE.

ARIES

MARCH 21 – APRIL 19

COURAGEOUS, BLUNT, AND DIRECT. THIS PERSON HAS THE COMPASSION OF A ROCK.

TAURUS

APRIL 20 – MAY 20

LIKES LIVING HIGH ON THE HOG. FULL OF BEAUTY, CHARM, AFFECTION... AND A LOT OF BULL.

GEMINI

MAY 21 – JUNE 20

ENTERTAINING, VERSATILE, WITTY, LOGICAL, SPONTANEOUS, AND CHARMING. THE KIND OF PERSON YOU WOULD LOVE... TO HATE.

CANCER

JUNE 21 – JULY 22

A VULNERABLE, DOMESTIC HOMEBODY WITH A GREAT SENSE OF FAMILY. NOT YOUR JET-SET MATERIAL.

LEO

JULY 23 – AUGUST 22

CREATIVE, ENTHUSIASTIC, FULL OF DETERMINATION. ALWAYS THE CENTER OF ATTENTION. A REAL HAM IN A CAT.

VIRGO

AUGUST 23 – SEPTEMBER 22

DISCRIMINATING, FINICKY, VERY METICULOUS AND ANALYTICAL. SIMPLY STATED—A PICKY WORRYWART.

LIBRA

SEPTEMBER 23 – OCTOBER 22

A HAPPY-GO-LUCKY CHARACTER WHO READS ROMANTIC NOVELS AND THINKS THAT LIFE SHOULD BE FAIR. WHAT A FOOL!

SCORPIO

OCTOBER 23 – NOVEMBER 21

A SELF-CENTERED PERSON WITH LOTS OF ENERGY AND PERSONAL MAGNETISM. ONE WHO ATTRACTS A LOT OF FRIENDS AND IRON FILINGS.

SAGITTARIUS

NOVEMBER 22 – DECEMBER 21

VERY EXPRESSIVE, HAS AN OPEN MIND, IS FRIENDLY AND SINCERE, CAN SOMETIMES BE IRRESPONSIBLE AND TACTLESS. OH WELL, NOBODY'S PERFECT.

CAPRICORN

DECEMBER 22 – JANUARY 19

AN AMBITIOUS, PRACTICAL PERSON WHO WILL CLIMB TO GREAT HEIGHTS. IT'S THE CLIMB DOWN THAT'S HARD FOR THIS SIGN.

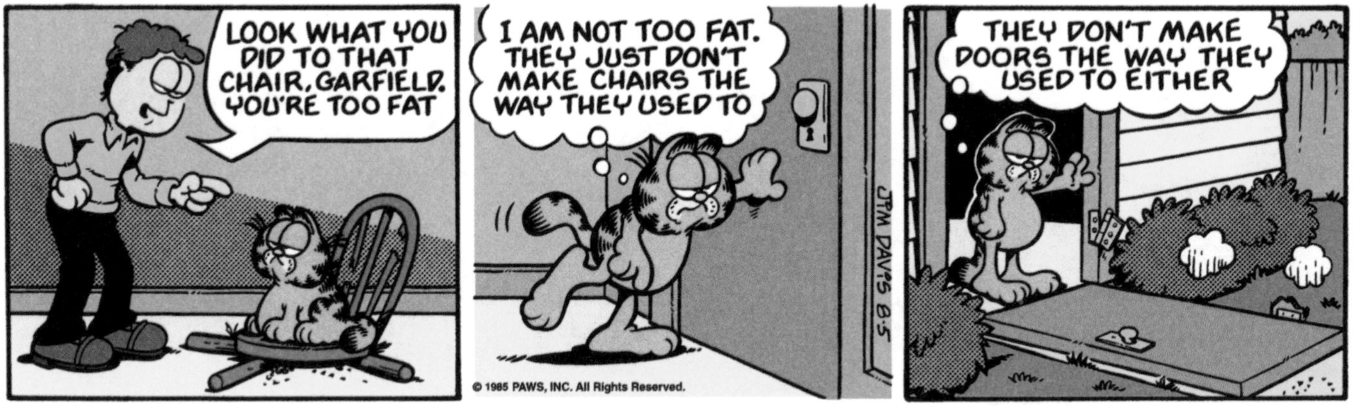
LOOK WHAT YOU DID TO THAT CHAIR, GARFIELD. YOU'RE TOO FAT
I AM NOT TOO FAT. THEY JUST DON'T MAKE CHAIRS THE WAY THEY USED TO
© 1985 PAWS, INC. All Rights Reserved.
JIM DAVIS 8-5
THEY DON'T MAKE DOORS THE WAY THEY USED TO EITHER

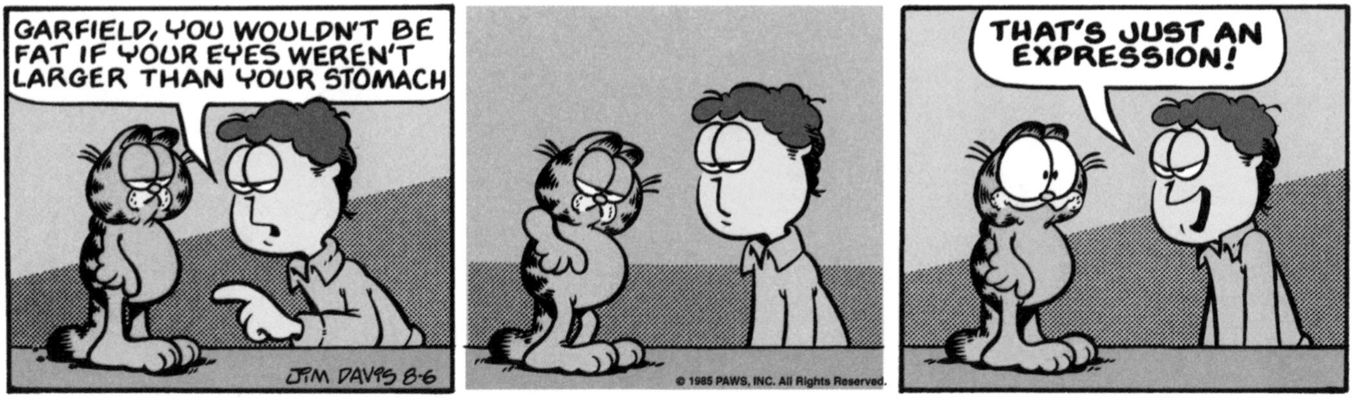
GARFIELD, YOU WOULDN'T BE FAT IF YOUR EYES WEREN'T LARGER THAN YOUR STOMACH
JIM DAVIS 8-6
© 1985 PAWS, INC. All Rights Reserved.
THAT'S JUST AN EXPRESSION!

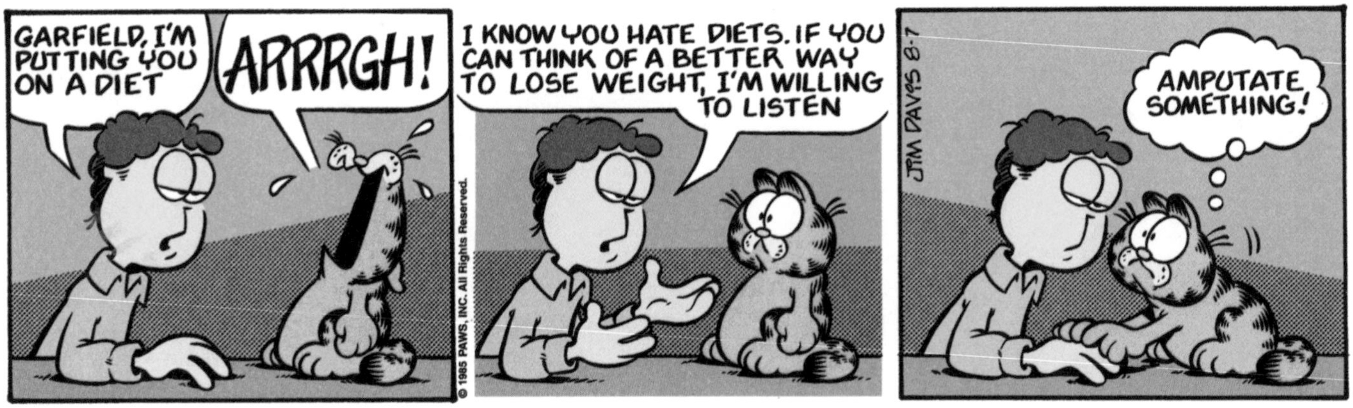
GARFIELD, I'M PUTTING YOU ON A DIET
ARRRGH!
© 1985 PAWS, INC. All Rights Reserved.
I KNOW YOU HATE DIETS. IF YOU CAN THINK OF A BETTER WAY TO LOSE WEIGHT, I'M WILLING TO LISTEN
JIM DAVIS 8-7
AMPUTATE SOMETHING!

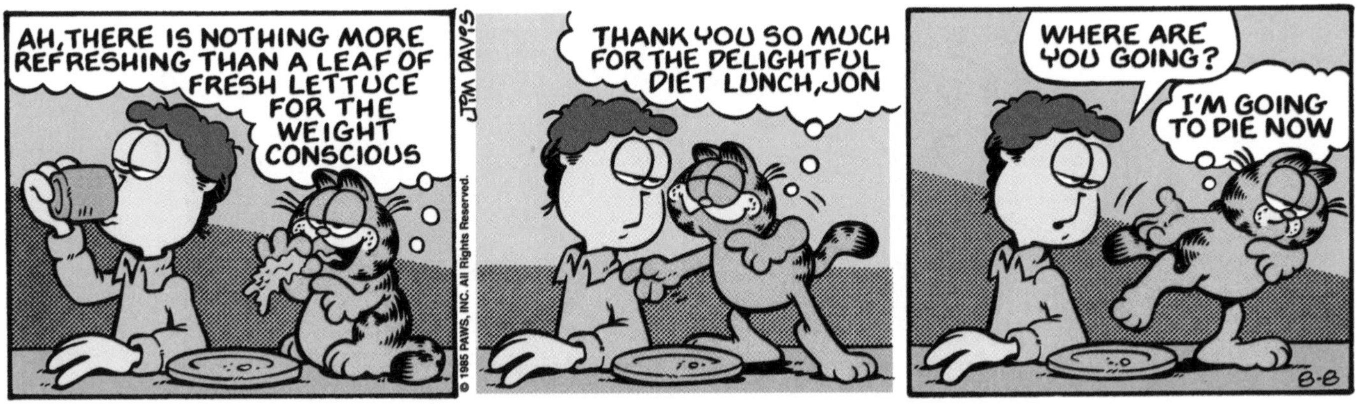
AH, THERE IS NOTHING MORE REFRESHING THAN A LEAF OF FRESH LETTUCE FOR THE WEIGHT CONSCIOUS
JIM DAVIS
© 1985 PAWS, INC. All Rights Reserved.
THANK YOU SO MUCH FOR THE DELIGHTFUL DIET LUNCH, JON
WHERE ARE YOU GOING?
I'M GOING TO DIE NOW
8-8

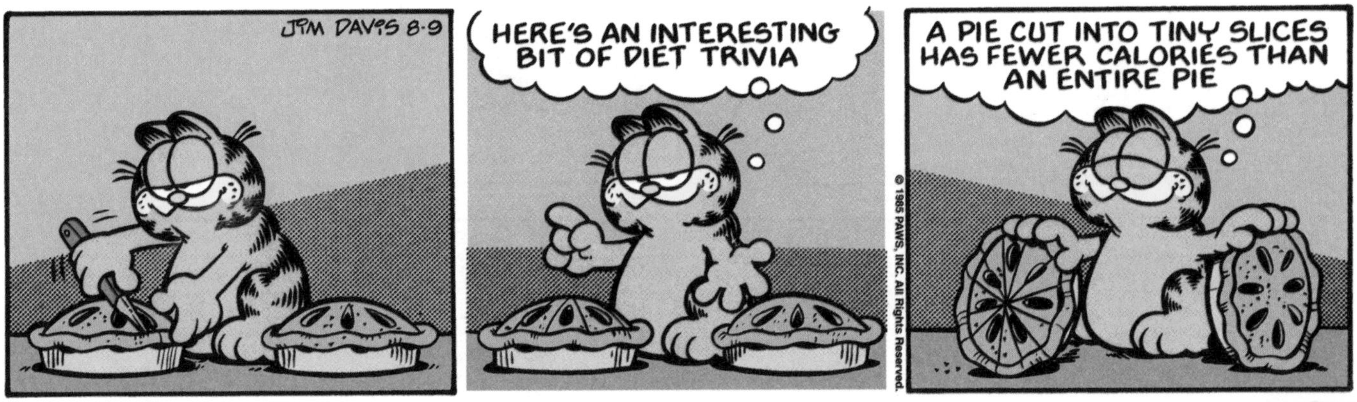
JIM DAVIS 8-9
HERE'S AN INTERESTING BIT OF DIET TRIVIA
© 1985 PAWS, INC. All Rights Reserved.
A PIE CUT INTO TINY SLICES HAS FEWER CALORIES THAN AN ENTIRE PIE

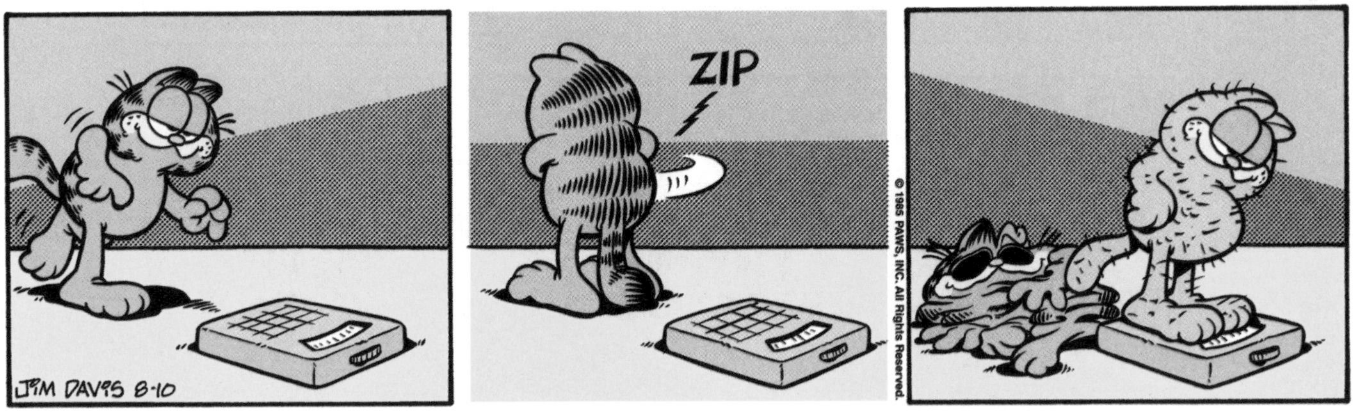
JIM DAVIS 8-10
ZIP
© 1985 PAWS, INC. All Rights Reserved.

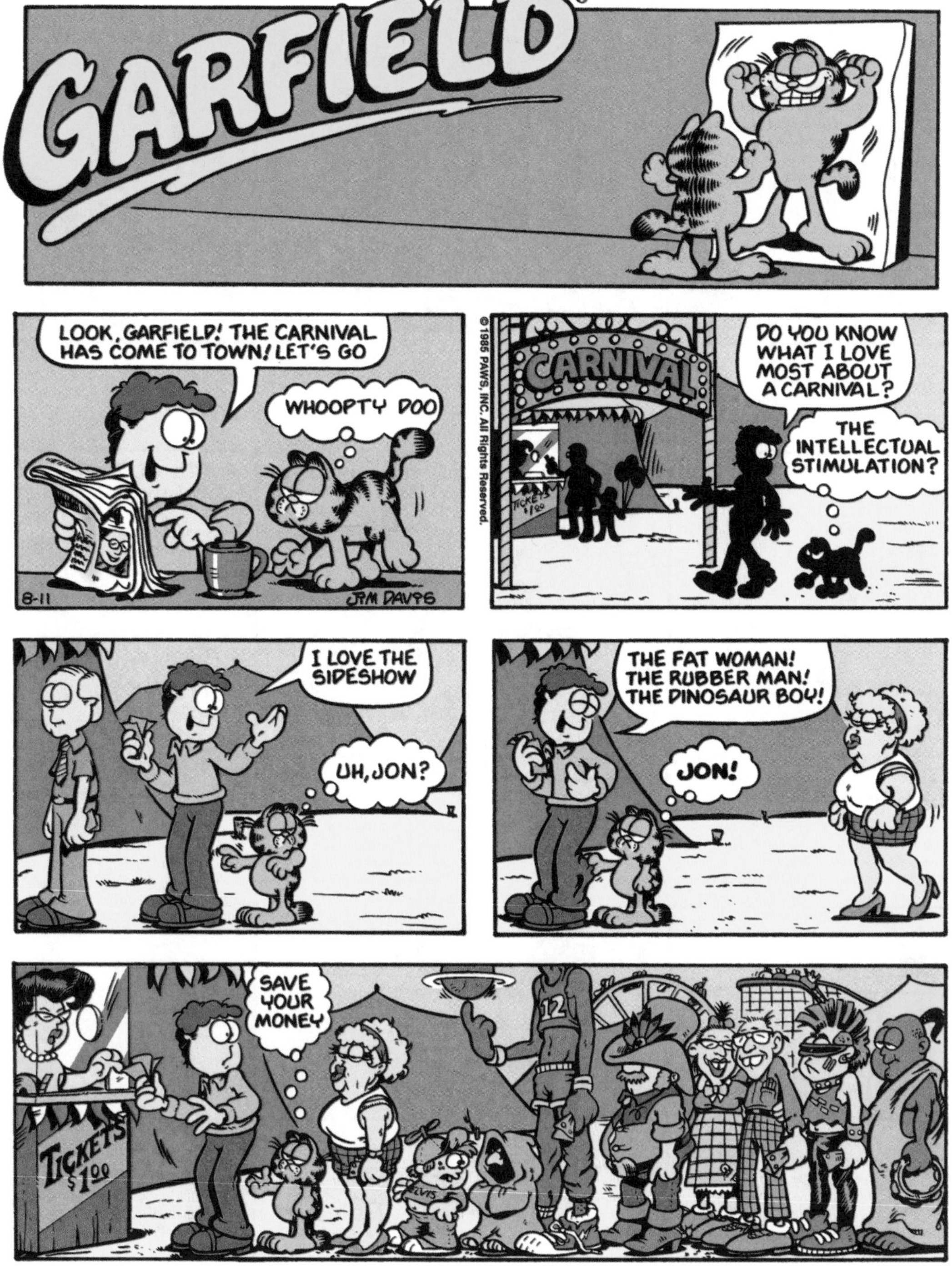
GARFIELD®
LOOK, GARFIELD! THE CARNIVAL HAS COME TO TOWN! LET'S GO
WHOOPTY DOO
8-11
JIM DAVIS
© 1985 PAWS, INC. All Rights Reserved.
CARNIVAL
DO YOU KNOW WHAT I LOVE MOST ABOUT A CARNIVAL?
THE INTELLECTUAL STIMULATION?
I LOVE THE SIDESHOW
UH, JON?
THE FAT WOMAN! THE RUBBER MAN! THE DINOSAUR BOY!
JON!
TICKETS $1.00
SAVE YOUR MONEY
12

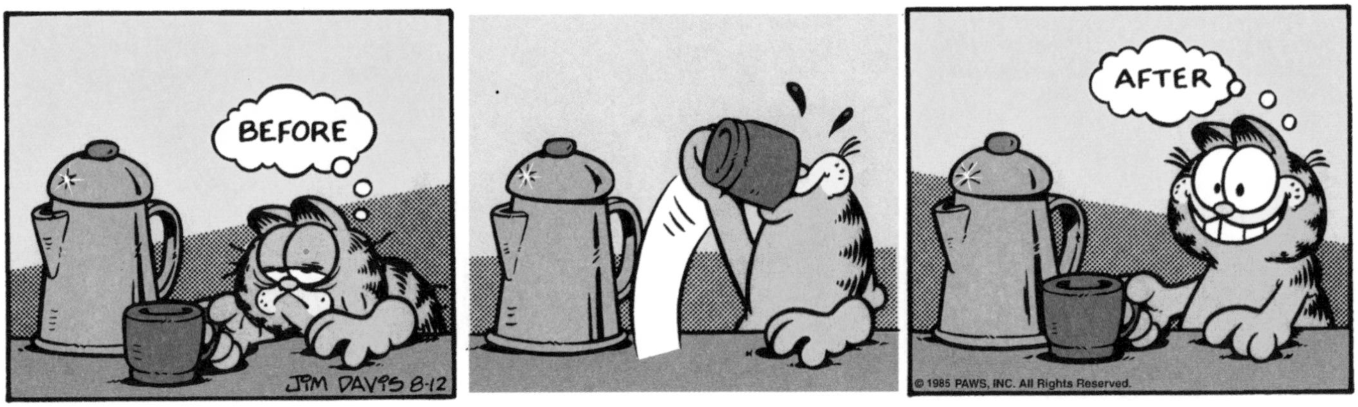
BEFORE
JIM DAVIS 8-12
AFTER
© 1985 PAWS, INC. All Rights Reserved.

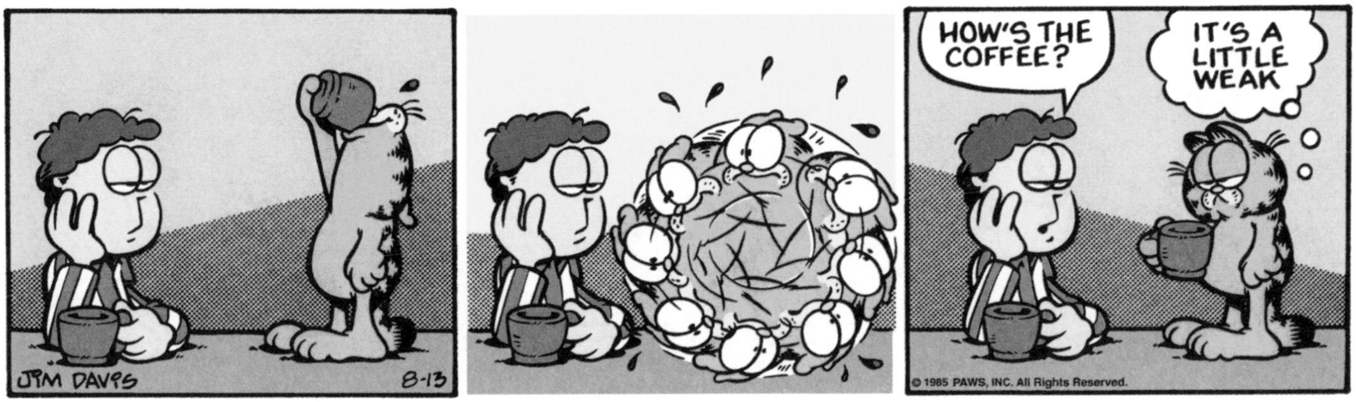
JIM DAVIS
8-13
HOW'S THE COFFEE?
IT'S A LITTLE WEAK
© 1985 PAWS, INC. All Rights Reserved.

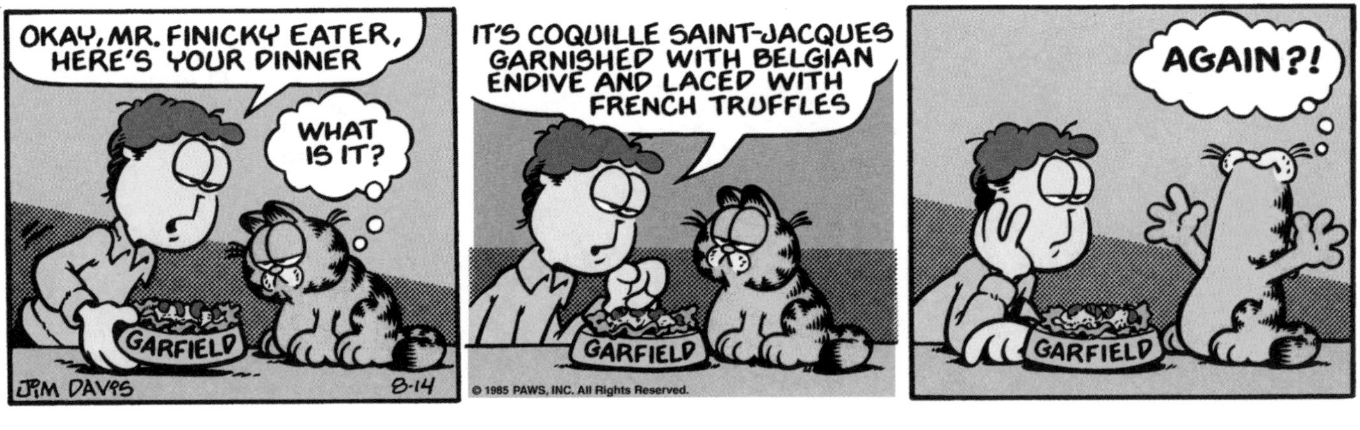
OKAY, MR. FINICKY EATER, HERE'S YOUR DINNER
WHAT IS IT?
GARFIELD
JIM DAVIS
8-14
IT'S COQUILLE SAINT-JACQUES GARNISHED WITH BELGIAN ENDIVE AND LACED WITH FRENCH TRUFFLES
GARFIELD
© 1985 PAWS, INC. All Rights Reserved.
AGAIN?!
GARFIELD

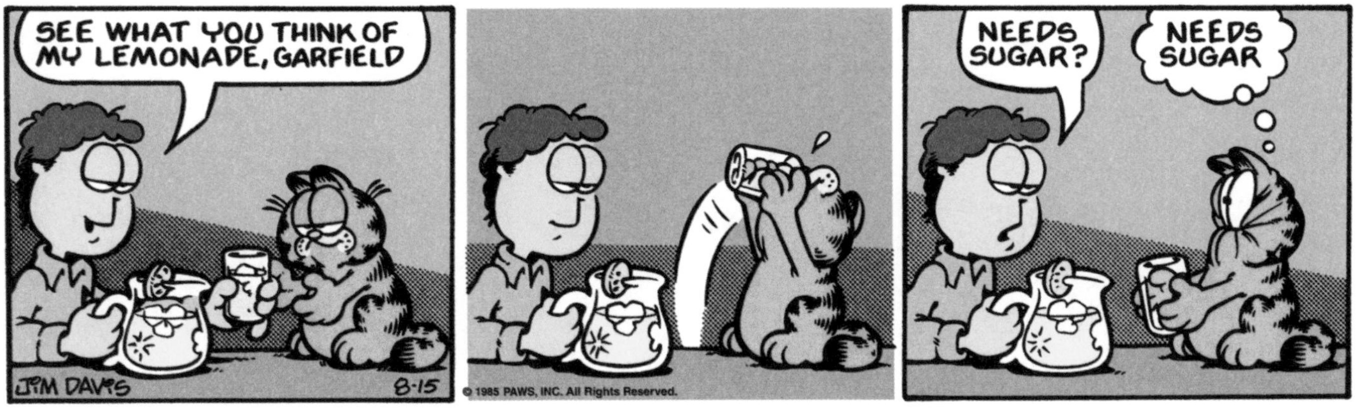
SEE WHAT YOU THINK OF MY LEMONADE, GARFIELD
JIM DAVIS
8-15
© 1985 PAWS, INC. All Rights Reserved.
NEEDS SUGAR?
NEEDS SUGAR

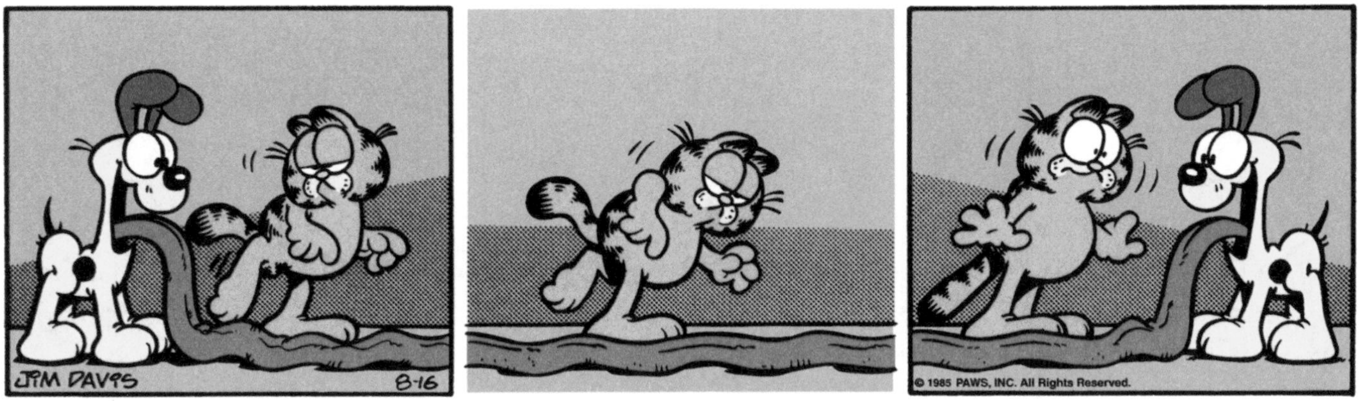
JIM DAVIS
8-16
© 1985 PAWS, INC. All Rights Reserved.

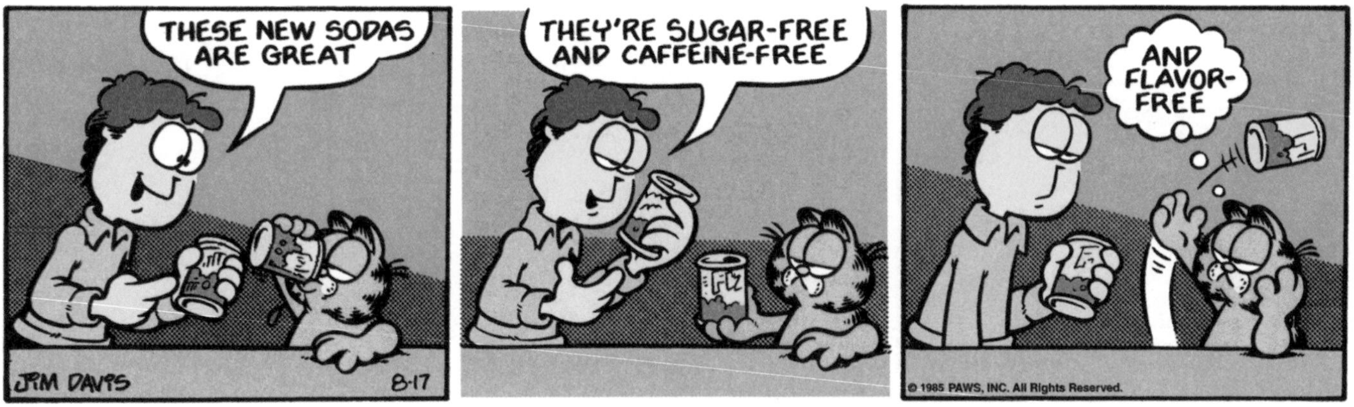
THESE NEW SODAS ARE GREAT
JIM DAVIS
8-17
THEY'RE SUGAR-FREE AND CAFFEINE-FREE
AND FLAVOR-FREE
© 1985 PAWS, INC. All Rights Reserved.

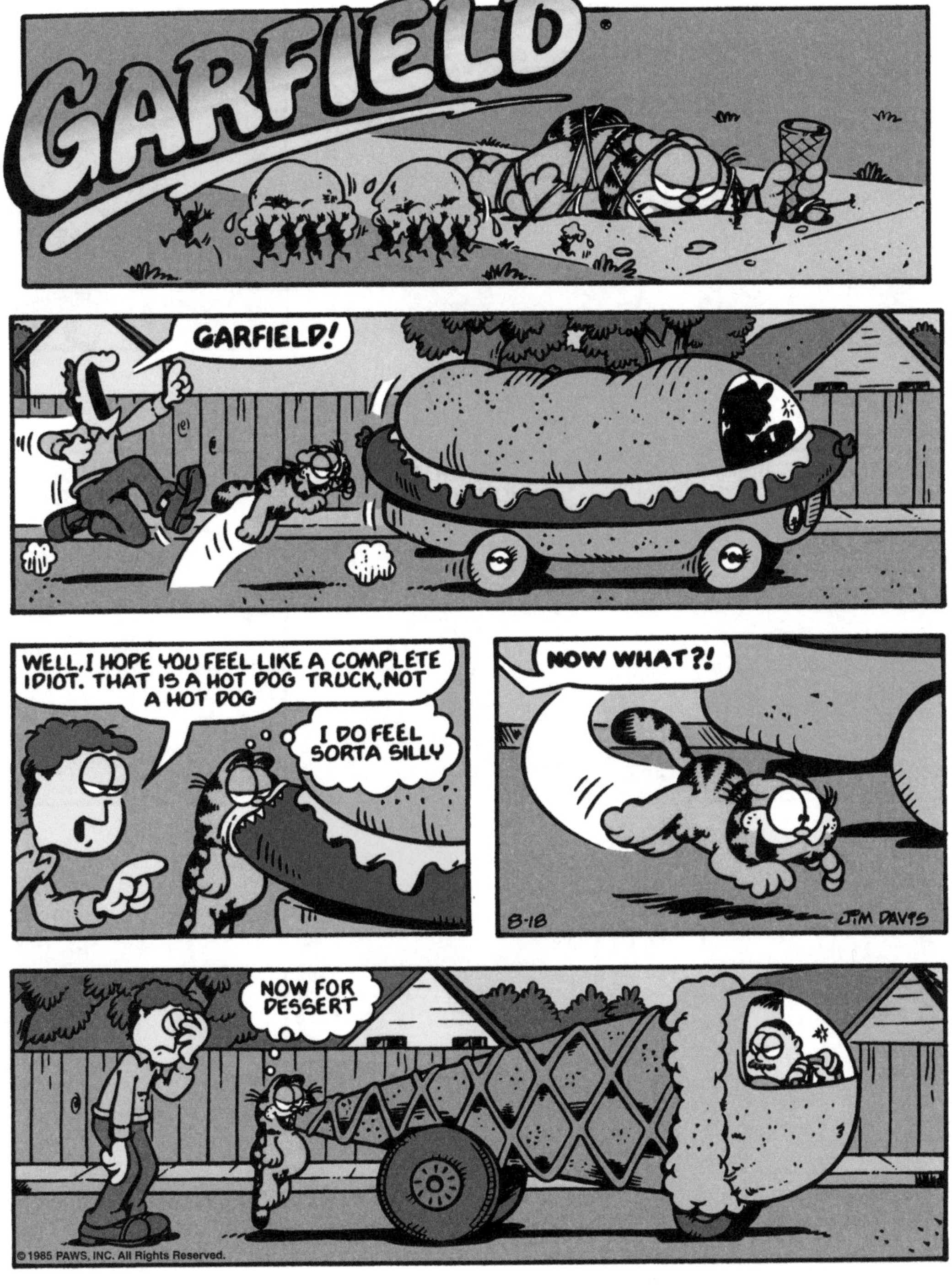
GARFIELD
GARFIELD!
WELL, I HOPE YOU FEEL LIKE A COMPLETE IDIOT. THAT IS A HOT DOG TRUCK, NOT A HOT DOG
I DO FEEL SORTA SILLY
NOW WHAT?!
8-18
JIM DAVIS
NOW FOR DESSERT

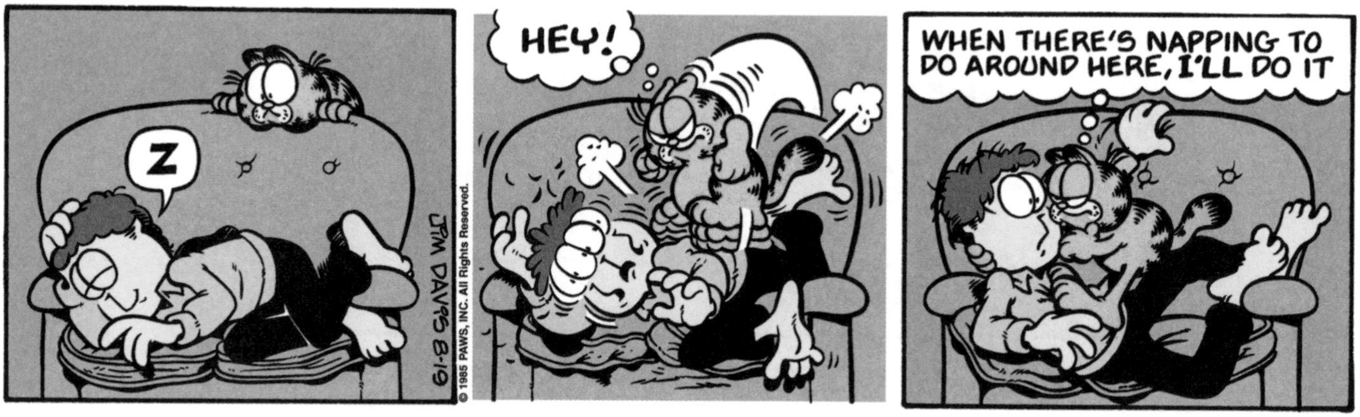
Z
JIM DAVIS 8-19
© 1985 PAWS, INC. All Rights Reserved.
HEY!
WHEN THERE'S NAPPING TO DO AROUND HERE, I'LL DO IT

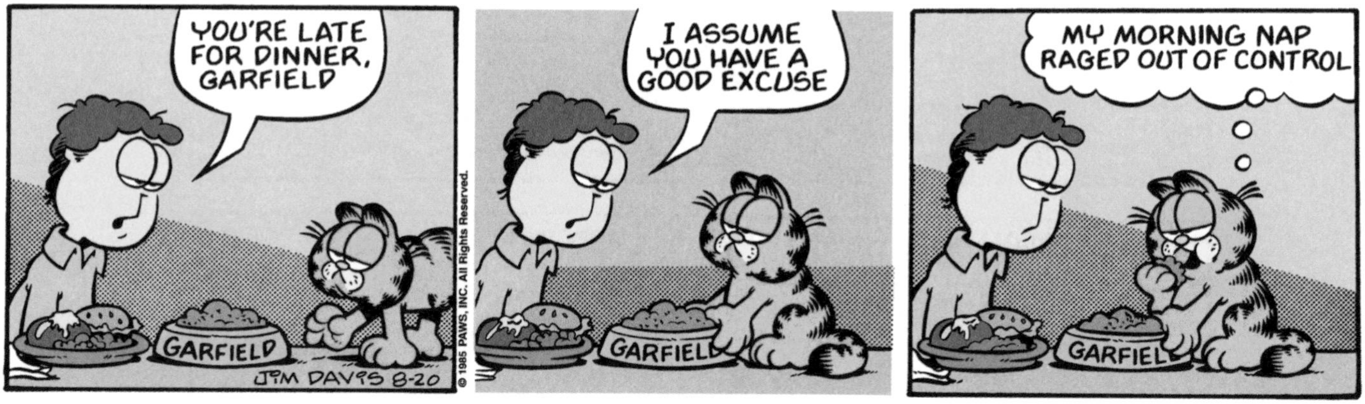
YOU'RE LATE FOR DINNER, GARFIELD
GARFIELD
JIM DAVIS 8-20
© 1985 PAWS, INC. All Rights Reserved.
I ASSUME YOU HAVE A GOOD EXCUSE
MY MORNING NAP RAGED OUT OF CONTROL

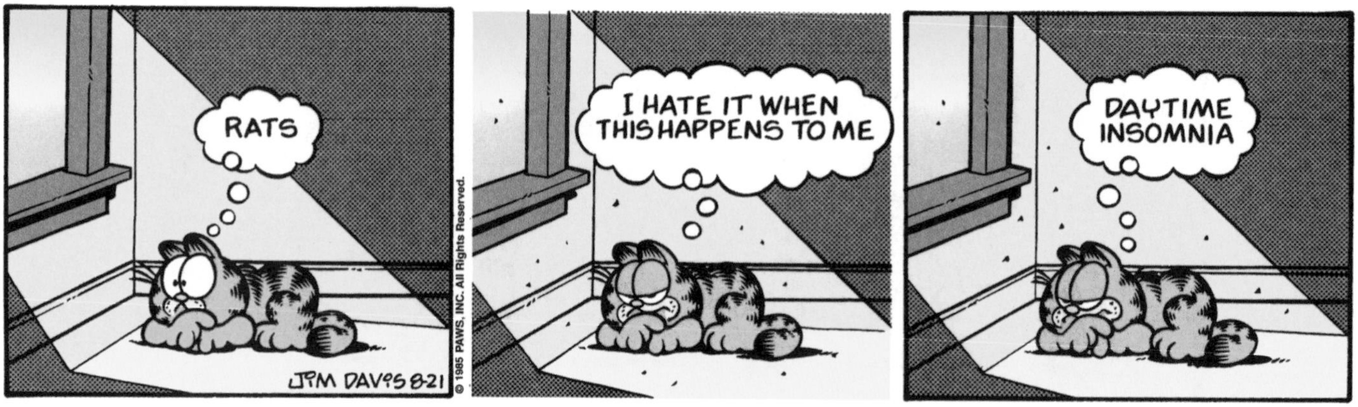
RATS
JIM DAVIS 8-21
© 1985 PAWS, INC. All Rights Reserved.
I HATE IT WHEN THIS HAPPENS TO ME
DAYTIME INSOMNIA

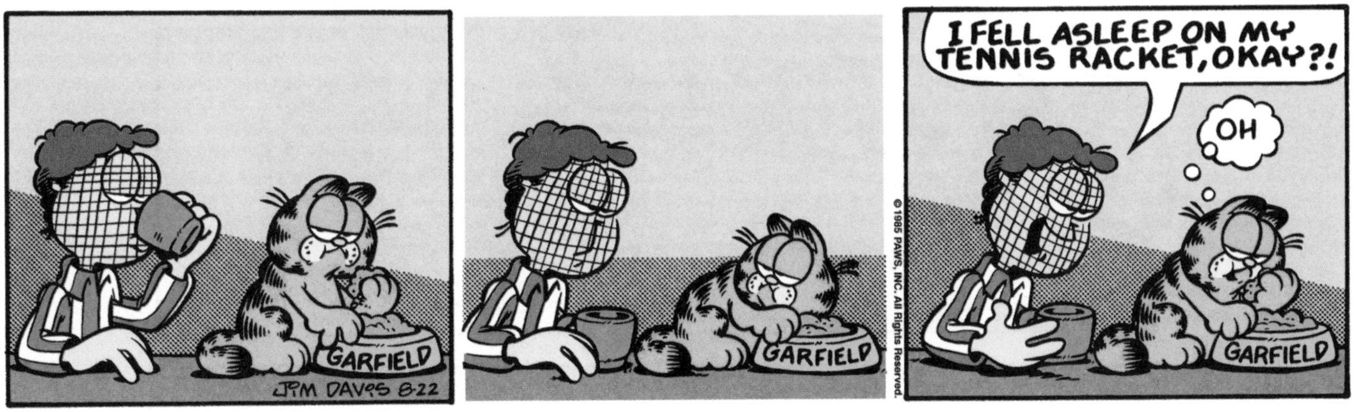
GARFIELD
JIM DAVIS 8-22
GARFIELD
© 1985 PAWS, INC. All Rights Reserved.
I FELL ASLEEP ON MY TENNIS RACKET, OKAY?!
OH
GARFIELD

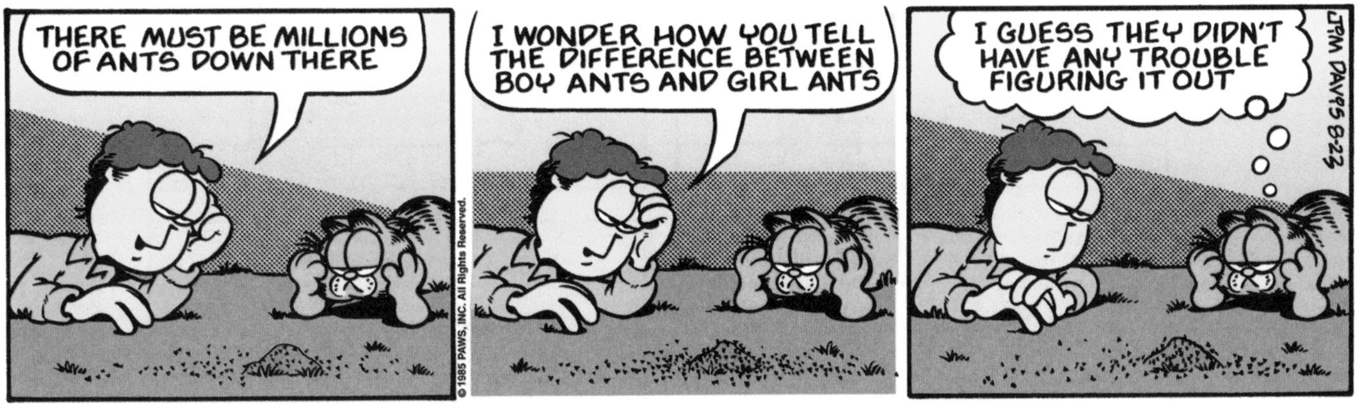
THERE MUST BE MILLIONS OF ANTS DOWN THERE
© 1985 PAWS, INC. All Rights Reserved.
I WONDER HOW YOU TELL THE DIFFERENCE BETWEEN BOY ANTS AND GIRL ANTS
I GUESS THEY DIDN'T HAVE ANY TROUBLE FIGURING IT OUT
JIM DAVIS 8-23

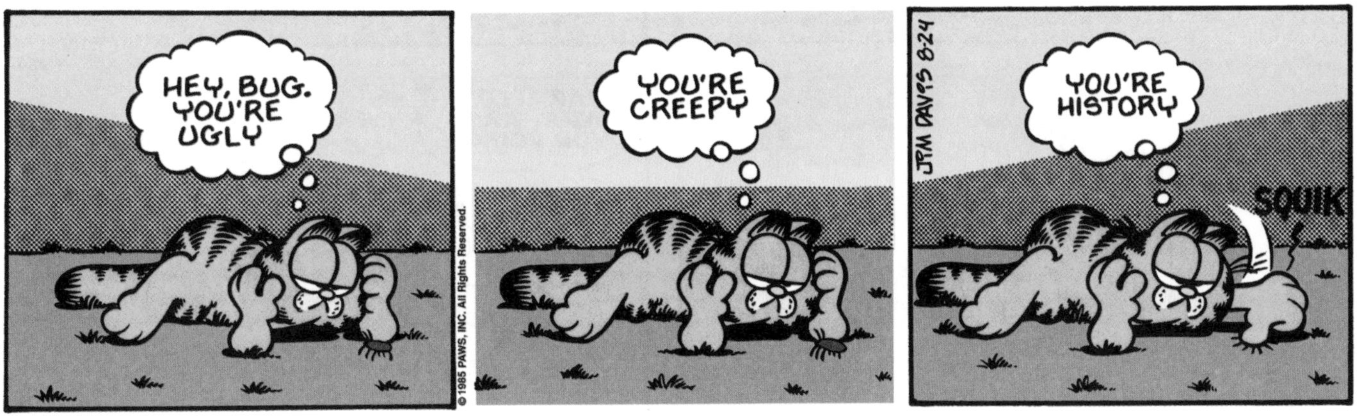
HEY, BUG. YOU'RE UGLY
© 1985 PAWS, INC. All Rights Reserved.
YOU'RE CREEPY
JIM DAVIS 8-24
YOU'RE HISTORY
SQUIK

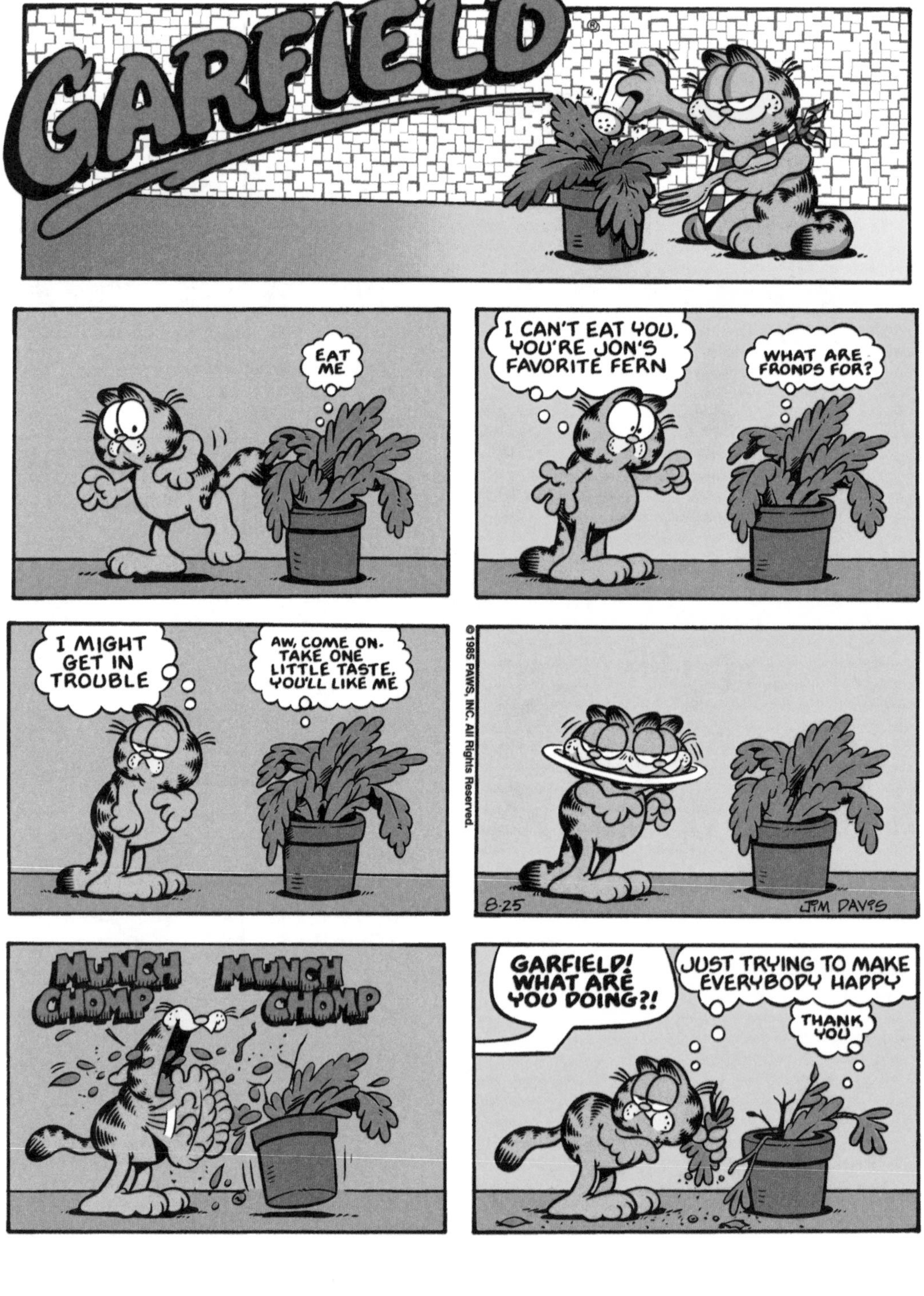
GARFIELD®
EAT ME
I CAN'T EAT YOU. YOU'RE JON'S FAVORITE FERN
WHAT ARE FRONDS FOR?
I MIGHT GET IN TROUBLE
AW, COME ON. TAKE ONE LITTLE TASTE. YOU'LL LIKE ME
© 1985 PAWS, INC. All Rights Reserved.
8-25
JIM DAVIS
MUNCH CHOMP
MUNCH CHOMP
GARFIELD! WHAT ARE YOU DOING?!
JUST TRYING TO MAKE EVERYBODY HAPPY
THANK YOU

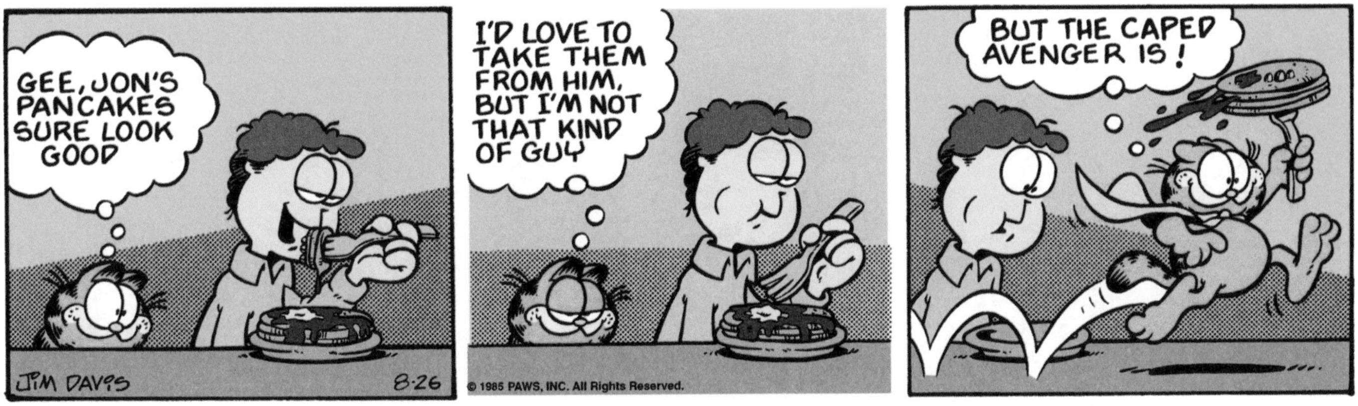
GEE, JON'S PANCAKES SURE LOOK GOOD
JIM DAVIS
8-26
I'D LOVE TO TAKE THEM FROM HIM, BUT I'M NOT THAT KIND OF GUY
© 1985 PAWS, INC. All Rights Reserved.
BUT THE CAPED AVENGER IS!

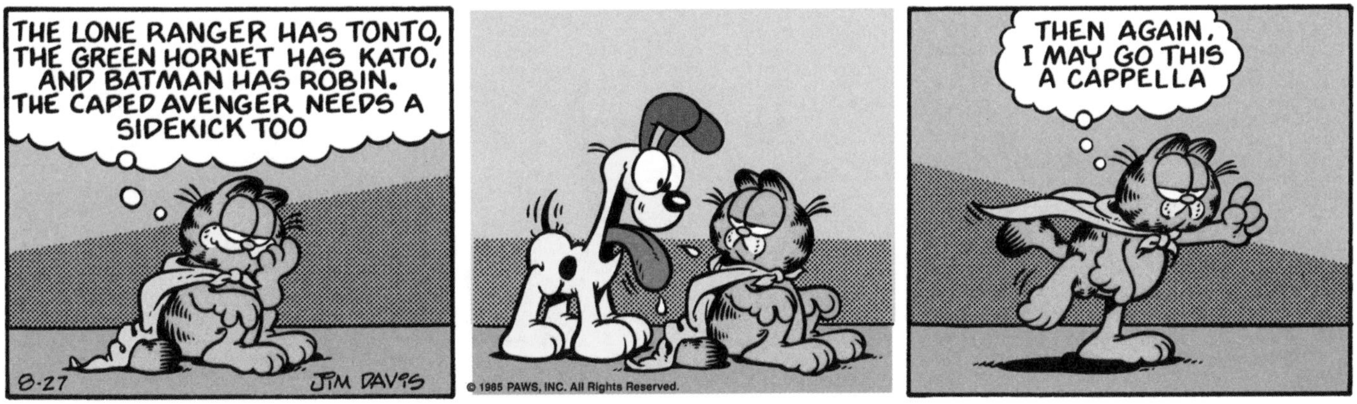
THE LONE RANGER HAS TONTO, THE GREEN HORNET HAS KATO, AND BATMAN HAS ROBIN. THE CAPED AVENGER NEEDS A SIDEKICK TOO
8-27
JIM DAVIS
© 1985 PAWS, INC. All Rights Reserved.
THEN AGAIN, I MAY GO THIS A CAPPELLA

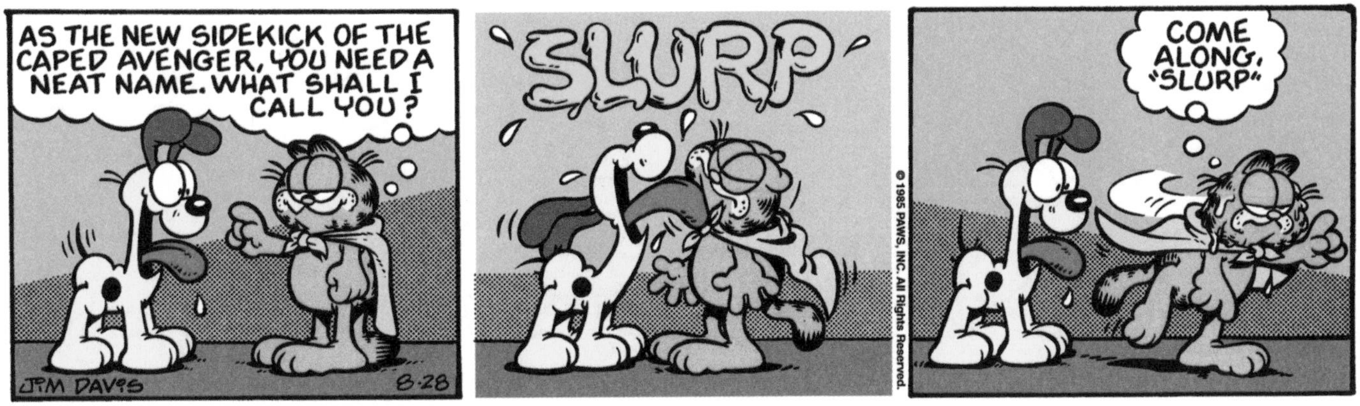
AS THE NEW SIDEKICK OF THE CAPED AVENGER, YOU NEED A NEAT NAME. WHAT SHALL I CALL YOU?
JIM DAVIS
8-28
SLURP
© 1985 PAWS, INC. All Rights Reserved.
COME ALONG, "SLURP"

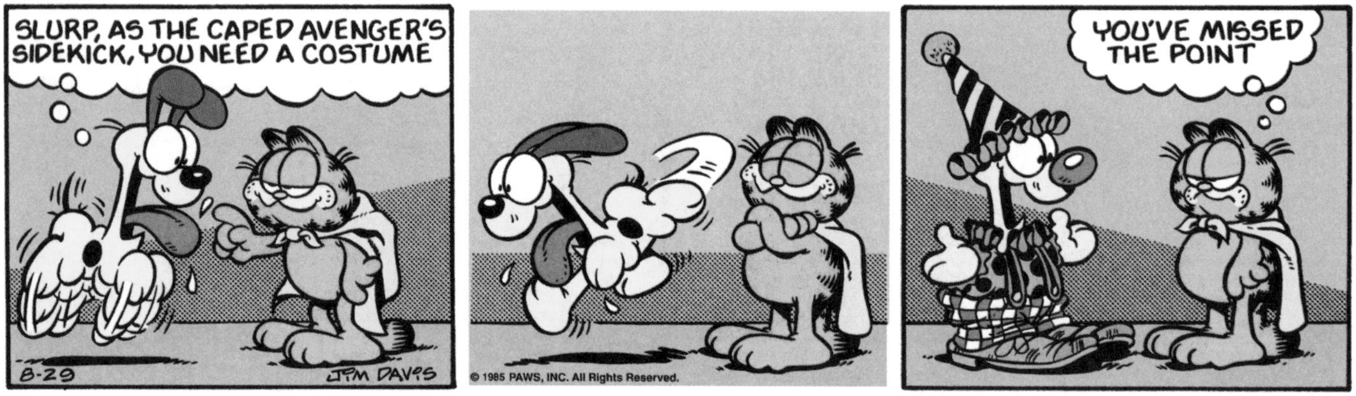
SLURP, AS THE CAPED AVENGER'S SIDEKICK, YOU NEED A COSTUME
8-29
JIM DAVIS
© 1985 PAWS, INC. All Rights Reserved.
YOU'VE MISSED THE POINT

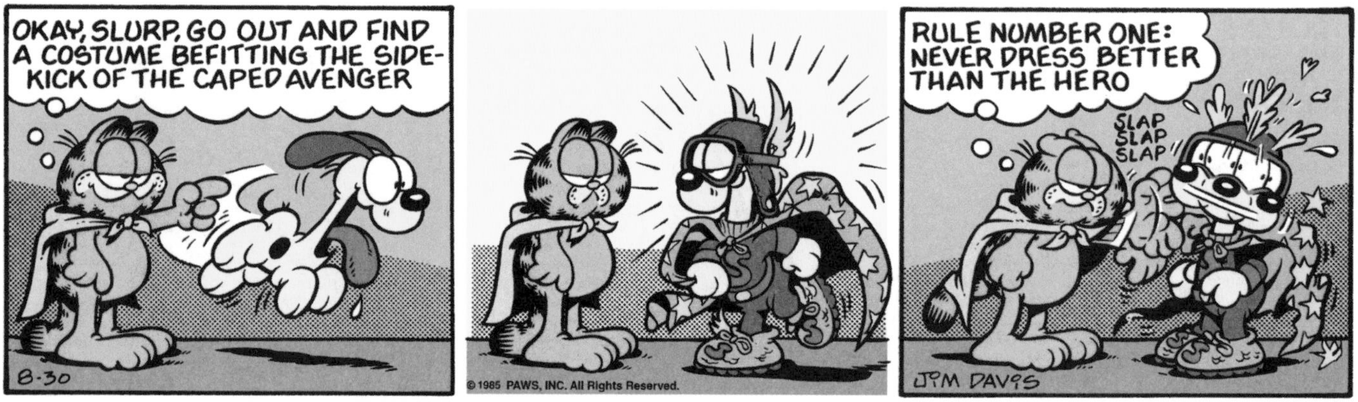
OKAY, SLURP, GO OUT AND FIND A COSTUME BEFITTING THE SIDE-KICK OF THE CAPED AVENGER
8-30
© 1985 PAWS, INC. All Rights Reserved.
RULE NUMBER ONE: NEVER DRESS BETTER THAN THE HERO
SLAP SLAP SLAP
JIM DAVIS

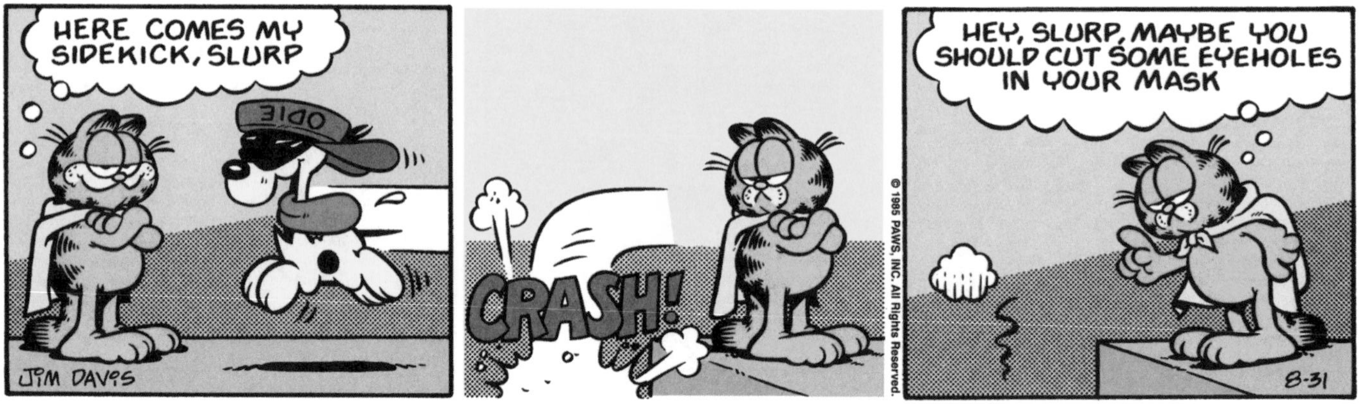
HERE COMES MY SIDEKICK, SLURP
ODIE
JIM DAVIS
CRASH!
© 1985 PAWS, INC. All Rights Reserved.
HEY, SLURP, MAYBE YOU SHOULD CUT SOME EYEHOLES IN YOUR MASK
8-31

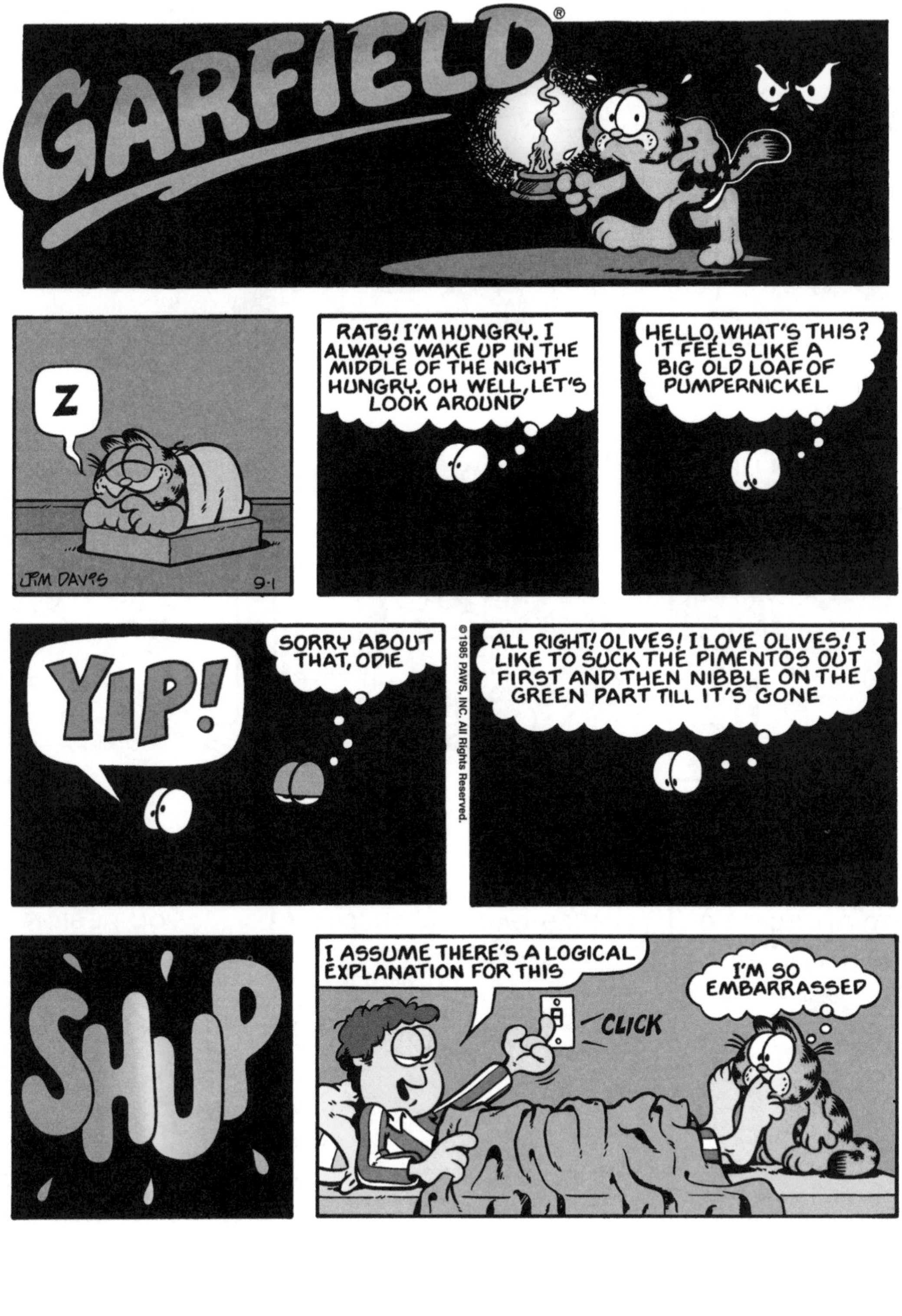
GARFIELD®
Z
JIM DAVIS
9-1
RATS! I'M HUNGRY. I ALWAYS WAKE UP IN THE MIDDLE OF THE NIGHT HUNGRY. OH WELL, LET'S LOOK AROUND
HELLO, WHAT'S THIS? IT FEELS LIKE A BIG OLD LOAF OF PUMPERNICKEL
YIP!
SORRY ABOUT THAT, ODIE
ALL RIGHT! OLIVES! I LOVE OLIVES! I LIKE TO SUCK THE PIMENTOS OUT FIRST AND THEN NIBBLE ON THE GREEN PART TILL IT'S GONE
SHUP
I ASSUME THERE'S A LOGICAL EXPLANATION FOR THIS
CLICK
I'M SO EMBARRASSED

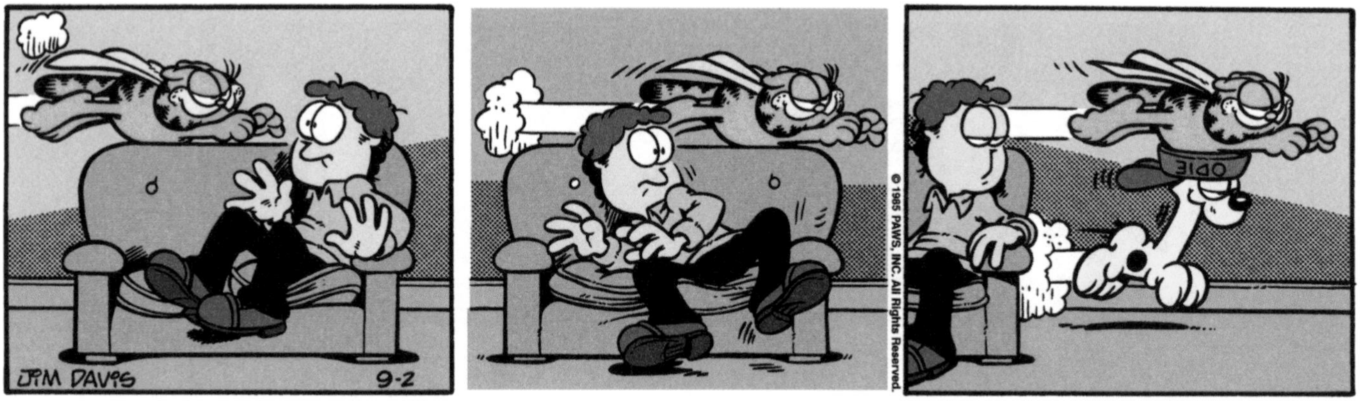
JIM DAVIS
9-2
© 1985 PAWS, INC. All Rights Reserved.
ODIE

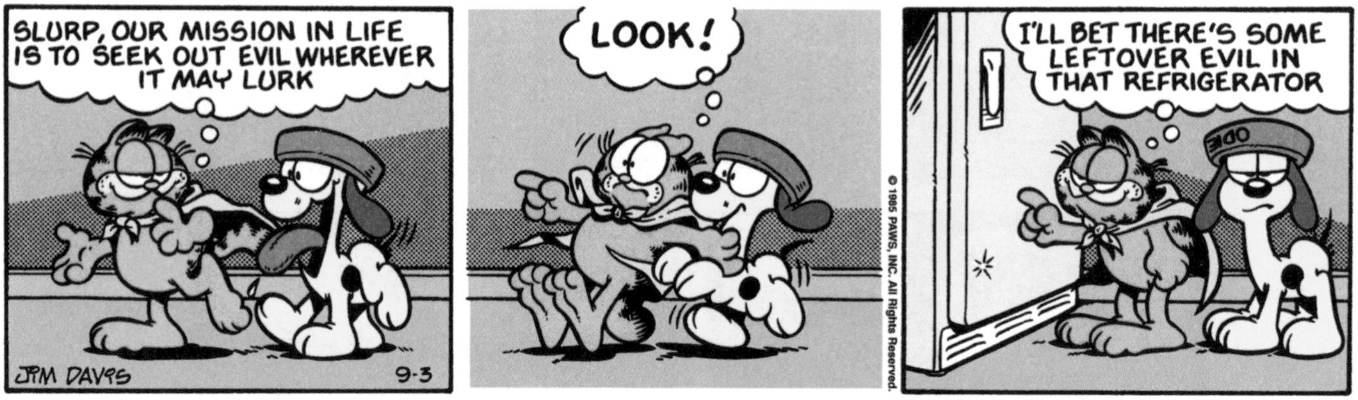
SLURP, OUR MISSION IN LIFE IS TO SEEK OUT EVIL WHEREVER IT MAY LURK
JIM DAVIS
9-3
LOOK!
© 1985 PAWS, INC. All Rights Reserved.
I'LL BET THERE'S SOME LEFTOVER EVIL IN THAT REFRIGERATOR
ODIE

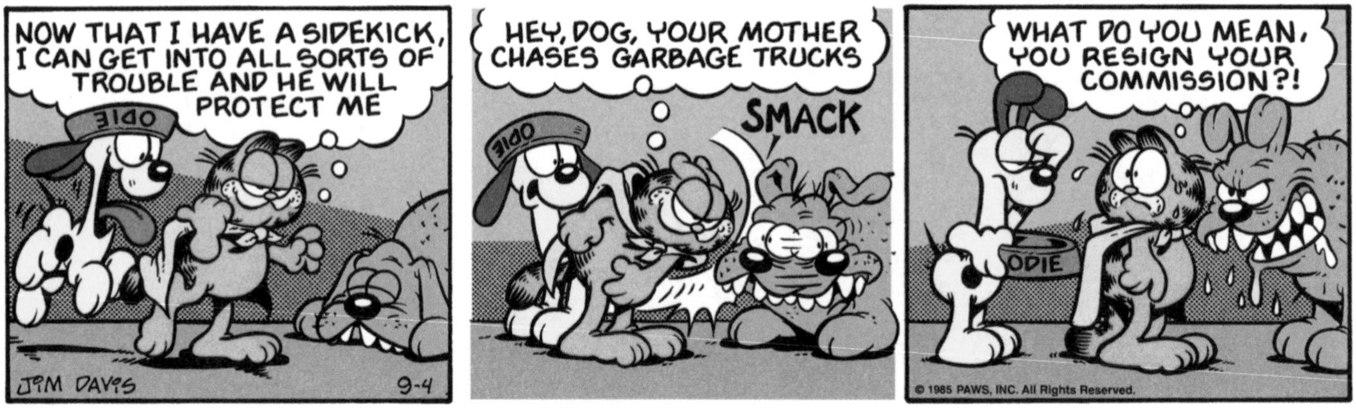
NOW THAT I HAVE A SIDEKICK, I CAN GET INTO ALL SORTS OF TROUBLE AND HE WILL PROTECT ME
ODIE
JIM DAVIS
9-4
HEY, DOG, YOUR MOTHER CHASES GARBAGE TRUCKS
ODIE
SMACK
WHAT DO YOU MEAN, YOU RESIGN YOUR COMMISSION?!
ODIE
© 1985 PAWS, INC. All Rights Reserved.

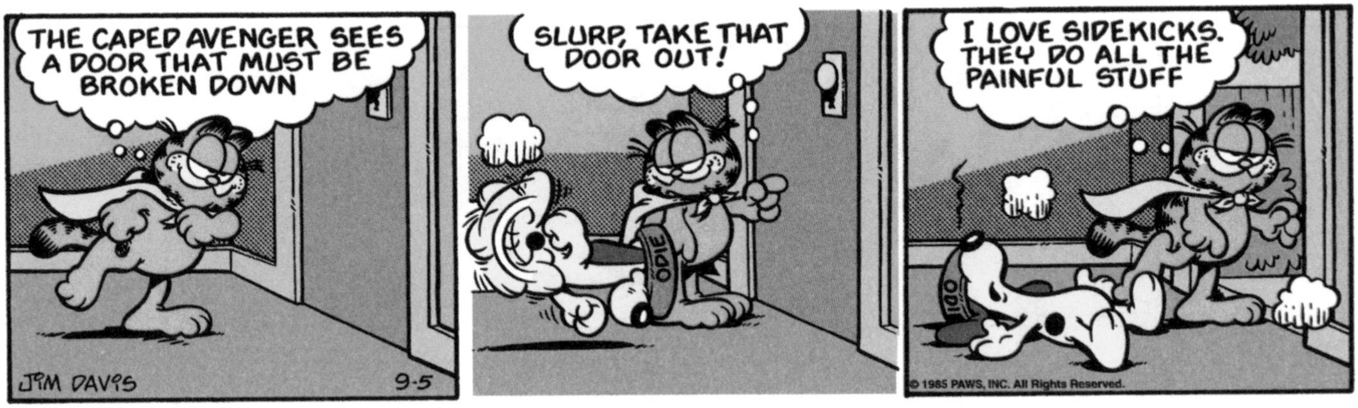
THE CAPED AVENGER SEES A DOOR THAT MUST BE BROKEN DOWN
JIM DAVIS
9-5
SLURP, TAKE THAT DOOR OUT!
ODIE
I LOVE SIDEKICKS. THEY DO ALL THE PAINFUL STUFF
© 1985 PAWS, INC. All Rights Reserved.

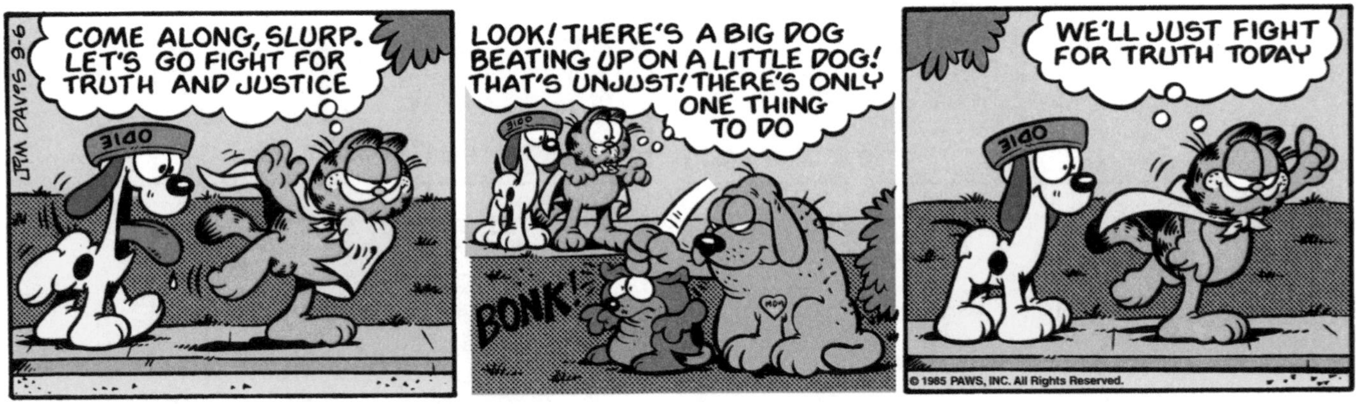
JIM DAVIS 9-6
COME ALONG, SLURP. LET'S GO FIGHT FOR TRUTH AND JUSTICE
LOOK! THERE'S A BIG DOG BEATING UP ON A LITTLE DOG! THAT'S UNJUST! THERE'S ONLY ONE THING TO DO
BONK!
WE'LL JUST FIGHT FOR TRUTH TODAY
© 1985 PAWS, INC. All Rights Reserved.

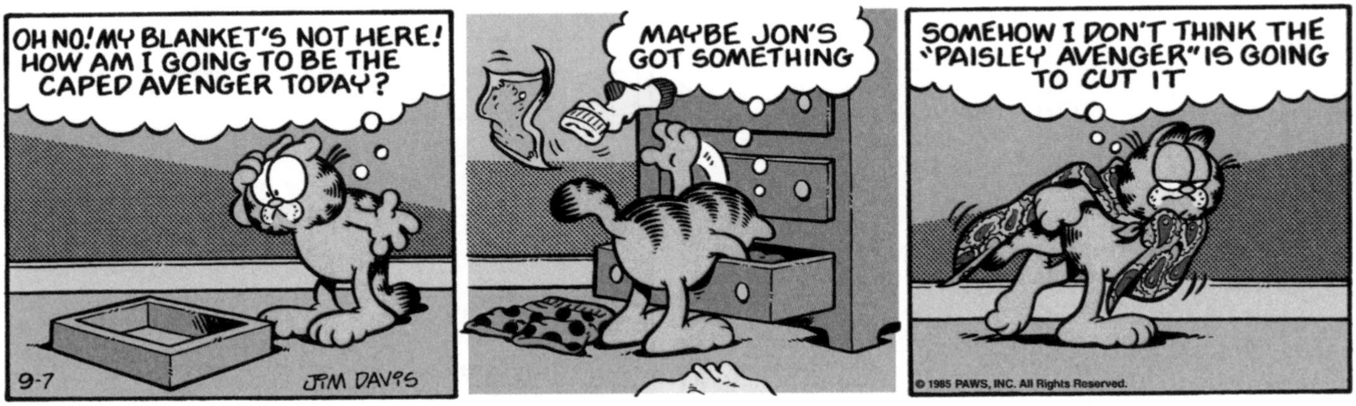
OH NO! MY BLANKET'S NOT HERE! HOW AM I GOING TO BE THE CAPED AVENGER TODAY?
9-7
JIM DAVIS
MAYBE JON'S GOT SOMETHING
SOMEHOW I DON'T THINK THE "PAISLEY AVENGER" IS GOING TO CUT IT
© 1985 PAWS, INC. All Rights Reserved.

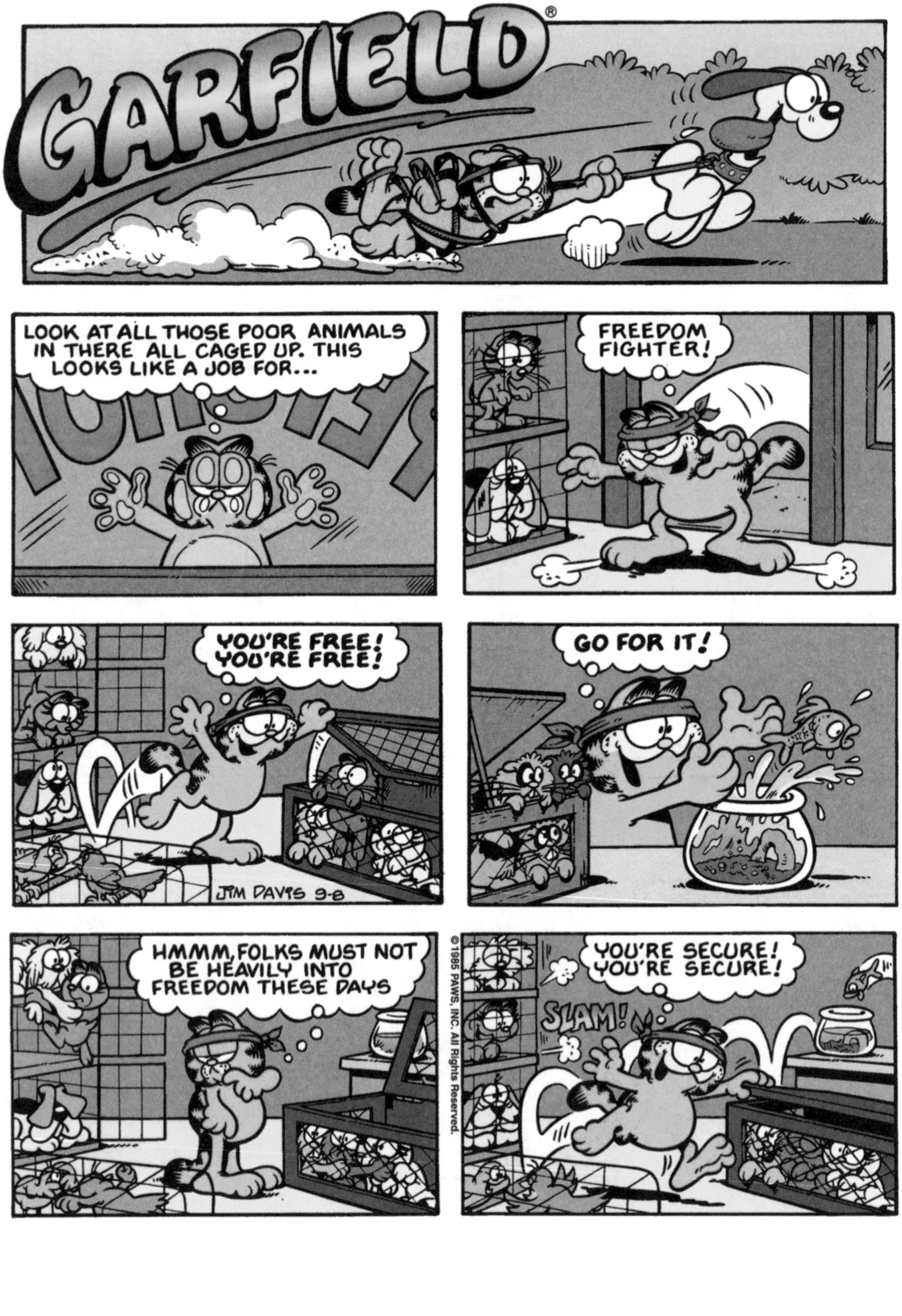
GARFIELD®
LOOK AT ALL THOSE POOR ANIMALS IN THERE ALL CAGED UP. THIS LOOKS LIKE A JOB FOR...
FREEDOM FIGHTER!
YOU'RE FREE! YOU'RE FREE!
JIM DAVIS 9-8
GO FOR IT!
HMMM, FOLKS MUST NOT BE HEAVILY INTO FREEDOM THESE DAYS
SLAM!
YOU'RE SECURE! YOU'RE SECURE!

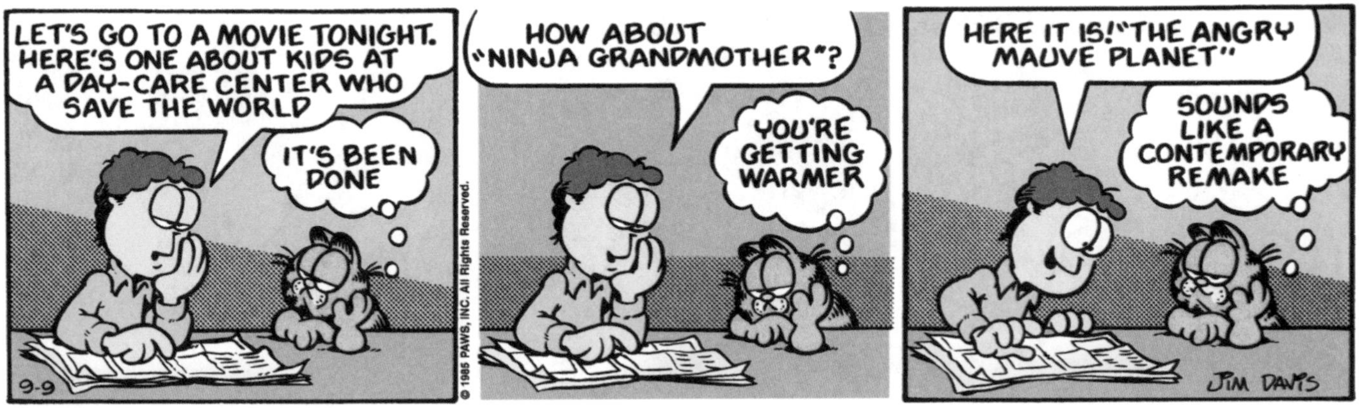
LET'S GO TO A MOVIE TONIGHT. HERE'S ONE ABOUT KIDS AT A DAY-CARE CENTER WHO SAVE THE WORLD
IT'S BEEN DONE
9-9
© 1985 PAWS, INC. All Rights Reserved.
HOW ABOUT "NINJA GRANDMOTHER"?
YOU'RE GETTING WARMER
HERE IT IS! "THE ANGRY MAUVE PLANET"
SOUNDS LIKE A CONTEMPORARY REMAKE
JIM DAVIS

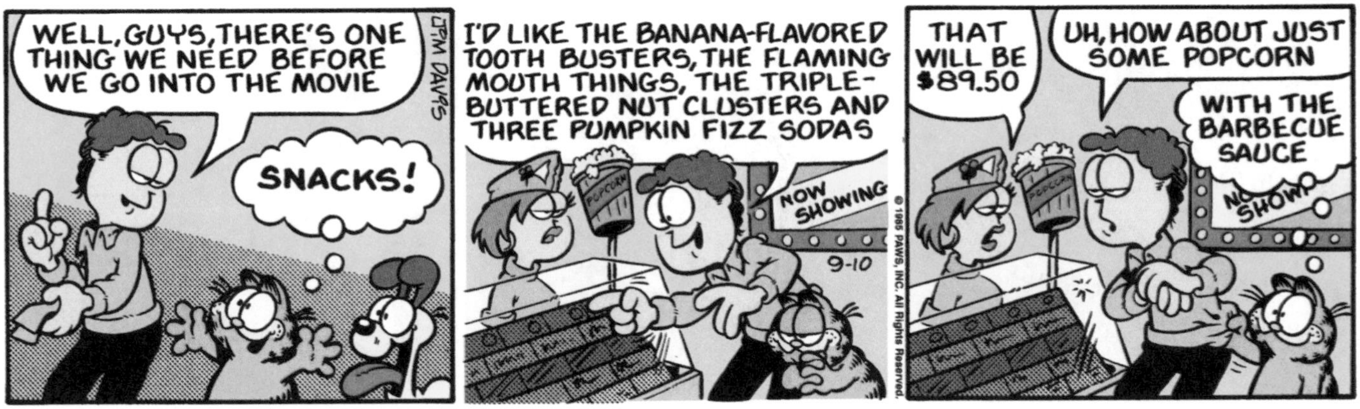
WELL, GUYS, THERE'S ONE THING WE NEED BEFORE WE GO INTO THE MOVIE
SNACKS!
JIM DAVIS
I'D LIKE THE BANANA-FLAVORED TOOTH BUSTERS, THE FLAMING MOUTH THINGS, THE TRIPLE-BUTTERED NUT CLUSTERS AND THREE PUMPKIN FIZZ SODAS
POPCORN
NOW SHOWING
9-10
© 1985 PAWS, INC. All Rights Reserved.
THAT WILL BE $89.50
UH, HOW ABOUT JUST SOME POPCORN
WITH THE BARBECUE SAUCE

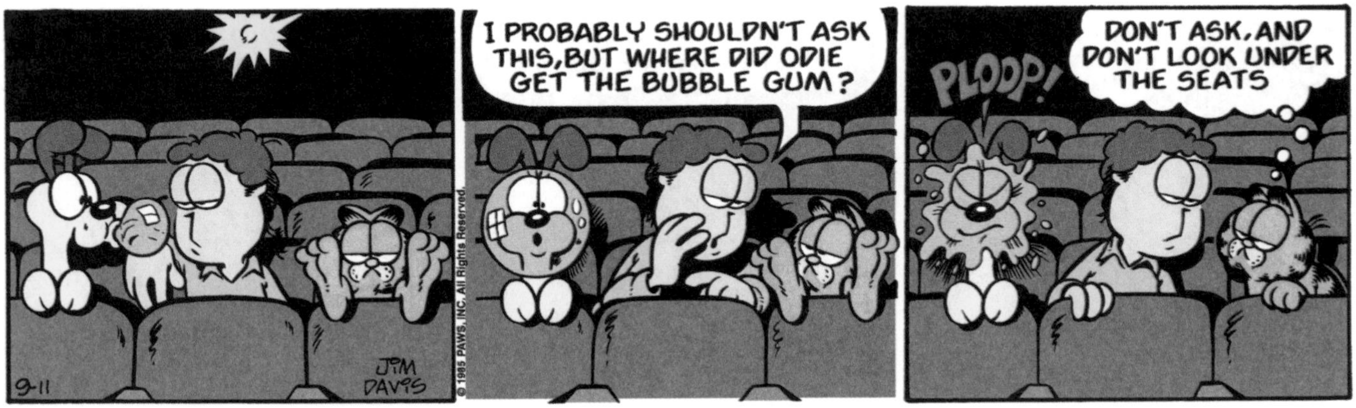
9-11
JIM DAVIS
© 1985 PAWS, INC. All Rights Reserved.
I PROBABLY SHOULDN'T ASK THIS, BUT WHERE DID ODIE GET THE BUBBLE GUM?
PLOOP!
DON'T ASK, AND DON'T LOOK UNDER THE SEATS

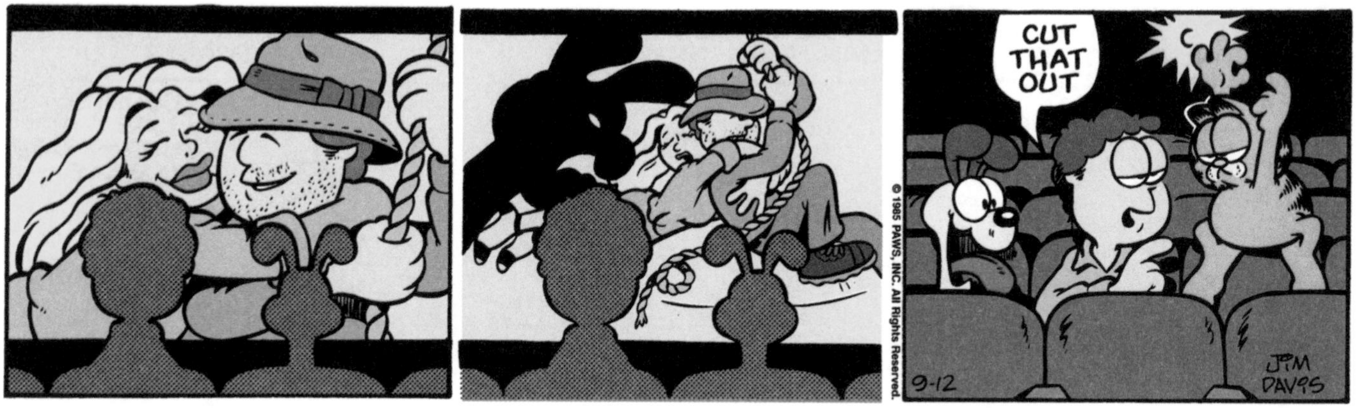
CUT THAT OUT
© 1985 PAWS, INC. All Rights Reserved.
JIM DAVIS
9-12

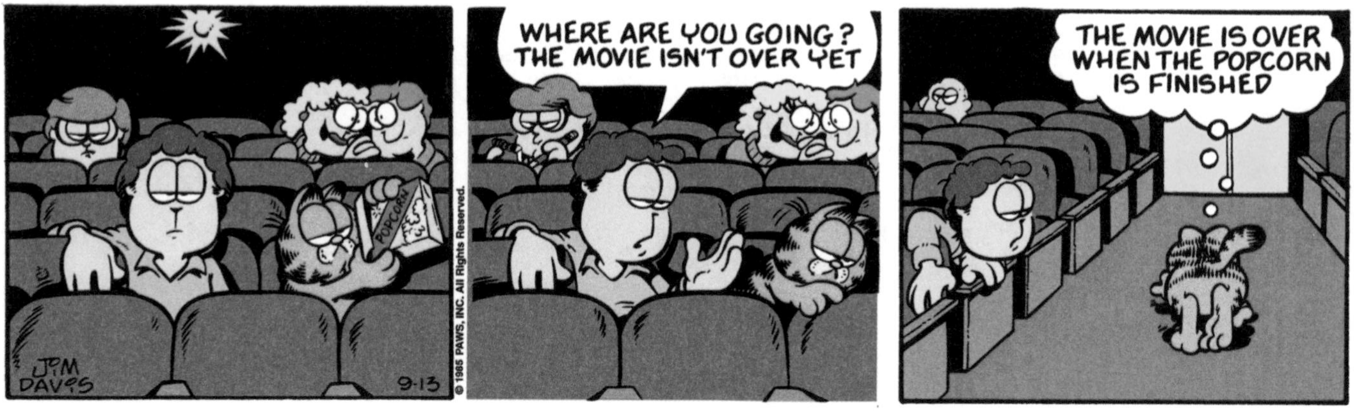
POPCORN
JIM DAVIS
9-13
© 1985 PAWS, INC. All Rights Reserved.
WHERE ARE YOU GOING? THE MOVIE ISN'T OVER YET
THE MOVIE IS OVER WHEN THE POPCORN IS FINISHED

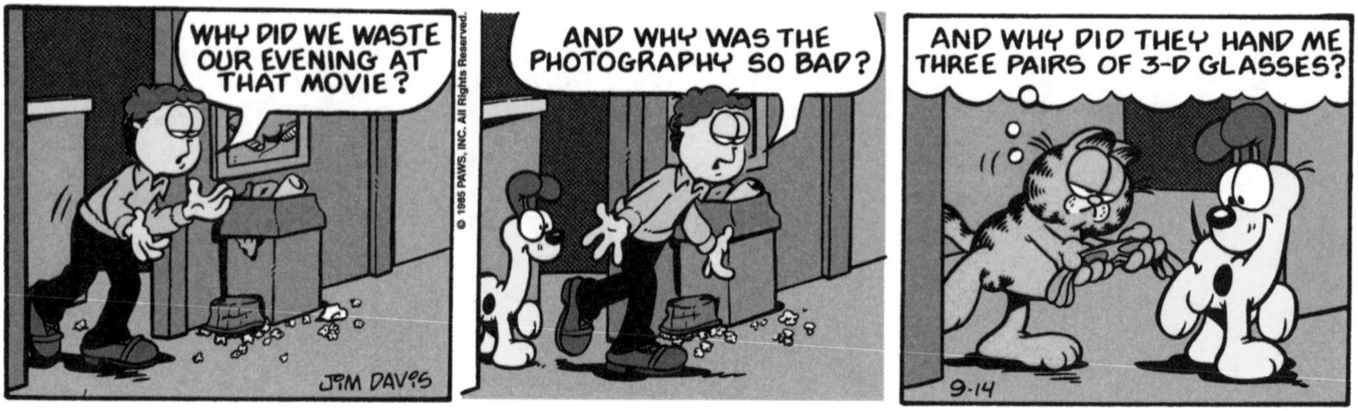
WHY DID WE WASTE OUR EVENING AT THAT MOVIE?
JIM DAVIS
© 1985 PAWS, INC. All Rights Reserved.
AND WHY WAS THE PHOTOGRAPHY SO BAD?
AND WHY DID THEY HAND ME THREE PAIRS OF 3-D GLASSES?
9-14

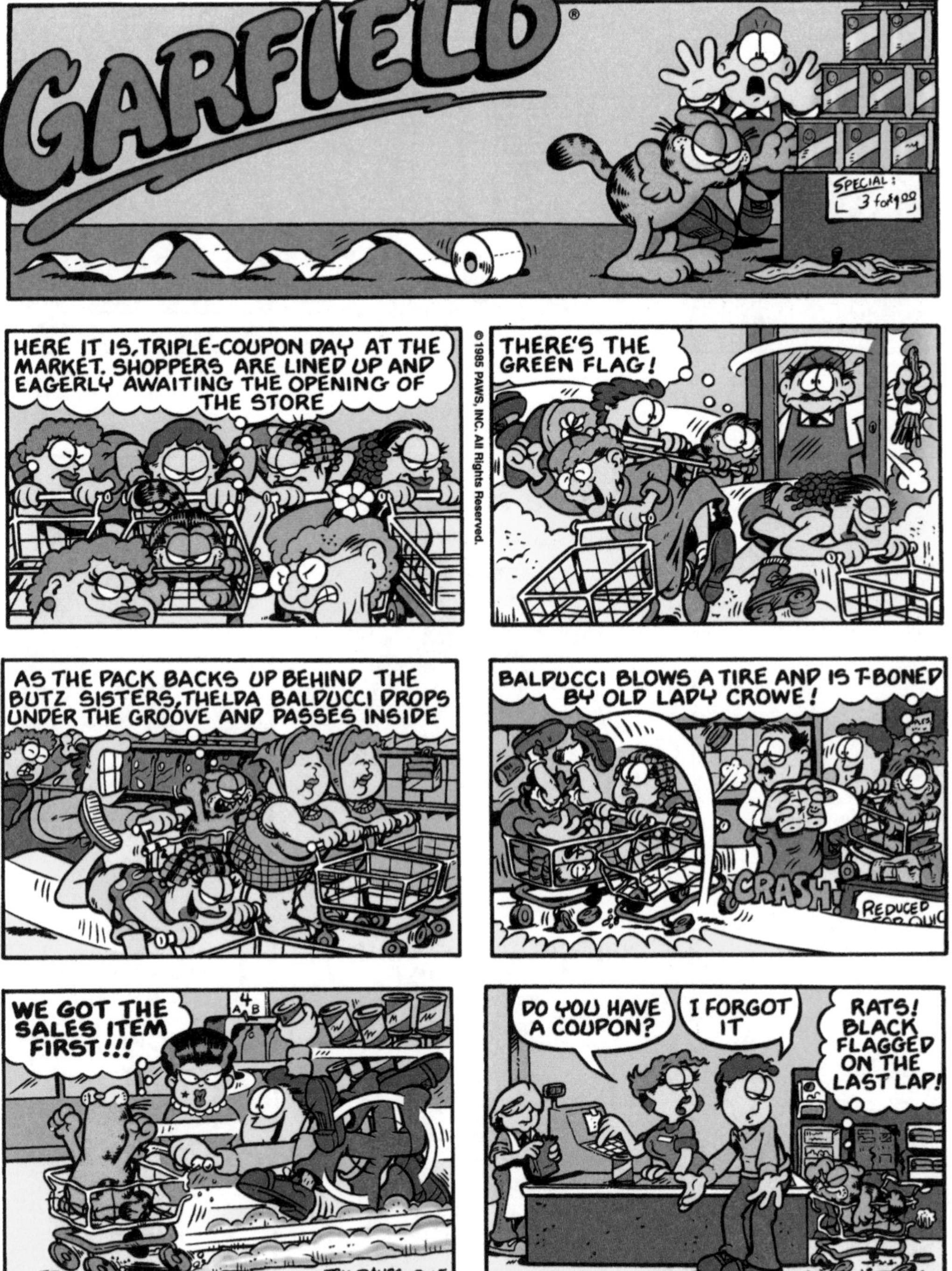
GARFIELD®
SPECIAL: 3 for $1.00
HERE IT IS, TRIPLE-COUPON DAY AT THE MARKET. SHOPPERS ARE LINED UP AND EAGERLY AWAITING THE OPENING OF THE STORE
© 1985 PAWS, INC. All Rights Reserved.
THERE'S THE GREEN FLAG!
AS THE PACK BACKS UP BEHIND THE BUTZ SISTERS, THELDA BALDUCCI DROPS UNDER THE GROOVE AND PASSES INSIDE
BALDUCCI BLOWS A TIRE AND IS T-BONED BY OLD LADY CROWE!
CRASH!
WE GOT THE SALES ITEM FIRST!!!
JIM DAVIS 9-15
DO YOU HAVE A COUPON?
I FORGOT IT
RATS! BLACK FLAGGED ON THE LAST LAP!

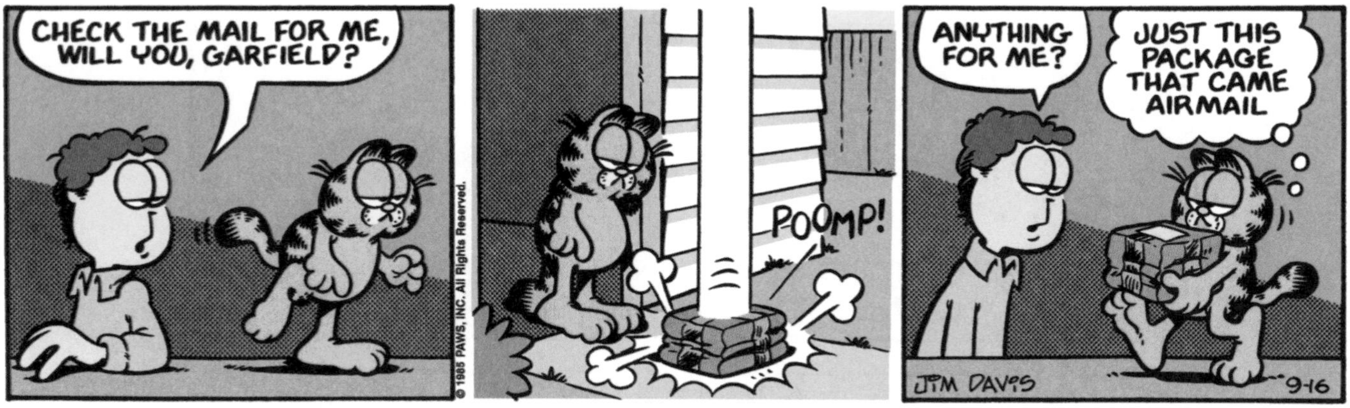
CHECK THE MAIL FOR ME, WILL YOU, GARFIELD?
© 1985 PAWS, INC. All Rights Reserved.
POOMP!
ANYTHING FOR ME?
JUST THIS PACKAGE THAT CAME AIRMAIL
JIM DAVIS
9-16

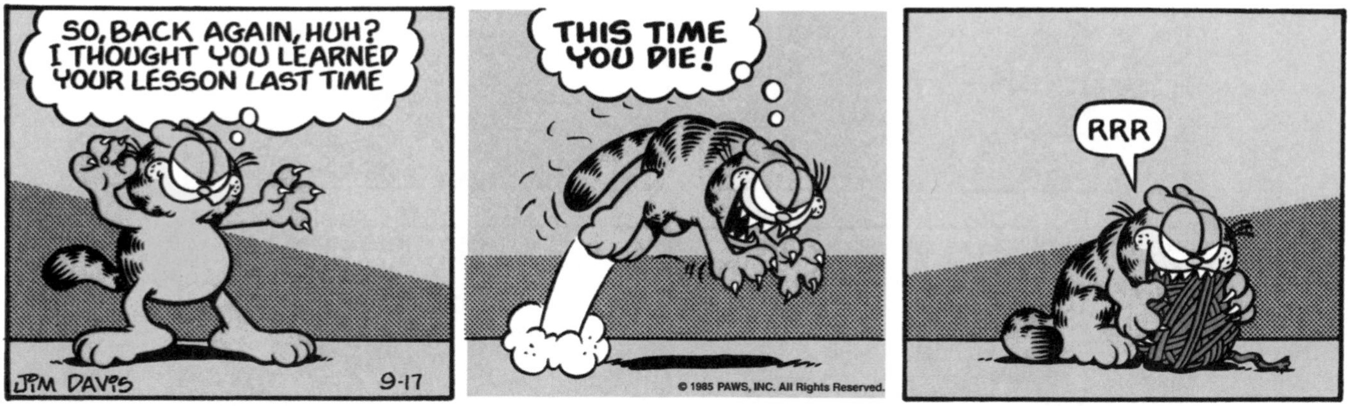
SO, BACK AGAIN, HUH? I THOUGHT YOU LEARNED YOUR LESSON LAST TIME
JIM DAVIS
9-17
THIS TIME YOU DIE!
© 1985 PAWS, INC. All Rights Reserved.
RRR

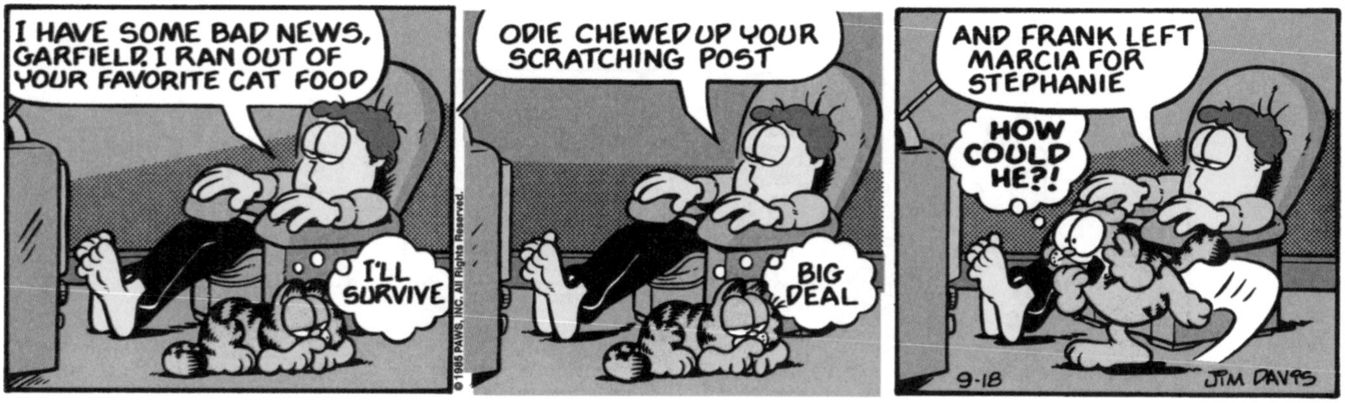
I HAVE SOME BAD NEWS, GARFIELD. I RAN OUT OF YOUR FAVORITE CAT FOOD
I'LL SURVIVE
© 1985 PAWS, INC. All Rights Reserved.
ODIE CHEWED UP YOUR SCRATCHING POST
BIG DEAL
AND FRANK LEFT MARCIA FOR STEPHANIE
HOW COULD HE?!
9-18
JIM DAVIS

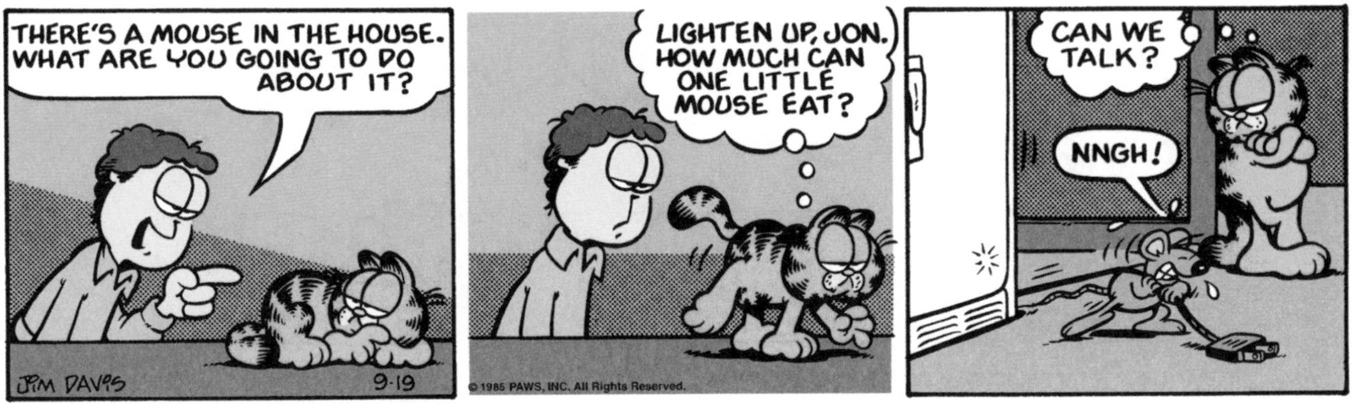
THERE'S A MOUSE IN THE HOUSE. WHAT ARE YOU GOING TO DO ABOUT IT?
JIM DAVIS
9-19
LIGHTEN UP, JON. HOW MUCH CAN ONE LITTLE MOUSE EAT?
© 1985 PAWS, INC. All Rights Reserved.
CAN WE TALK?
NNGH!

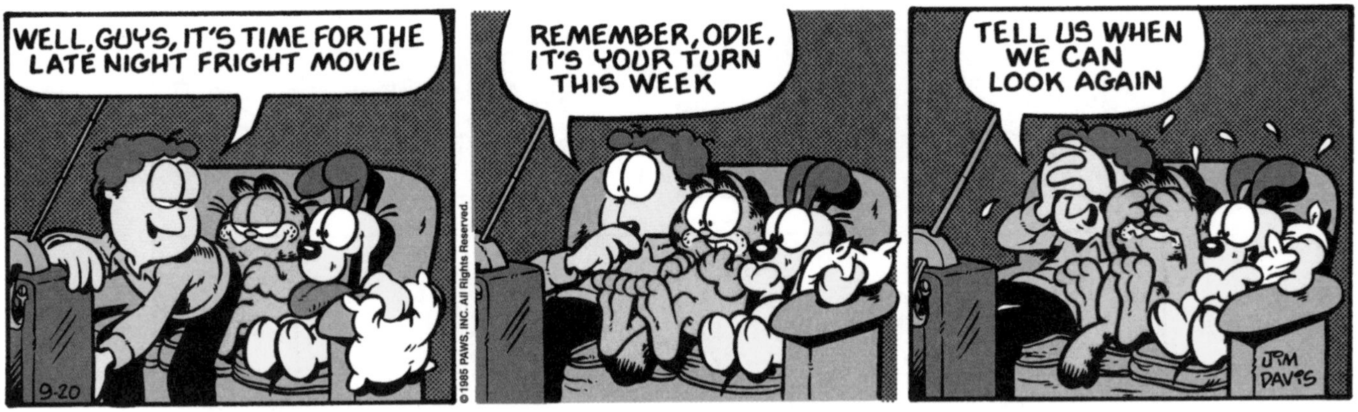
WELL, GUYS, IT'S TIME FOR THE LATE NIGHT FRIGHT MOVIE
9-20
© 1985 PAWS, INC. All Rights Reserved.
REMEMBER, ODIE, IT'S YOUR TURN THIS WEEK
TELL US WHEN WE CAN LOOK AGAIN
JIM DAVIS

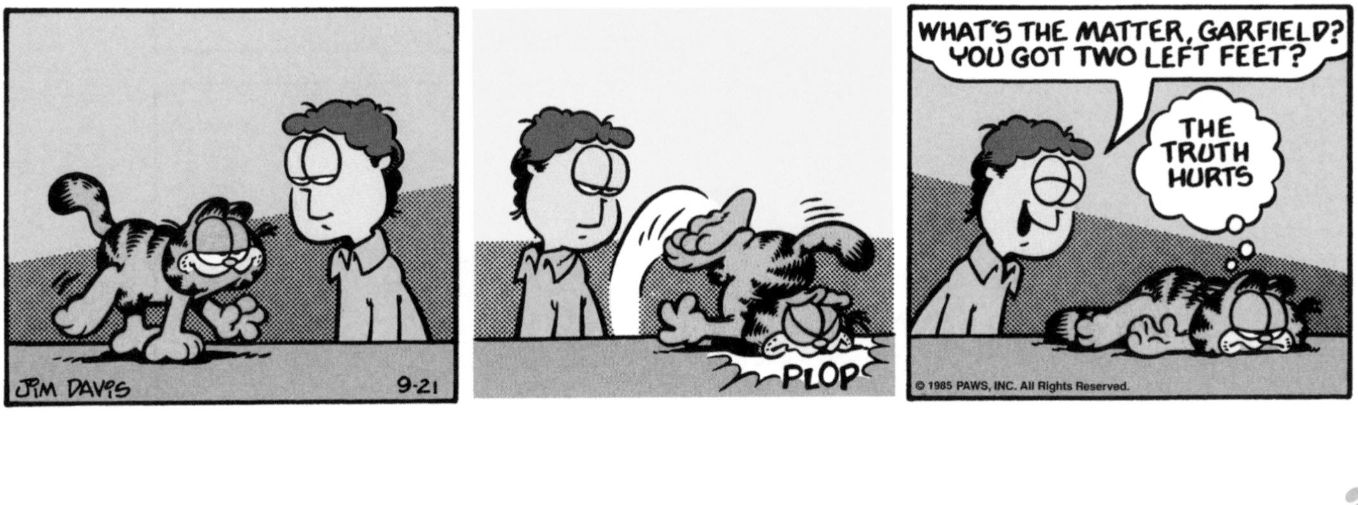
JIM DAVIS
9-21
PLOP
WHAT'S THE MATTER, GARFIELD? YOU GOT TWO LEFT FEET?
THE TRUTH HURTS
© 1985 PAWS, INC. All Rights Reserved.

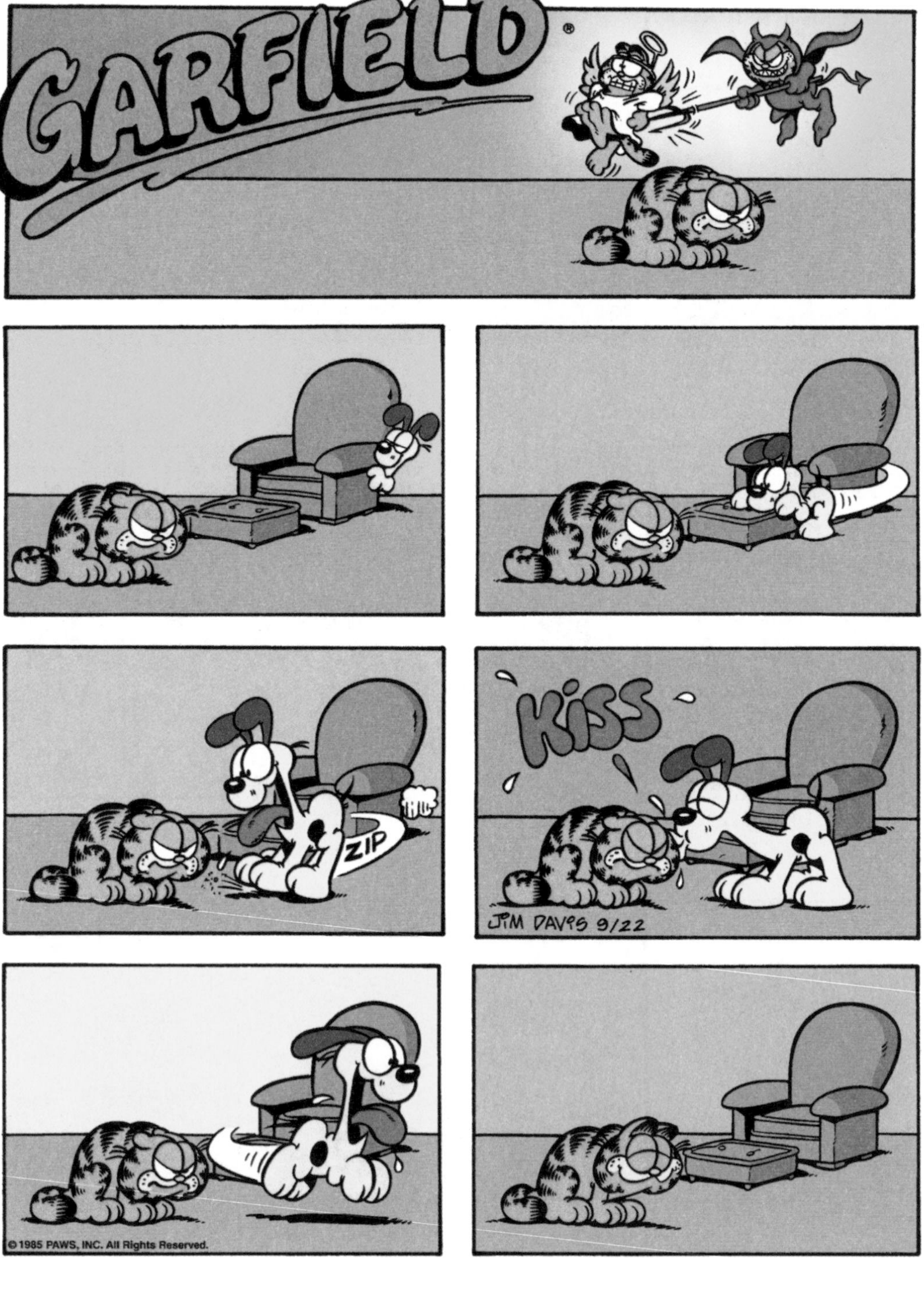
GARFIELD®
KISS
ZIP
JIM DAVIS 9/22
© 1985 PAWS, INC. All Rights Reserved.

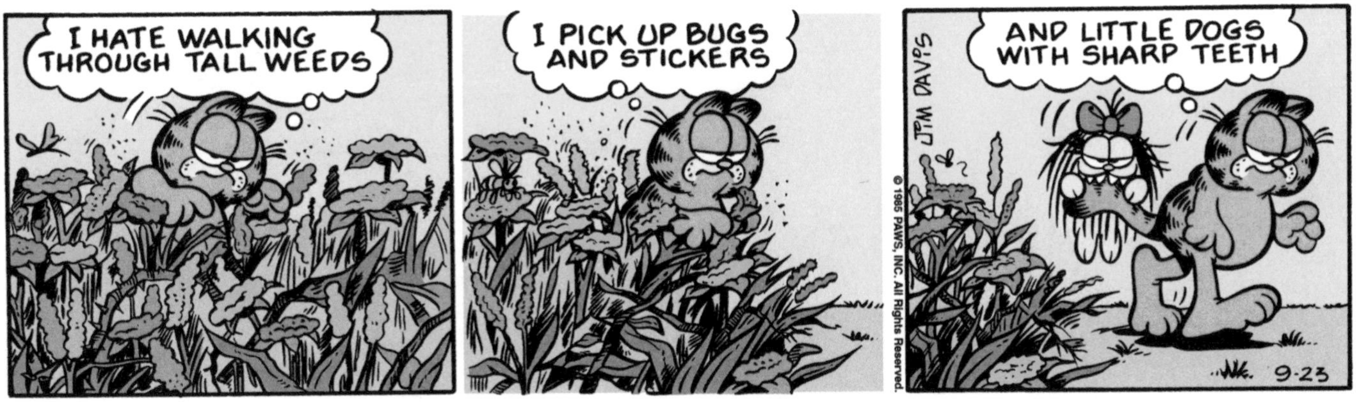
I HATE WALKING THROUGH TALL WEEDS
I PICK UP BUGS AND STICKERS
AND LITTLE DOGS WITH SHARP TEETH
JIM DAVIS
© 1985 PAWS, INC. All Rights Reserved.
9-23

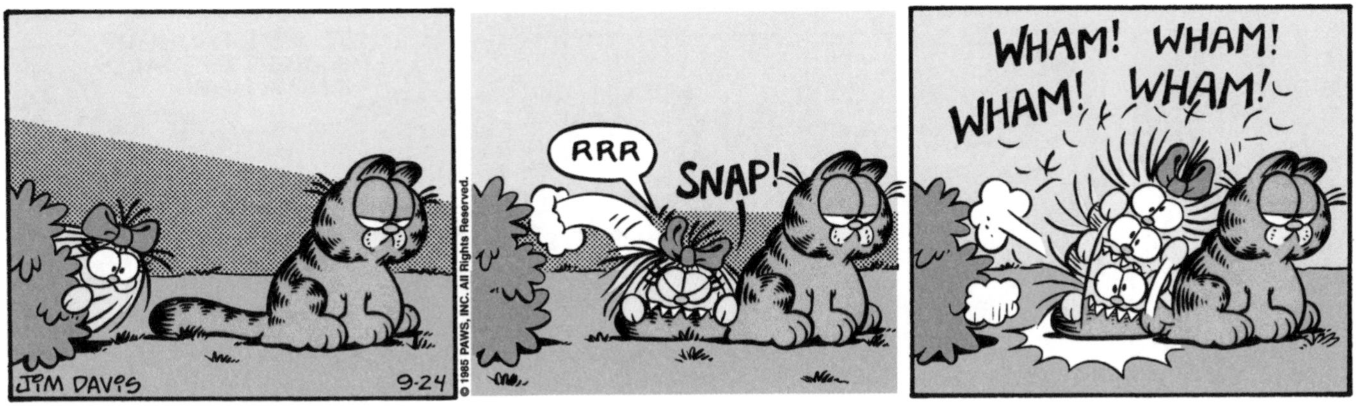
JIM DAVIS
9-24
© 1985 PAWS, INC. All Rights Reserved.
RRR
SNAP!
WHAM! WHAM!
WHAM! WHAM!

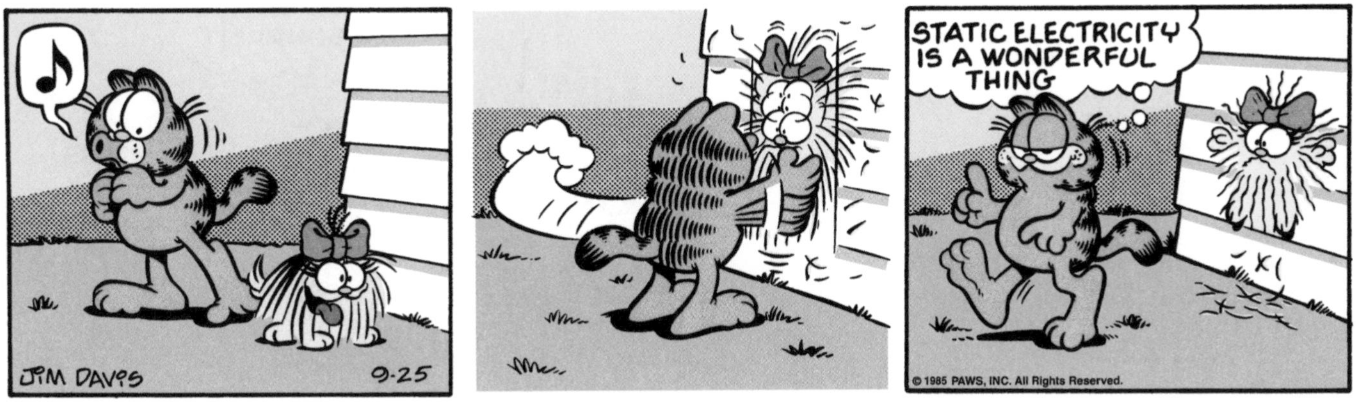
♪
JIM DAVIS
9-25
STATIC ELECTRICITY IS A WONDERFUL THING
© 1985 PAWS, INC. All Rights Reserved.

HEY, ODIE
JIM DAVIS
DO ME A FAVOR, WILL YOU
© 1985 PAWS, INC. All Rights Reserved.
THANKS
9-26

9-27
JIM DAVIS
GOOSH!
© 1985 PAWS, INC. All Rights Reserved.
JUST AS I THOUGHT. IT'S JUST EYEBALLS AND A BOW

HEY, DOG, HOW ABOUT SOME PEPPER TO GO WITH THAT TAIL
JIM DAVIS
9-28
© 1985 PAWS, INC. All Rights Reserved.
WAH-CHOO!
GESUNDHEIT

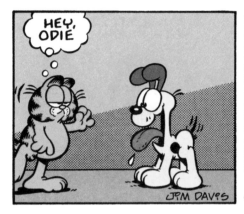

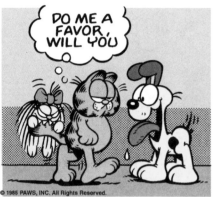

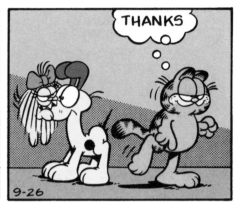

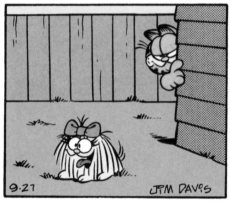

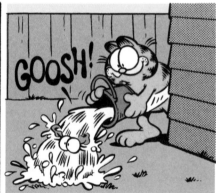

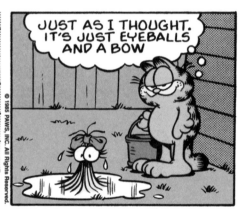

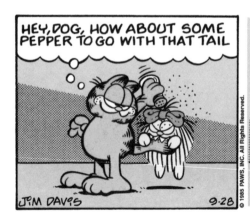

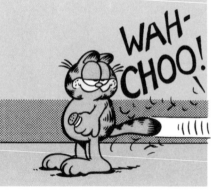

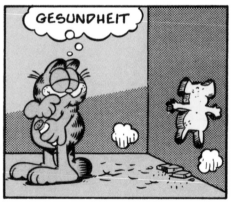

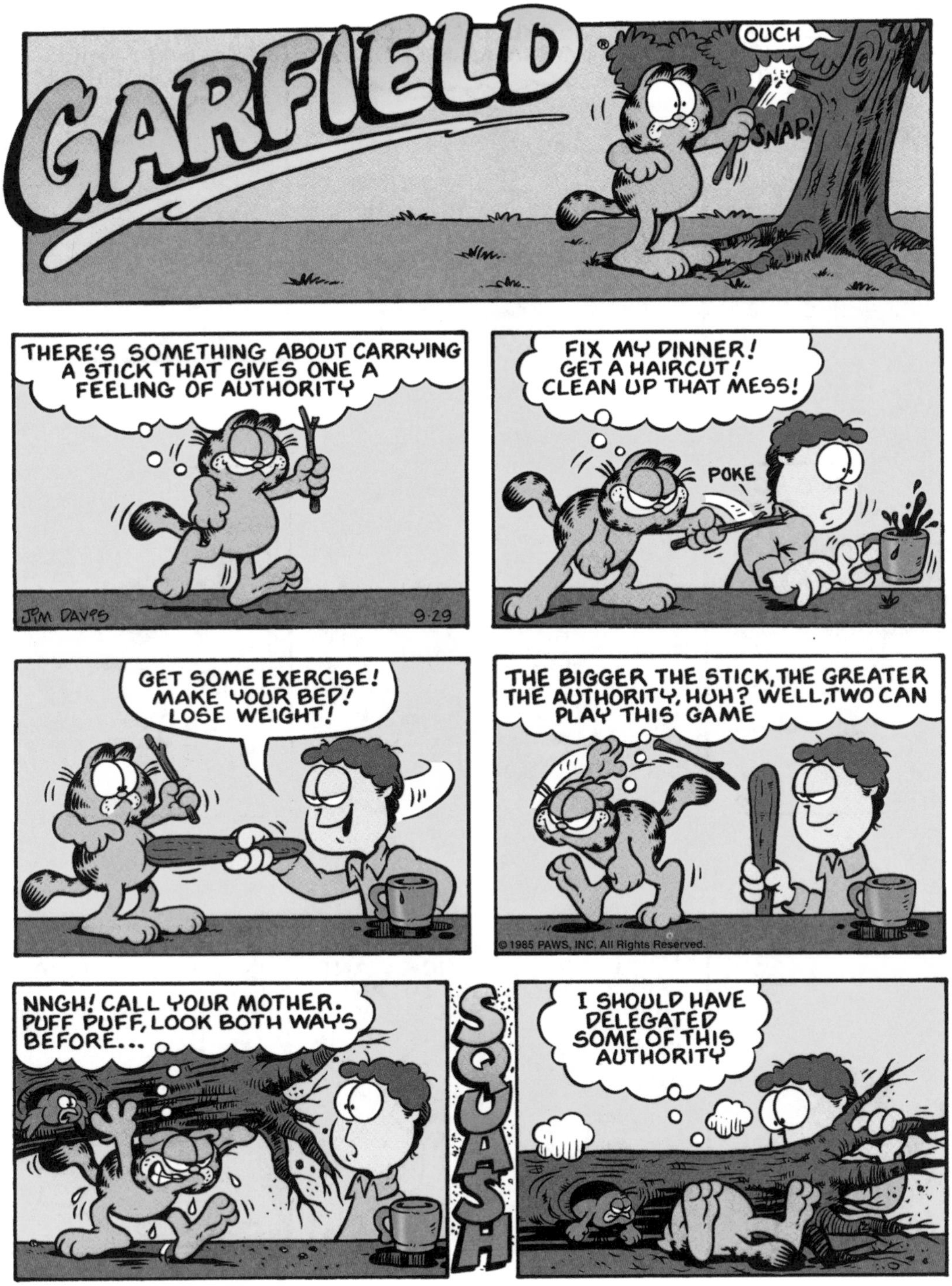
GARFIELD®
OUCH
SNAP!
THERE'S SOMETHING ABOUT CARRYING A STICK THAT GIVES ONE A FEELING OF AUTHORITY
JIM DAVIS
9-29
FIX MY DINNER! GET A HAIRCUT! CLEAN UP THAT MESS!
POKE
GET SOME EXERCISE! MAKE YOUR BED! LOSE WEIGHT!
THE BIGGER THE STICK, THE GREATER THE AUTHORITY, HUH? WELL, TWO CAN PLAY THIS GAME
© 1985 PAWS, INC. All Rights Reserved.
NNGH! CALL YOUR MOTHER. PUFF PUFF, LOOK BOTH WAYS BEFORE...
SQUASH
I SHOULD HAVE DELEGATED SOME OF THIS AUTHORITY

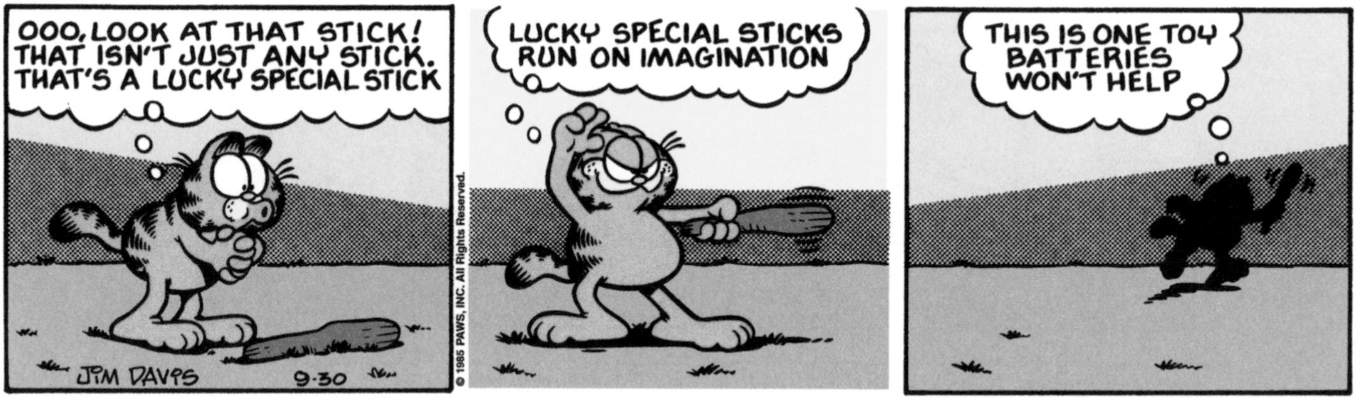
OOO, LOOK AT THAT STICK! THAT ISN'T JUST ANY STICK. THAT'S A LUCKY SPECIAL STICK
JIM DAVIS 9-30
© 1985 PAWS, INC. All Rights Reserved.
LUCKY SPECIAL STICKS RUN ON IMAGINATION
THIS IS ONE TOY BATTERIES WON'T HELP

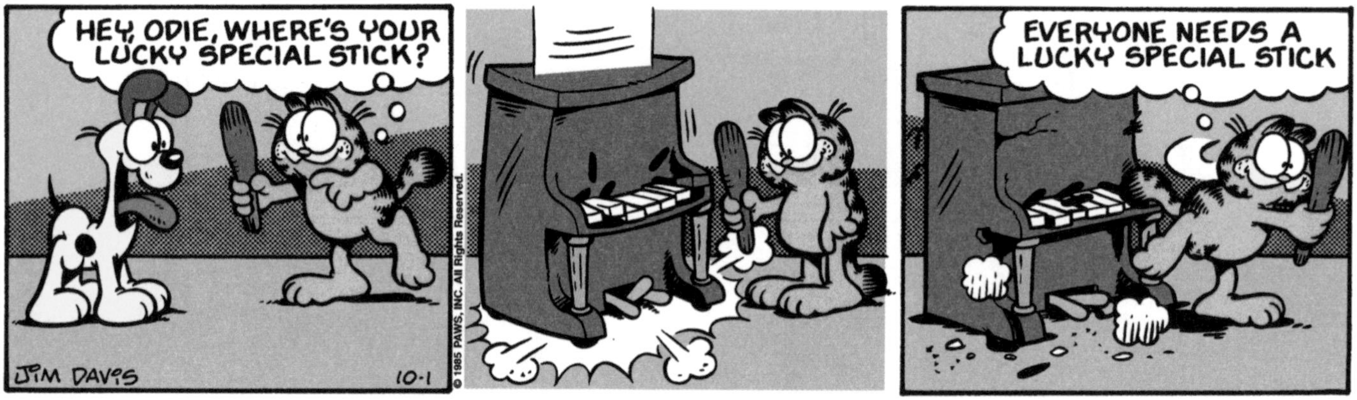
HEY, ODIE, WHERE'S YOUR LUCKY SPECIAL STICK?
JIM DAVIS 10-1
© 1985 PAWS, INC. All Rights Reserved.
EVERYONE NEEDS A LUCKY SPECIAL STICK

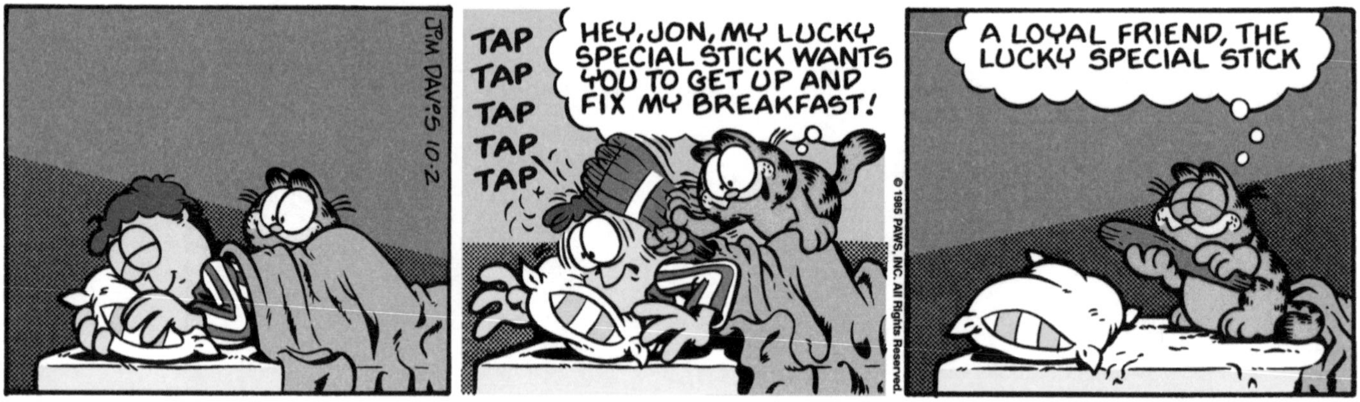
JIM DAVIS 10-2
TAP TAP TAP TAP TAP
HEY, JON, MY LUCKY SPECIAL STICK WANTS YOU TO GET UP AND FIX MY BREAKFAST!
© 1985 PAWS, INC. All Rights Reserved.
A LOYAL FRIEND, THE LUCKY SPECIAL STICK

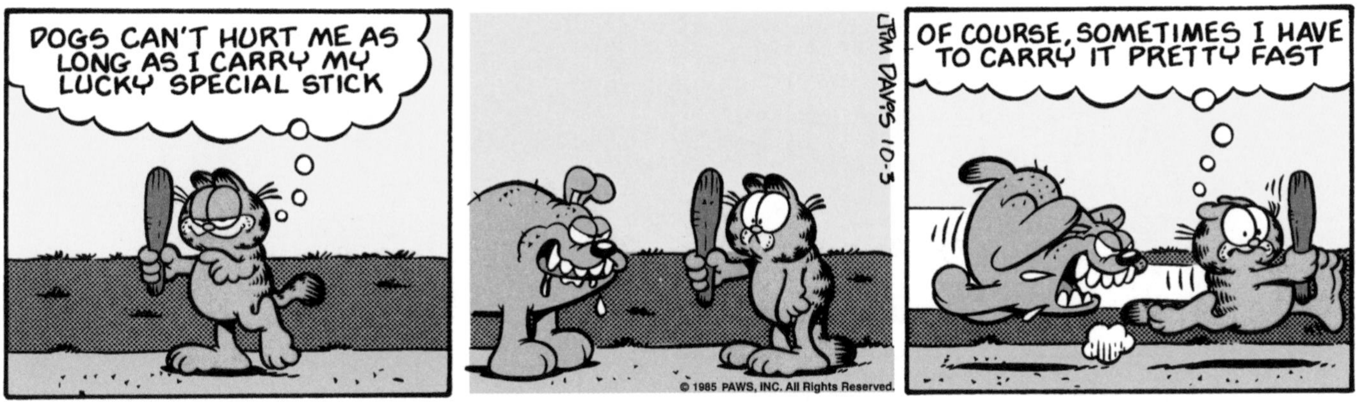
DOGS CAN'T HURT ME AS LONG AS I CARRY MY LUCKY SPECIAL STICK
JIM DAVIS 10-3
© 1985 PAWS, INC. All Rights Reserved.
OF COURSE, SOMETIMES I HAVE TO CARRY IT PRETTY FAST

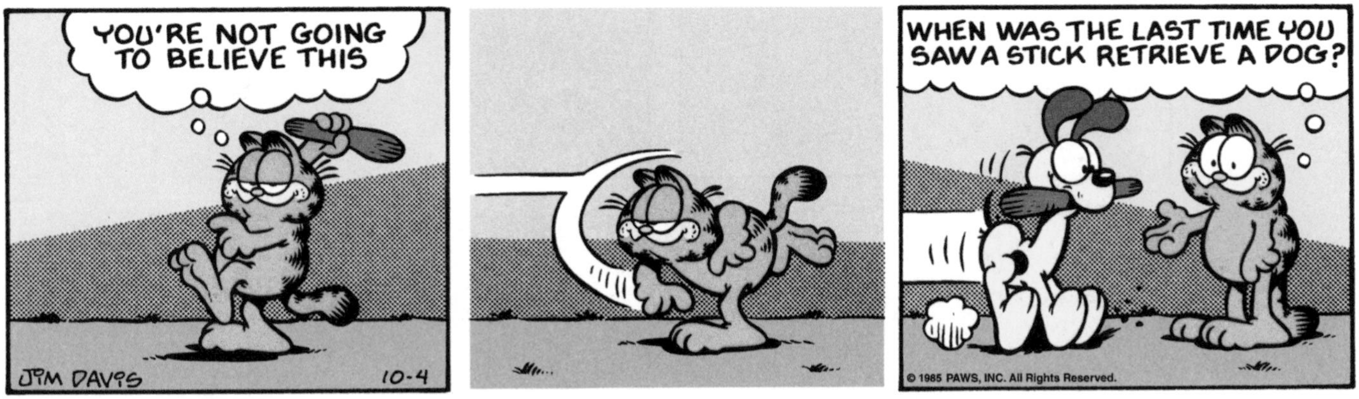
YOU'RE NOT GOING TO BELIEVE THIS
JIM DAVIS 10-4
WHEN WAS THE LAST TIME YOU SAW A STICK RETRIEVE A DOG?
© 1985 PAWS, INC. All Rights Reserved.

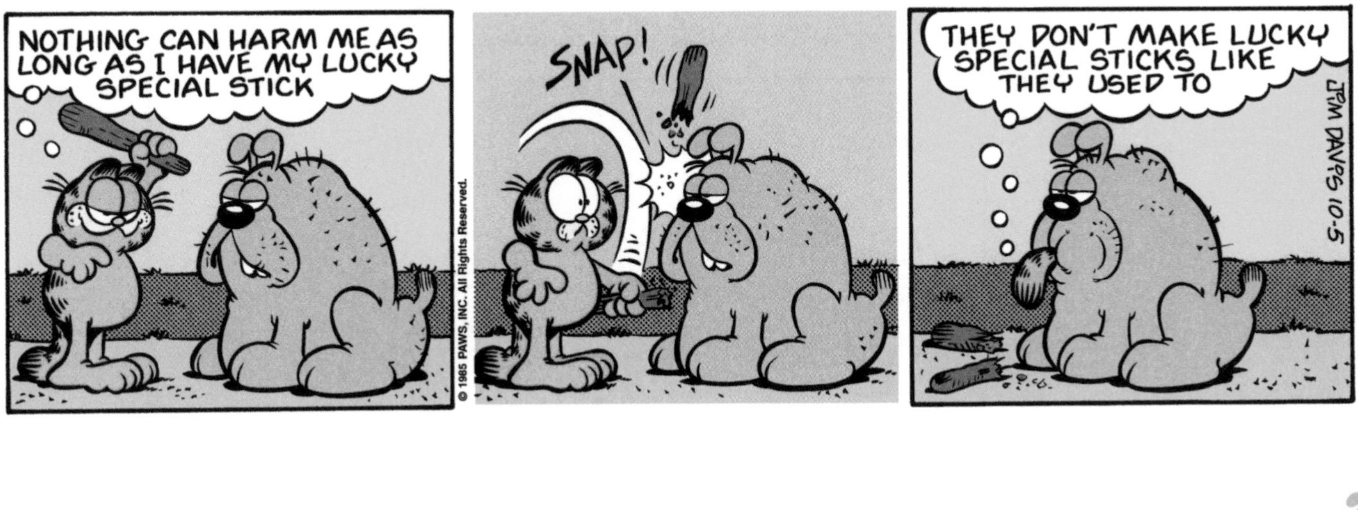
NOTHING CAN HARM ME AS LONG AS I HAVE MY LUCKY SPECIAL STICK
© 1985 PAWS, INC. All Rights Reserved.
SNAP!
THEY DON'T MAKE LUCKY SPECIAL STICKS LIKE THEY USED TO
JIM DAVIS 10-5

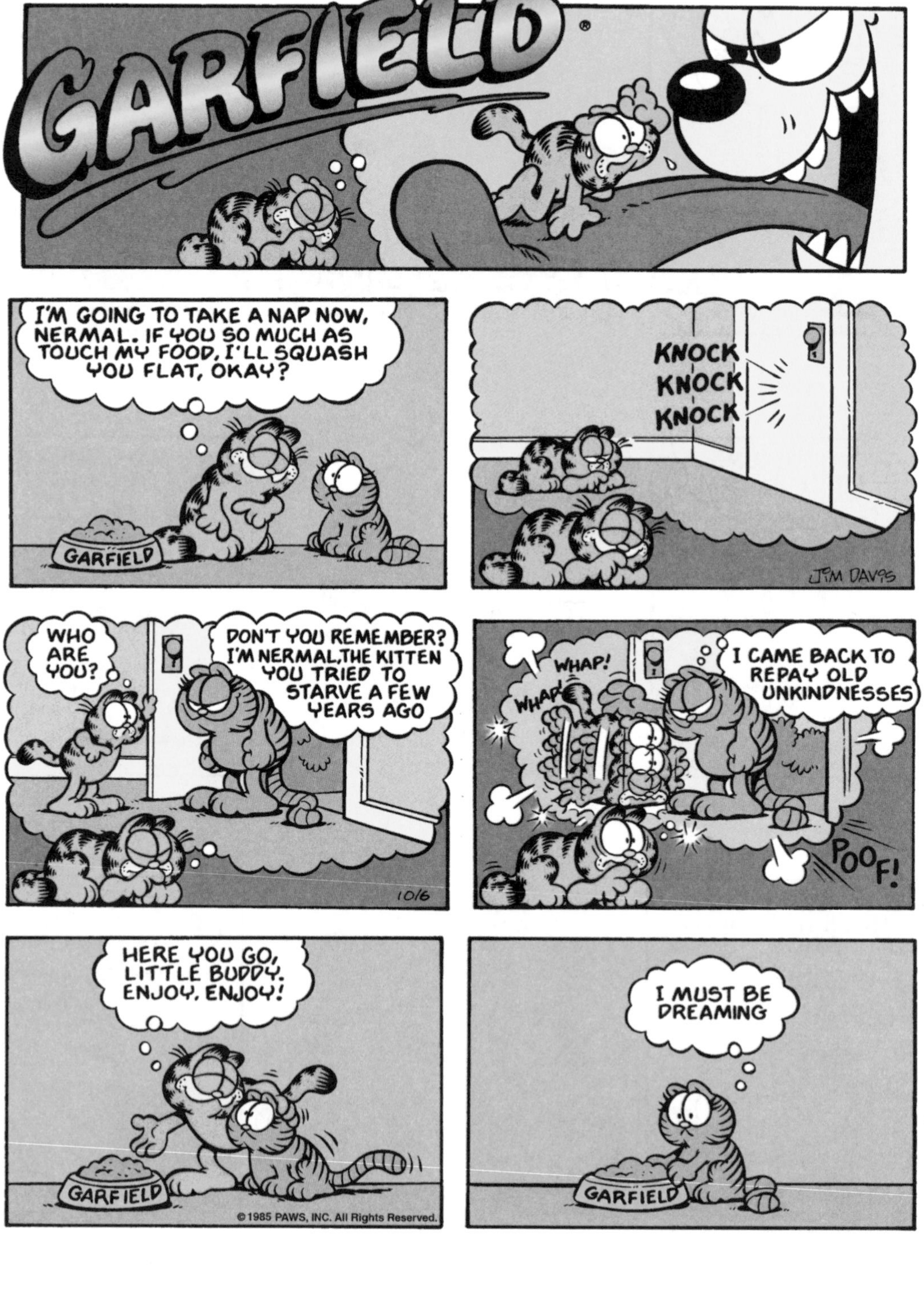
GARFIELD
I'M GOING TO TAKE A NAP NOW, NERMAL. IF YOU SO MUCH AS TOUCH MY FOOD, I'LL SQUASH YOU FLAT, OKAY?
GARFIELD
KNOCK KNOCK KNOCK
JIM DAVIS
WHO ARE YOU?
DON'T YOU REMEMBER? I'M NERMAL, THE KITTEN YOU TRIED TO STARVE A FEW YEARS AGO
10/6
WHAP! WHAP!
I CAME BACK TO REPAY OLD UNKINDNESSES
POOF!
HERE YOU GO, LITTLE BUDDY. ENJOY, ENJOY!
GARFIELD
I MUST BE DREAMING
GARFIELD

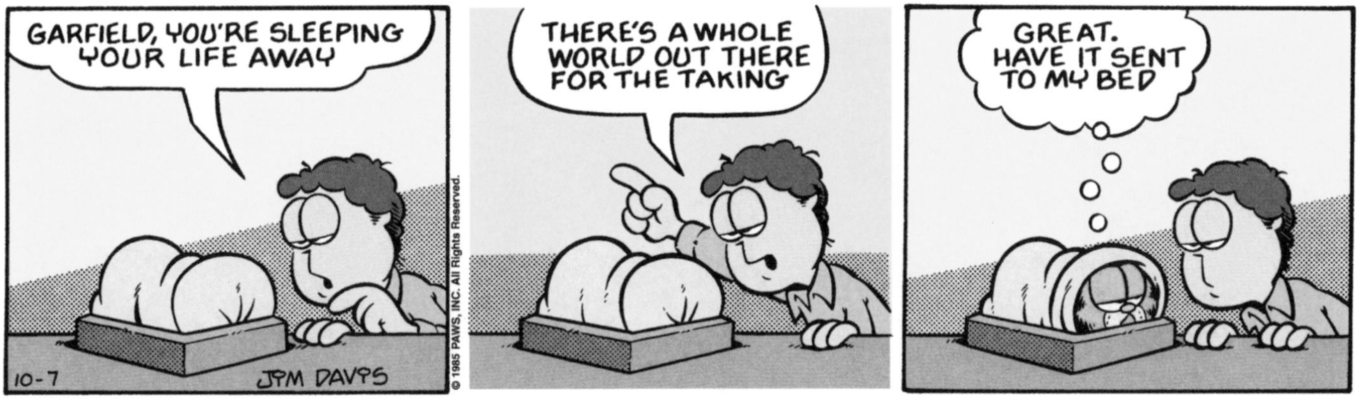
GARFIELD, YOU'RE SLEEPING YOUR LIFE AWAY
10-7
JIM DAVIS
© 1985 PAWS, INC. All Rights Reserved.
THERE'S A WHOLE WORLD OUT THERE FOR THE TAKING
GREAT. HAVE IT SENT TO MY BED

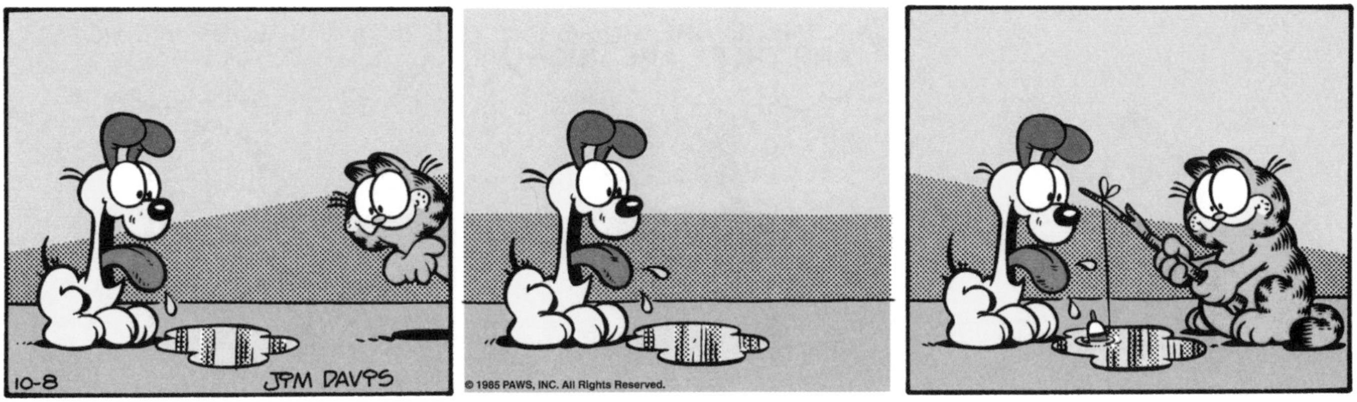
10-8
JIM DAVIS
© 1985 PAWS, INC. All Rights Reserved.

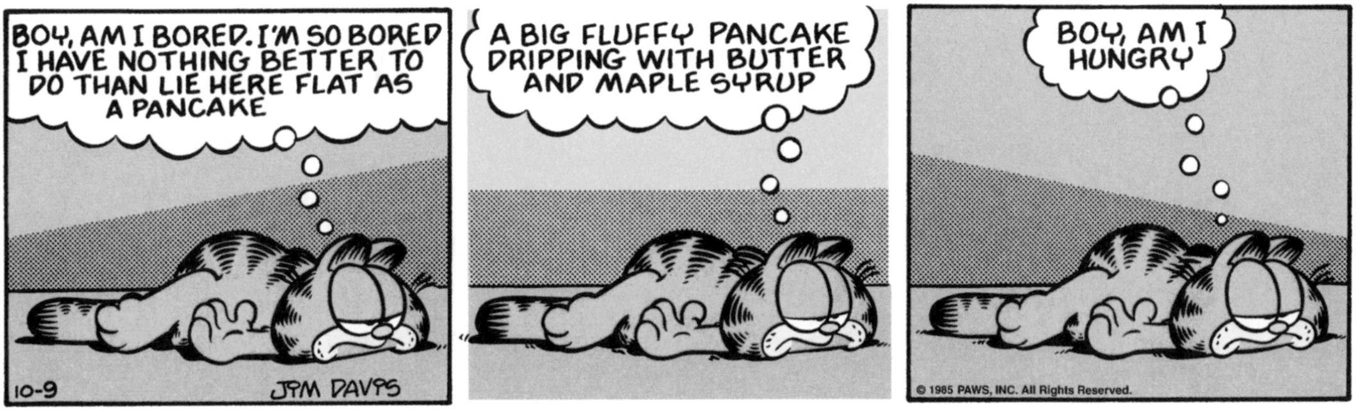
BOY, AM I BORED. I'M SO BORED I HAVE NOTHING BETTER TO DO THAN LIE HERE FLAT AS A PANCAKE
10-9
JIM DAVIS
A BIG FLUFFY PANCAKE DRIPPING WITH BUTTER AND MAPLE SYRUP
BOY, AM I HUNGRY
© 1985 PAWS, INC. All Rights Reserved.

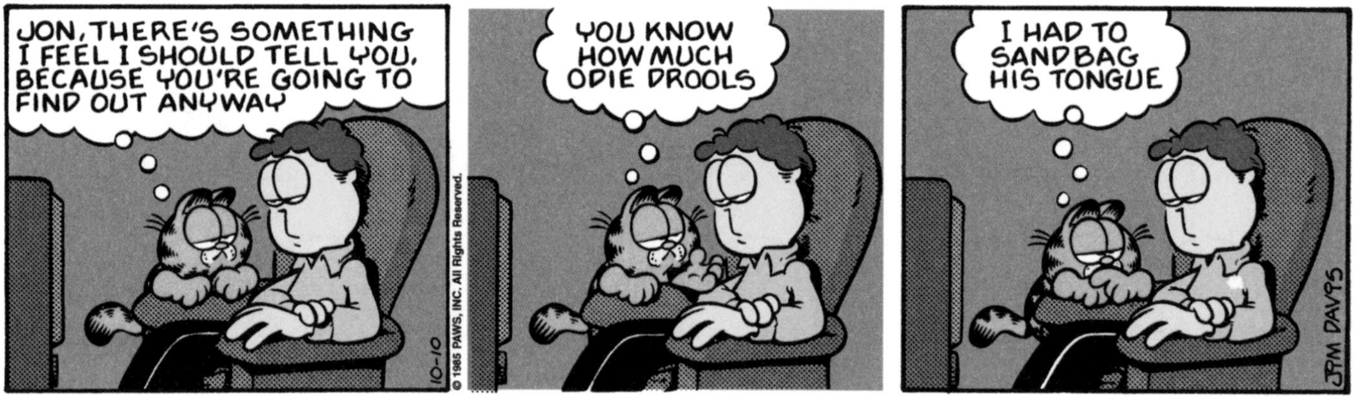
JON, THERE'S SOMETHING I FEEL I SHOULD TELL YOU, BECAUSE YOU'RE GOING TO FIND OUT ANYWAY
YOU KNOW HOW MUCH ODIE DROOLS
I HAD TO SANDBAG HIS TONGUE
10-10
© 1985 PAWS, INC. All Rights Reserved.
JIM DAVIS

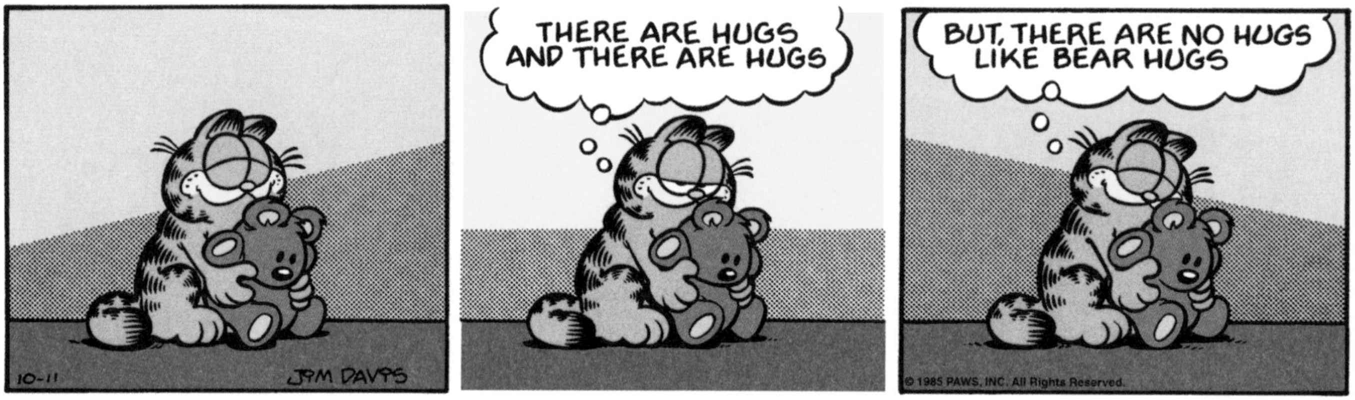
10-11
JIM DAVIS
THERE ARE HUGS AND THERE ARE HUGS
BUT, THERE ARE NO HUGS LIKE BEAR HUGS
© 1985 PAWS, INC. All Rights Reserved.

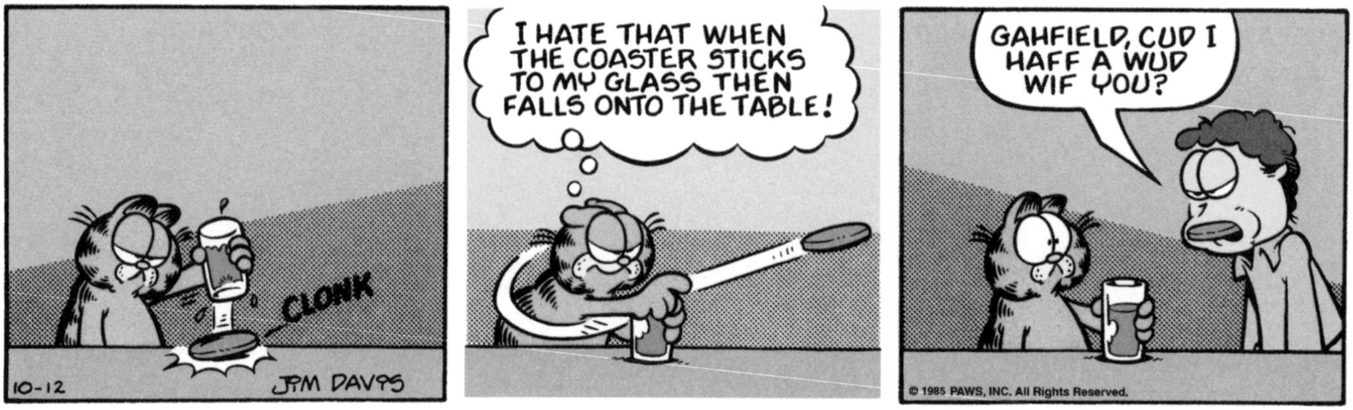
CLONK
10-12
JIM DAVIS
I HATE THAT WHEN THE COASTER STICKS TO MY GLASS THEN FALLS ONTO THE TABLE!
GAHFIELD, CUD I HAFF A WUD WIF YOU?
© 1985 PAWS, INC. All Rights Reserved.

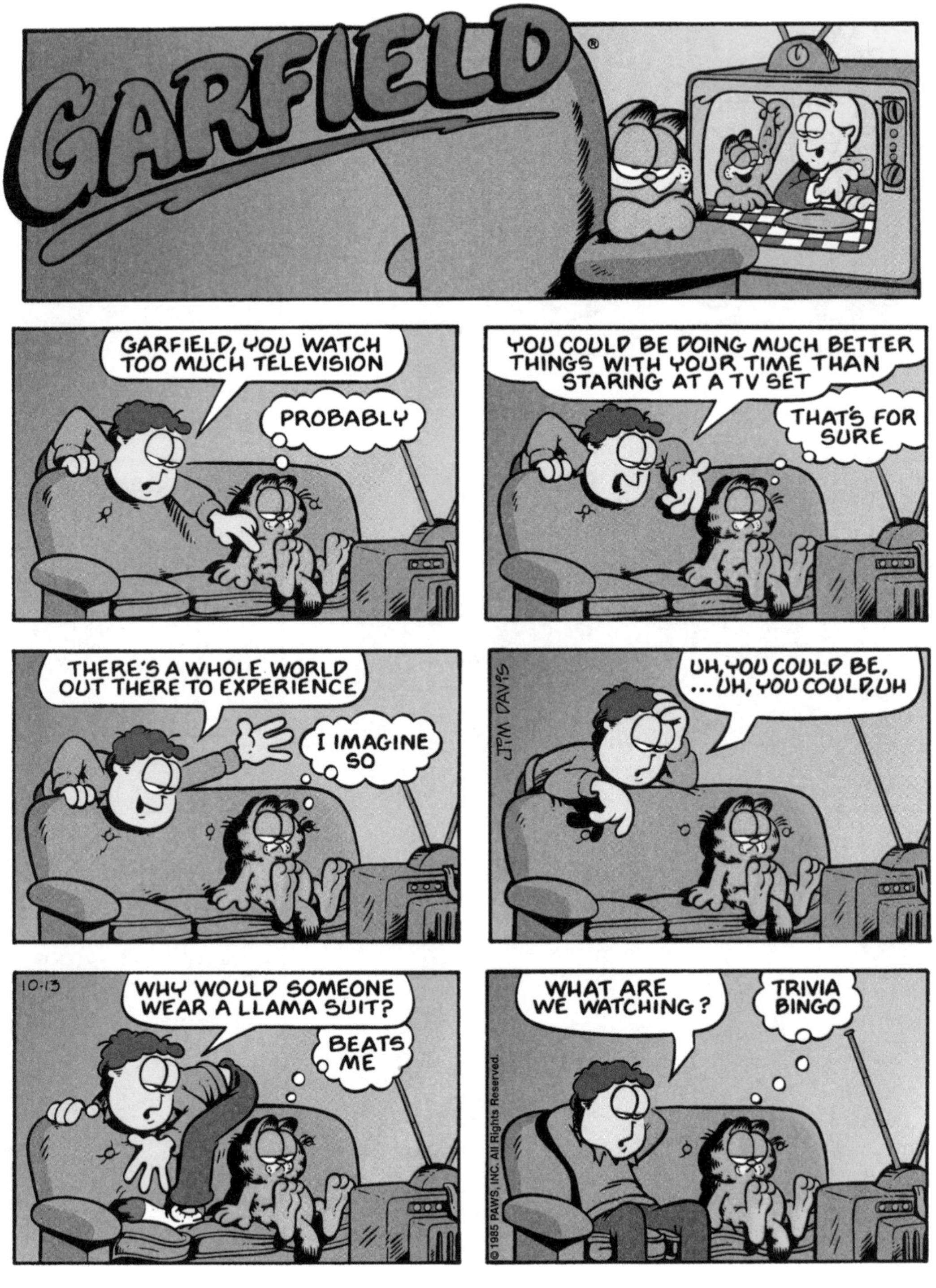
GARFIELD®
GARFIELD, YOU WATCH TOO MUCH TELEVISION
PROBABLY
YOU COULD BE DOING MUCH BETTER THINGS WITH YOUR TIME THAN STARING AT A TV SET
THAT'S FOR SURE
THERE'S A WHOLE WORLD OUT THERE TO EXPERIENCE
I IMAGINE SO
JPM DAVIS
UH, YOU COULD BE, ...UH, YOU COULD, UH
10-13
WHY WOULD SOMEONE WEAR A LLAMA SUIT?
BEATS ME
© 1985 PAWS, INC. All Rights Reserved.
WHAT ARE WE WATCHING?
TRIVIA BINGO

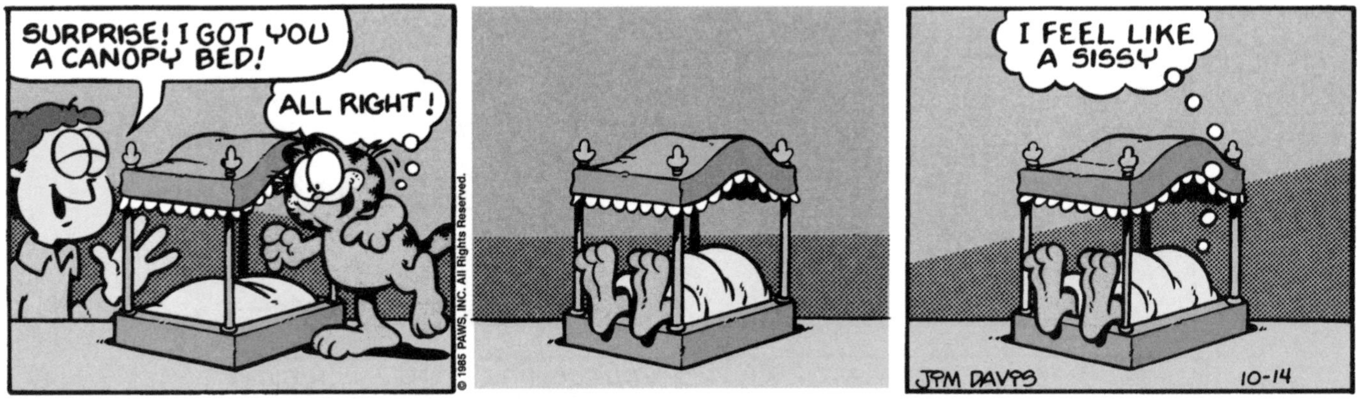
SURPRISE! I GOT YOU A CANOPY BED!
ALL RIGHT!
© 1985 PAWS, INC. All Rights Reserved.
I FEEL LIKE A SISSY
JIM DAVIS
10-14

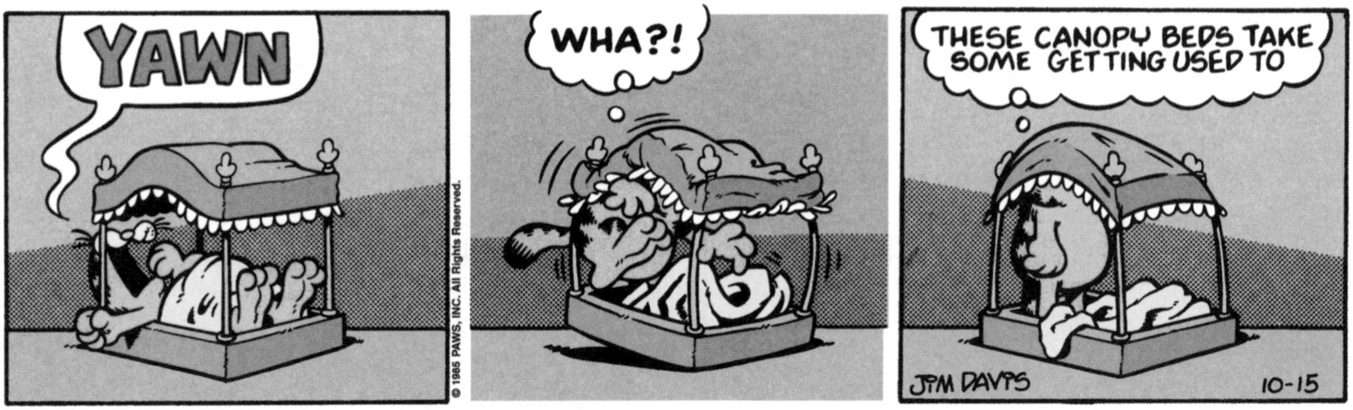
YAWN
© 1985 PAWS, INC. All Rights Reserved.
WHA?!
THESE CANOPY BEDS TAKE SOME GETTING USED TO
JIM DAVIS
10-15

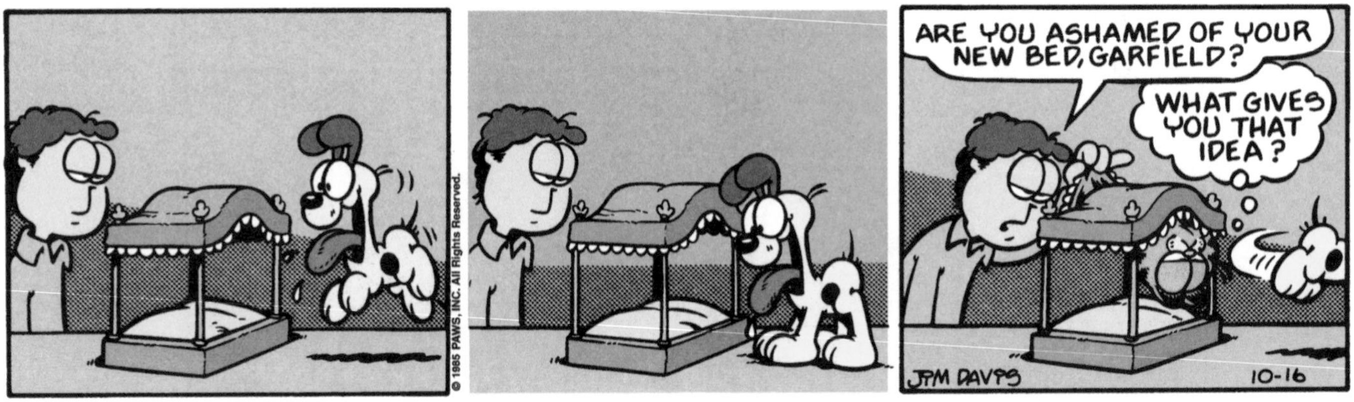
© 1985 PAWS, INC. All Rights Reserved.
ARE YOU ASHAMED OF YOUR NEW BED, GARFIELD?
WHAT GIVES YOU THAT IDEA?
JIM DAVIS
10-16

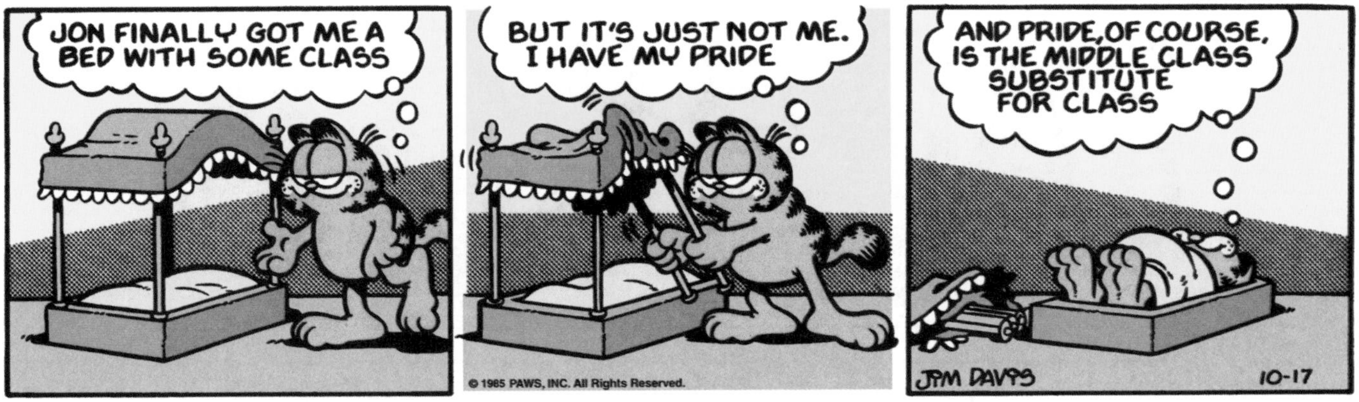
JON FINALLY GOT ME A BED WITH SOME CLASS
BUT IT'S JUST NOT ME. I HAVE MY PRIDE
AND PRIDE, OF COURSE, IS THE MIDDLE CLASS SUBSTITUTE FOR CLASS
© 1985 PAWS, INC. All Rights Reserved.
JIM DAVIS
10-17

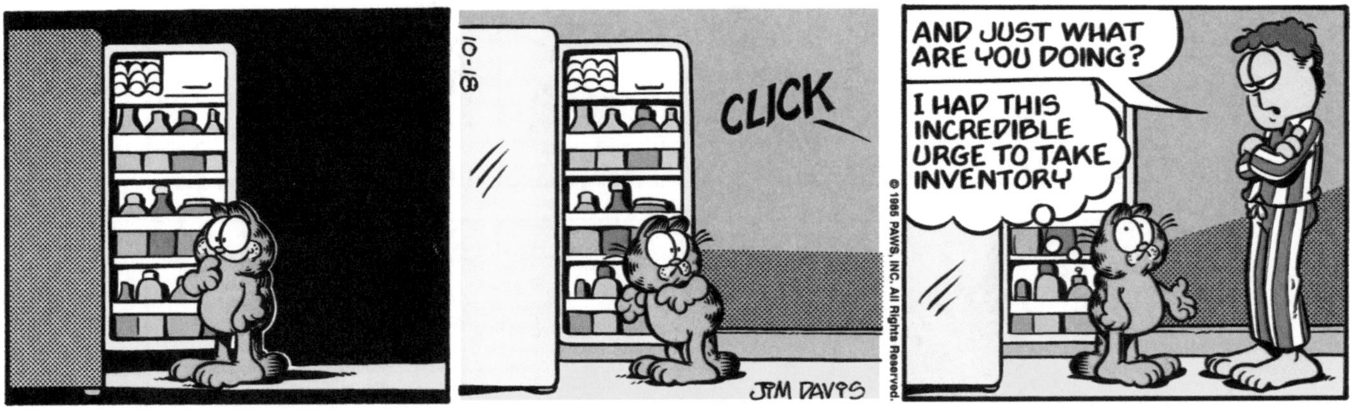
10-18
CLICK
JIM DAVIS
© 1985 PAWS, INC. All Rights Reserved.
AND JUST WHAT ARE YOU DOING?
I HAD THIS INCREDIBLE URGE TO TAKE INVENTORY

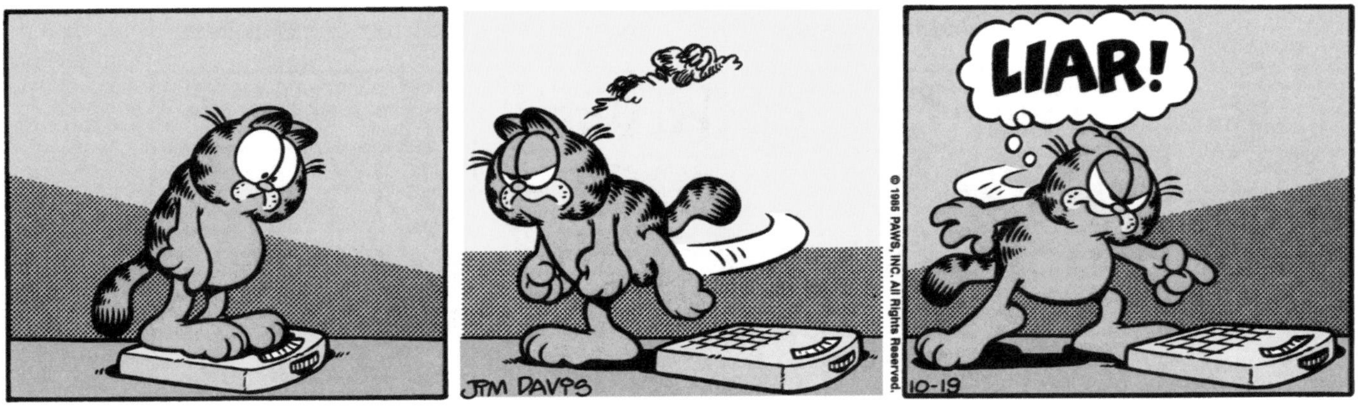
JIM DAVIS
© 1985 PAWS, INC. All Rights Reserved.
LIAR!
10-19

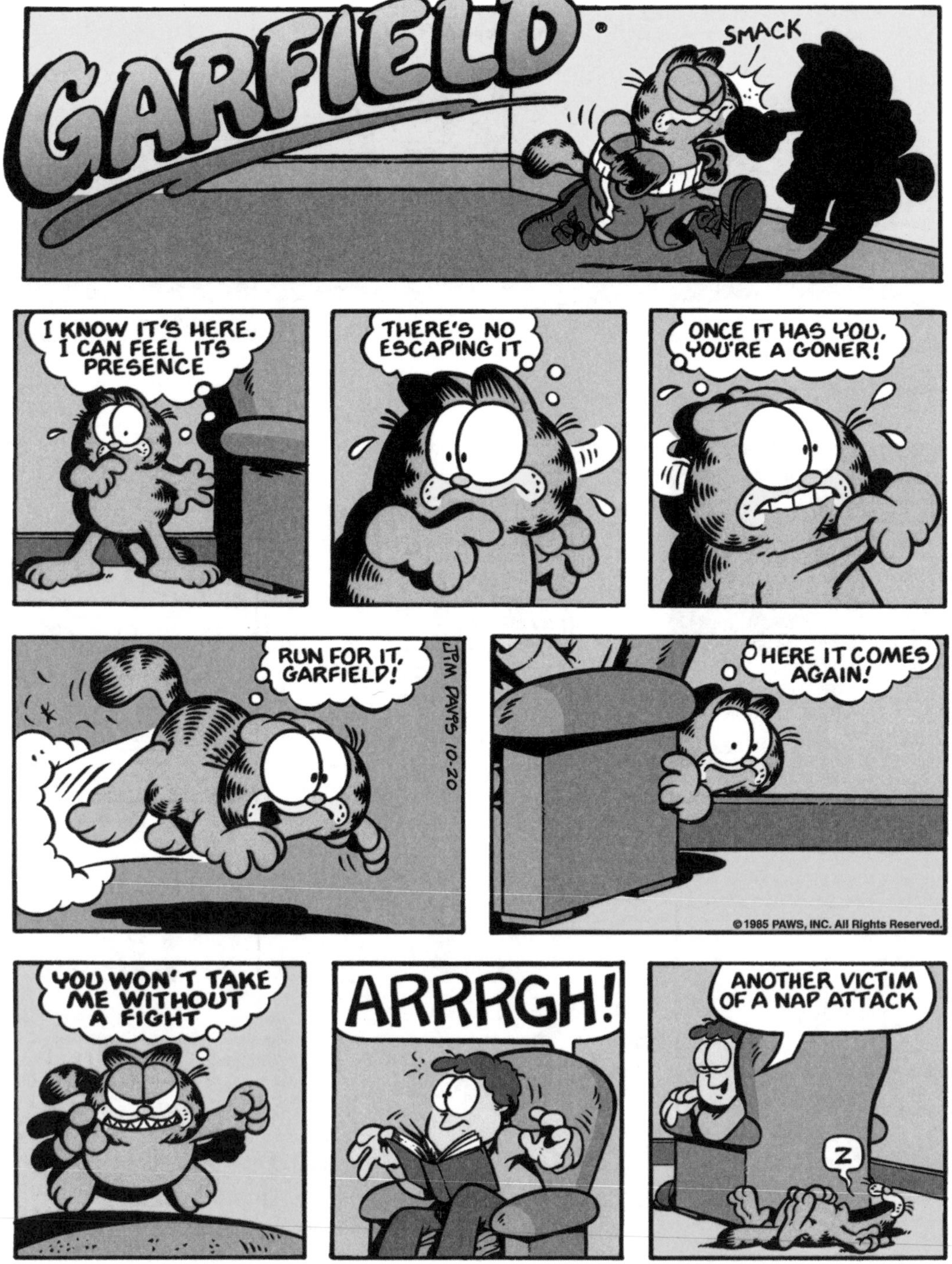
GARFIELD®
SMACK
I KNOW IT'S HERE. I CAN FEEL ITS PRESENCE
THERE'S NO ESCAPING IT
ONCE IT HAS YOU, YOU'RE A GONER!
RUN FOR IT, GARFIELD!
JIM DAVIS 10-20
HERE IT COMES AGAIN!
©1985 PAWS, INC. All Rights Reserved.
YOU WON'T TAKE ME WITHOUT A FIGHT
ARRRGH!
ANOTHER VICTIM OF A NAP ATTACK
Z

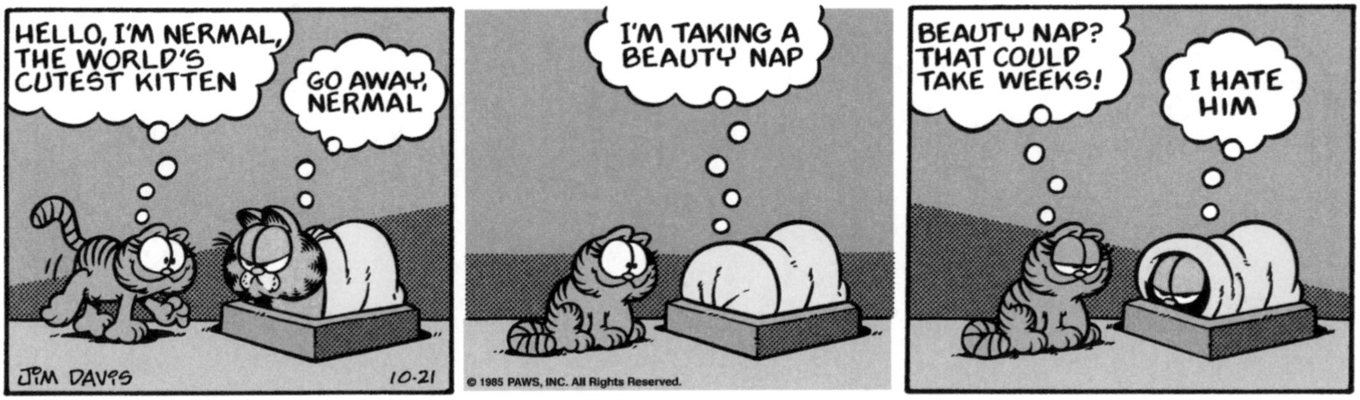
HELLO, I'M NERMAL, THE WORLD'S CUTEST KITTEN
GO AWAY, NERMAL
JIM DAVIS
10-21
I'M TAKING A BEAUTY NAP
© 1985 PAWS, INC. All Rights Reserved.
BEAUTY NAP? THAT COULD TAKE WEEKS!
I HATE HIM

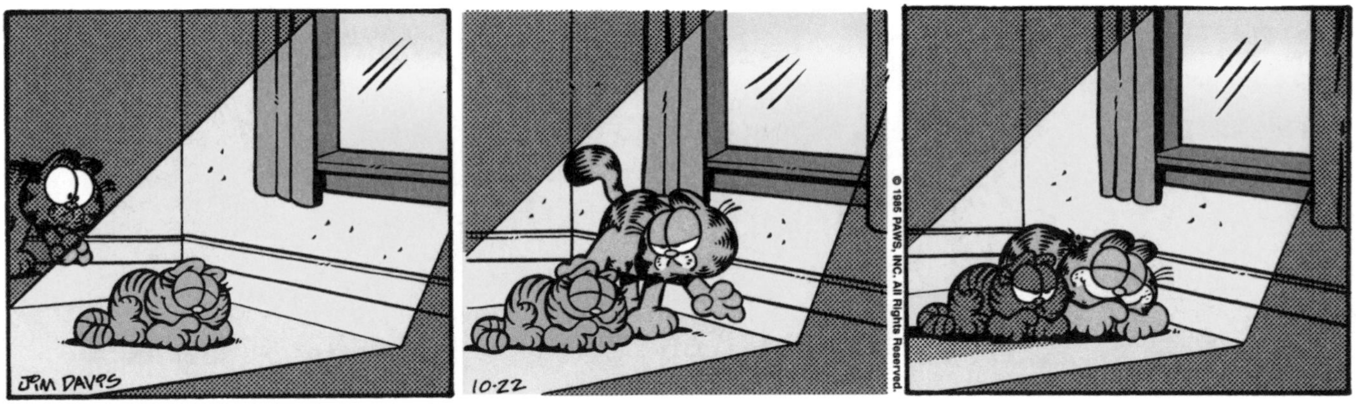
JIM DAVIS
10-22
© 1985 PAWS, INC. All Rights Reserved.

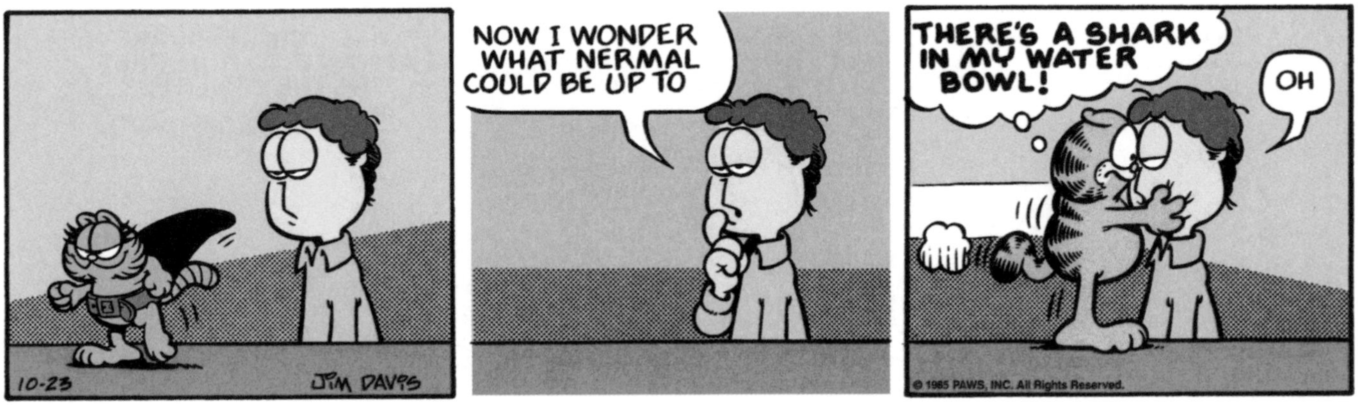
10-23
JIM DAVIS
NOW I WONDER WHAT NERMAL COULD BE UP TO
THERE'S A SHARK IN MY WATER BOWL!
OH
© 1985 PAWS, INC. All Rights Reserved.

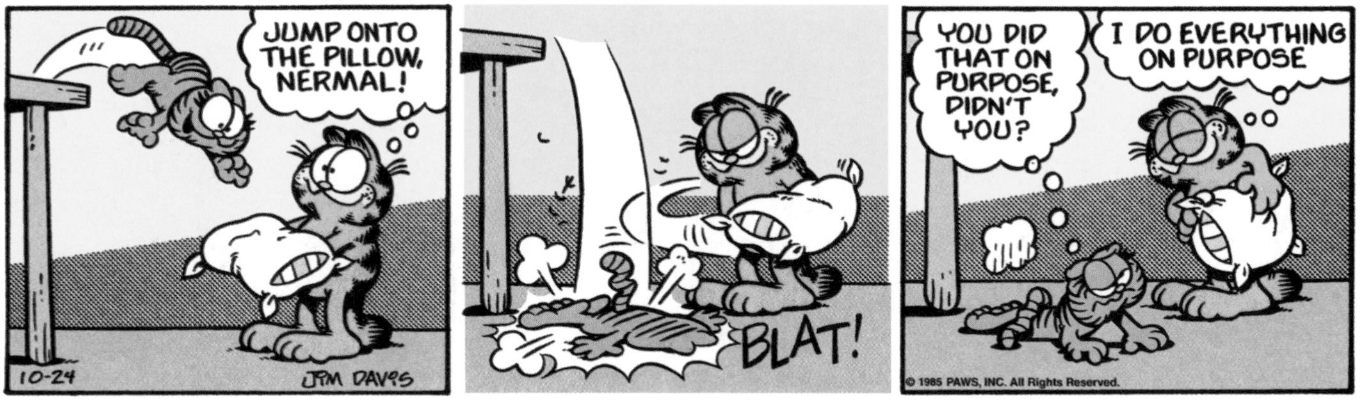
JUMP ONTO THE PILLOW, NERMAL!
10-24
JIM DAVIS
BLAT!
YOU DID THAT ON PURPOSE, DIDN'T YOU?
I DO EVERYTHING ON PURPOSE
© 1985 PAWS, INC. All Rights Reserved.

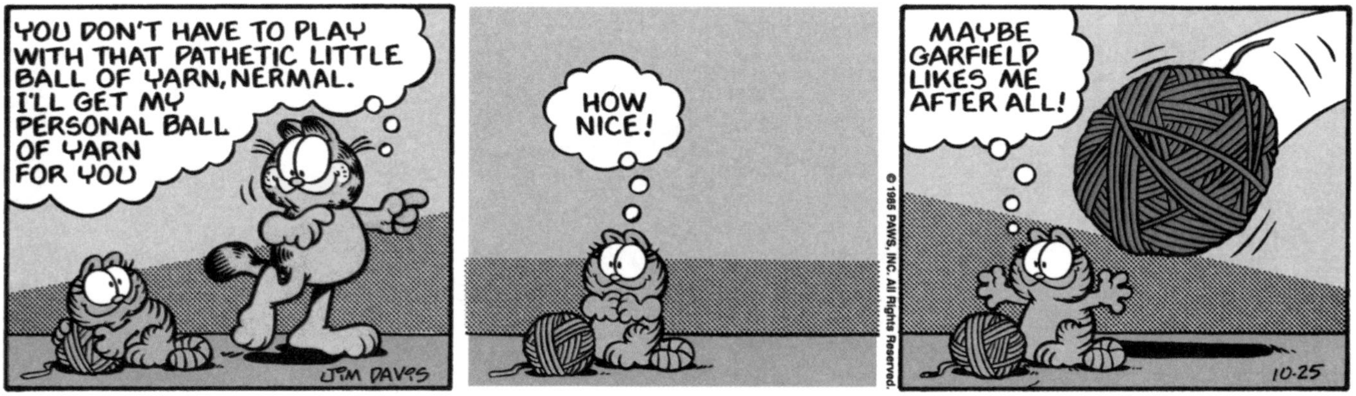
YOU DON'T HAVE TO PLAY WITH THAT PATHETIC LITTLE BALL OF YARN, NERMAL. I'LL GET MY PERSONAL BALL OF YARN FOR YOU
JIM DAVIS
HOW NICE!
© 1985 PAWS, INC. All Rights Reserved.
MAYBE GARFIELD LIKES ME AFTER ALL!
10-25

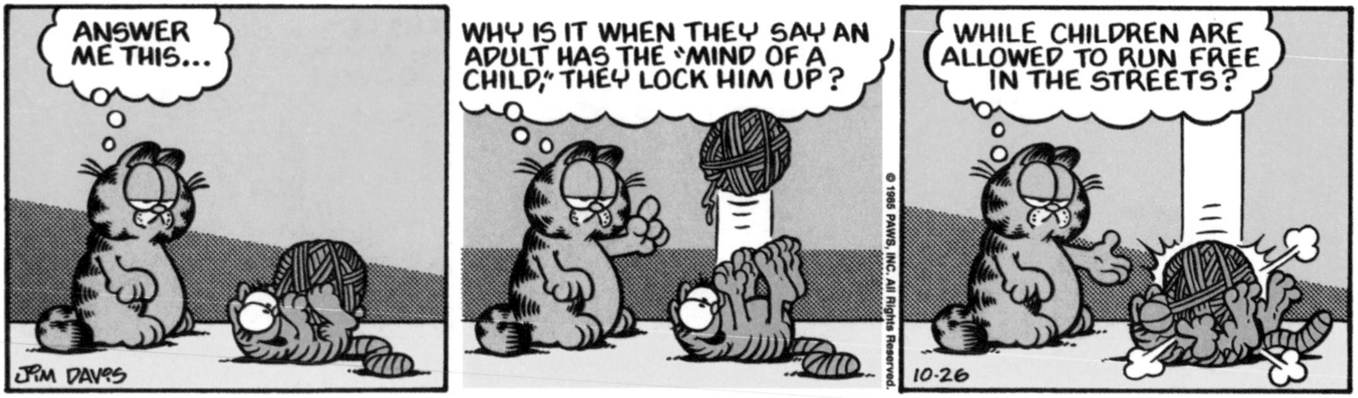
ANSWER ME THIS...
JIM DAVIS
WHY IS IT WHEN THEY SAY AN ADULT HAS THE "MIND OF A CHILD," THEY LOCK HIM UP?
© 1985 PAWS, INC. All Rights Reserved.
WHILE CHILDREN ARE ALLOWED TO RUN FREE IN THE STREETS?
10-26

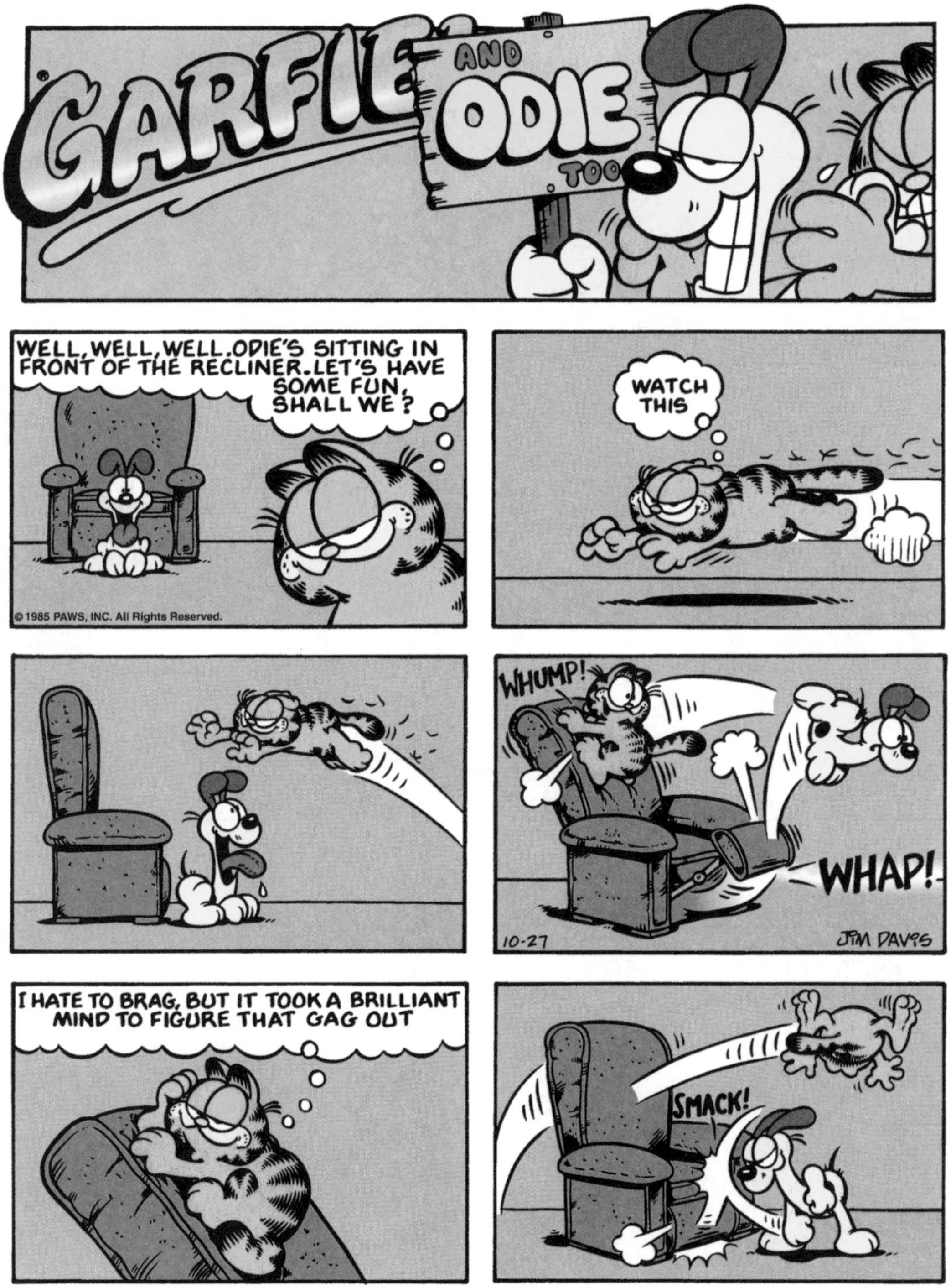
GARFIELD
AND
ODIE
TOO
WELL, WELL, WELL. ODIE'S SITTING IN FRONT OF THE RECLINER. LET'S HAVE SOME FUN, SHALL WE?
© 1985 PAWS, INC. All Rights Reserved.
WATCH THIS
WHUMP!
WHAP!
10-27
JIM DAVIS
I HATE TO BRAG, BUT IT TOOK A BRILLIANT MIND TO FIGURE THAT GAG OUT
SMACK!

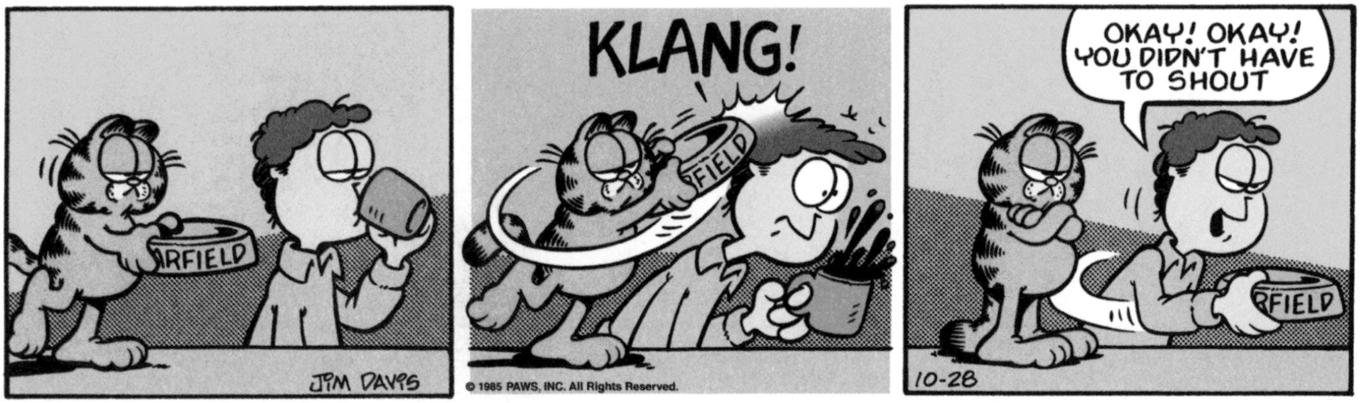
RFIELD
JIM DAVIS
KLANG!
FIELD
RFIELD
© 1985 PAWS, INC. All Rights Reserved.
OKAY! OKAY! YOU DIDN'T HAVE TO SHOUT
RFIELD
10-28

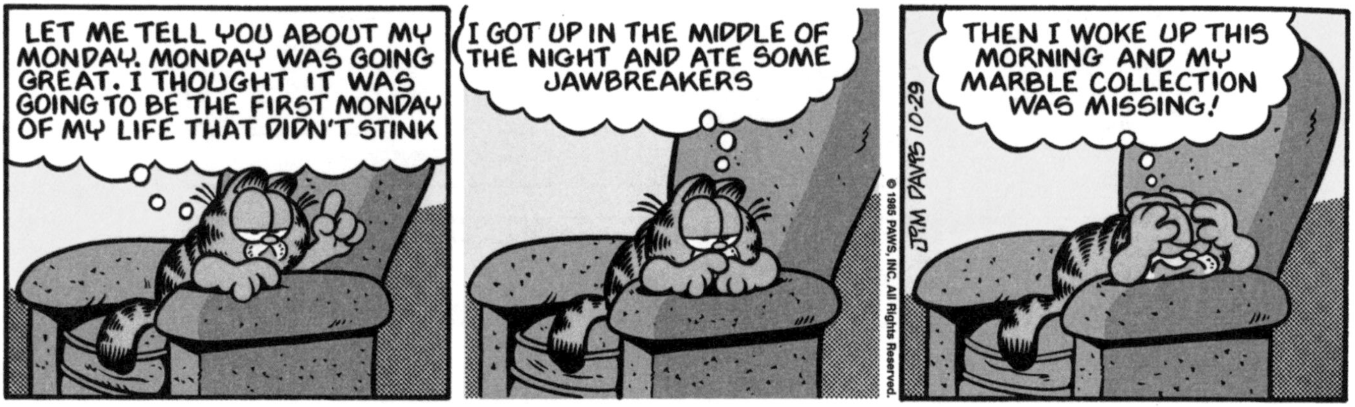
LET ME TELL YOU ABOUT MY MONDAY. MONDAY WAS GOING GREAT. I THOUGHT IT WAS GOING TO BE THE FIRST MONDAY OF MY LIFE THAT DIDN'T STINK
I GOT UP IN THE MIDDLE OF THE NIGHT AND ATE SOME JAWBREAKERS
© 1985 PAWS, INC. All Rights Reserved.
JIM DAVIS 10-29
THEN I WOKE UP THIS MORNING AND MY MARBLE COLLECTION WAS MISSING!

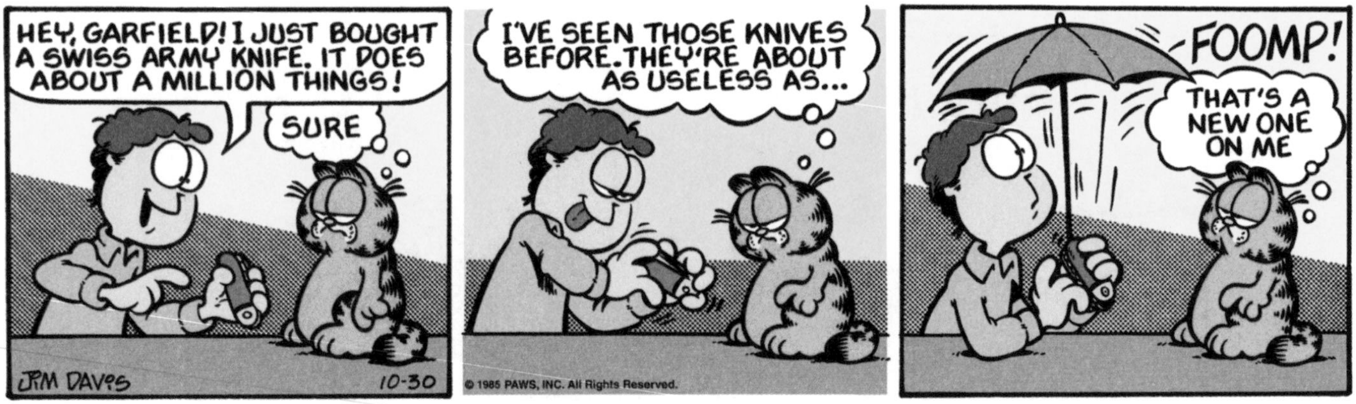
HEY, GARFIELD! I JUST BOUGHT A SWISS ARMY KNIFE. IT DOES ABOUT A MILLION THINGS!
SURE
JIM DAVIS
10-30
I'VE SEEN THOSE KNIVES BEFORE. THEY'RE ABOUT AS USELESS AS...
© 1985 PAWS, INC. All Rights Reserved.
FOOMP!
THAT'S A NEW ONE ON ME

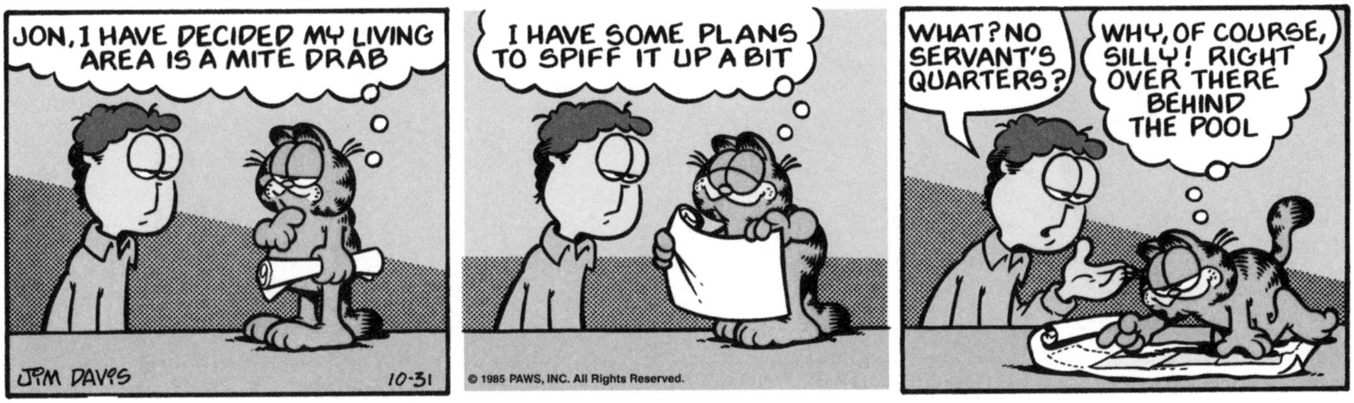
JON, I HAVE DECIDED MY LIVING AREA IS A MITE DRAB
JIM DAVIS
10-31
I HAVE SOME PLANS TO SPIFF IT UP A BIT
© 1985 PAWS, INC. All Rights Reserved.
WHAT? NO SERVANT'S QUARTERS?
WHY, OF COURSE, SILLY! RIGHT OVER THERE BEHIND THE POOL

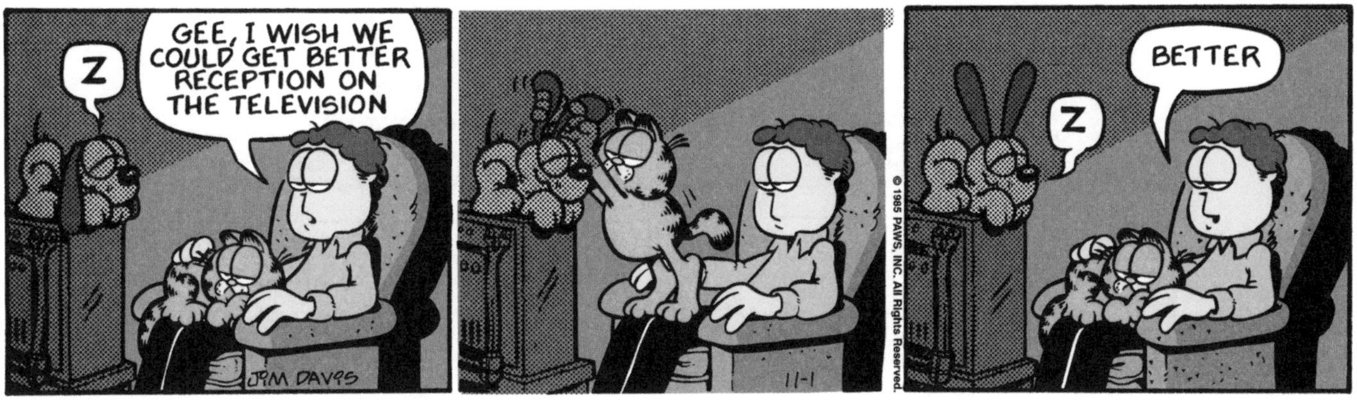
Z
GEE, I WISH WE COULD GET BETTER RECEPTION ON THE TELEVISION
JIM DAVIS
11-1
© 1985 PAWS, INC. All Rights Reserved.
Z
BETTER

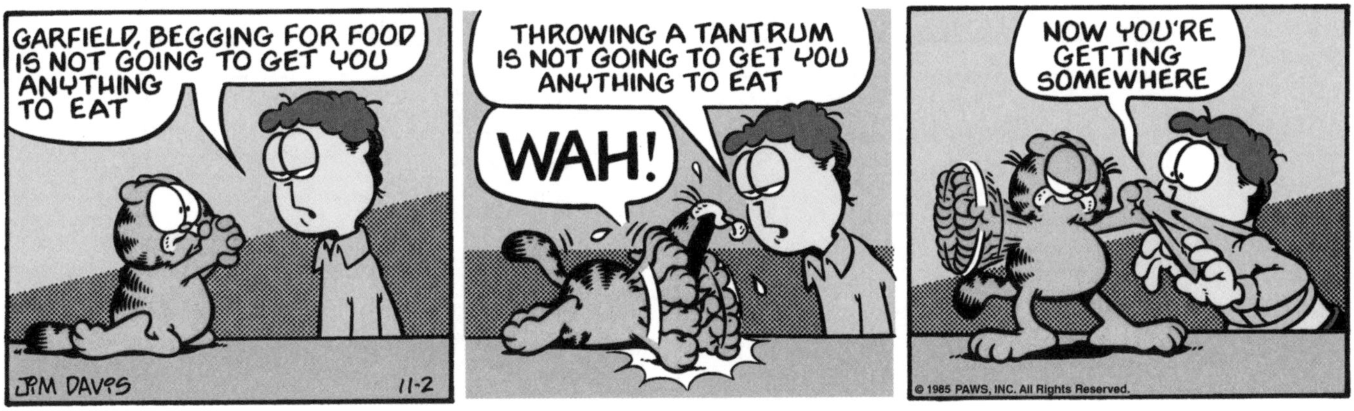
GARFIELD, BEGGING FOR FOOD IS NOT GOING TO GET YOU ANYTHING TO EAT
JIM DAVIS
11-2
THROWING A TANTRUM IS NOT GOING TO GET YOU ANYTHING TO EAT
WAH!
NOW YOU'RE GETTING SOMEWHERE
© 1985 PAWS, INC. All Rights Reserved.

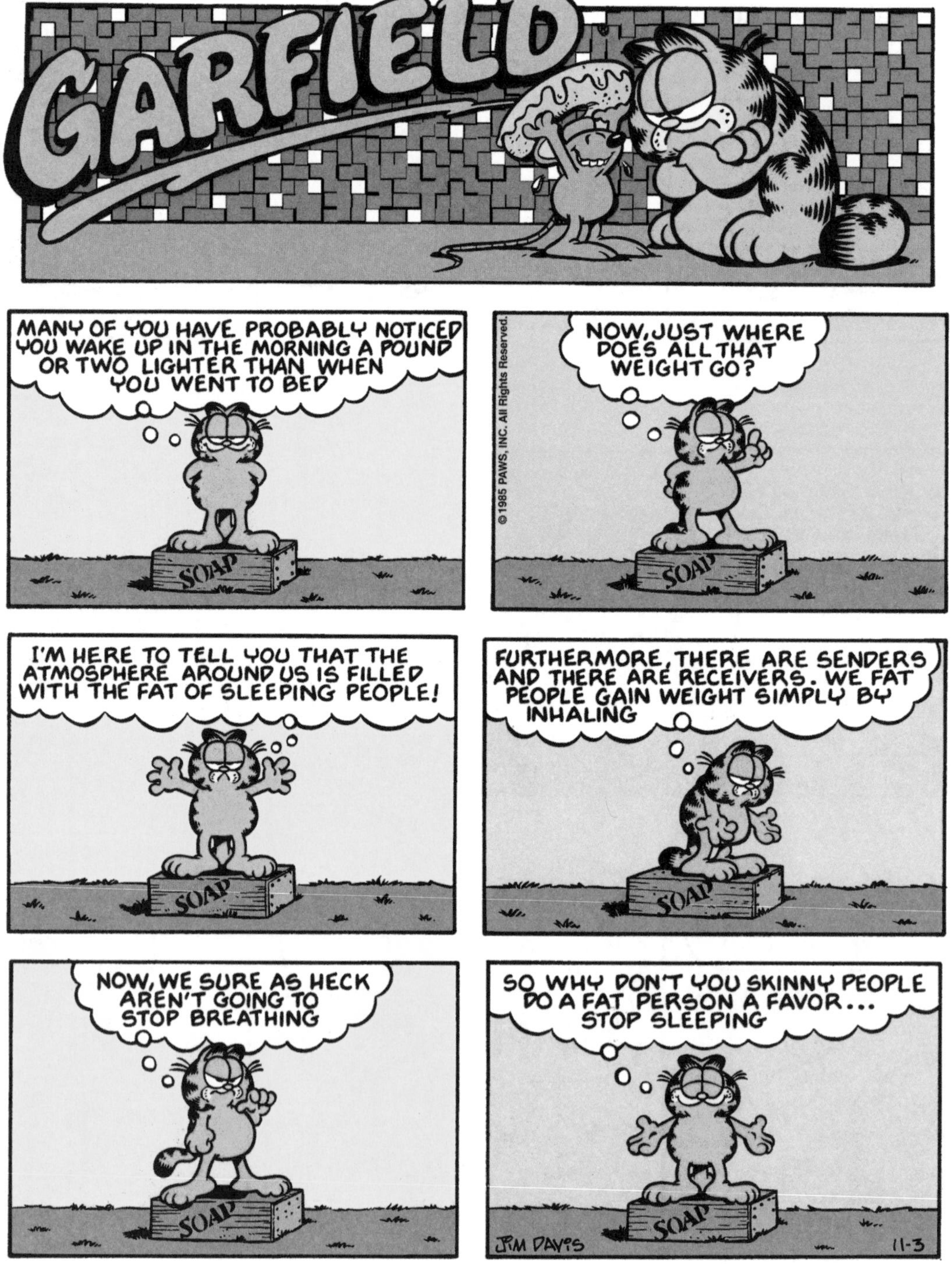
GARFIELD
MANY OF YOU HAVE PROBABLY NOTICED YOU WAKE UP IN THE MORNING A POUND OR TWO LIGHTER THAN WHEN YOU WENT TO BED
SOAP
NOW, JUST WHERE DOES ALL THAT WEIGHT GO?
©1985 PAWS, INC. All Rights Reserved.
I'M HERE TO TELL YOU THAT THE ATMOSPHERE AROUND US IS FILLED WITH THE FAT OF SLEEPING PEOPLE!
FURTHERMORE, THERE ARE SENDERS AND THERE ARE RECEIVERS. WE FAT PEOPLE GAIN WEIGHT SIMPLY BY INHALING
NOW, WE SURE AS HECK AREN'T GOING TO STOP BREATHING
SO WHY DON'T YOU SKINNY PEOPLE DO A FAT PERSON A FAVOR... STOP SLEEPING
JIM DAVIS
11-3

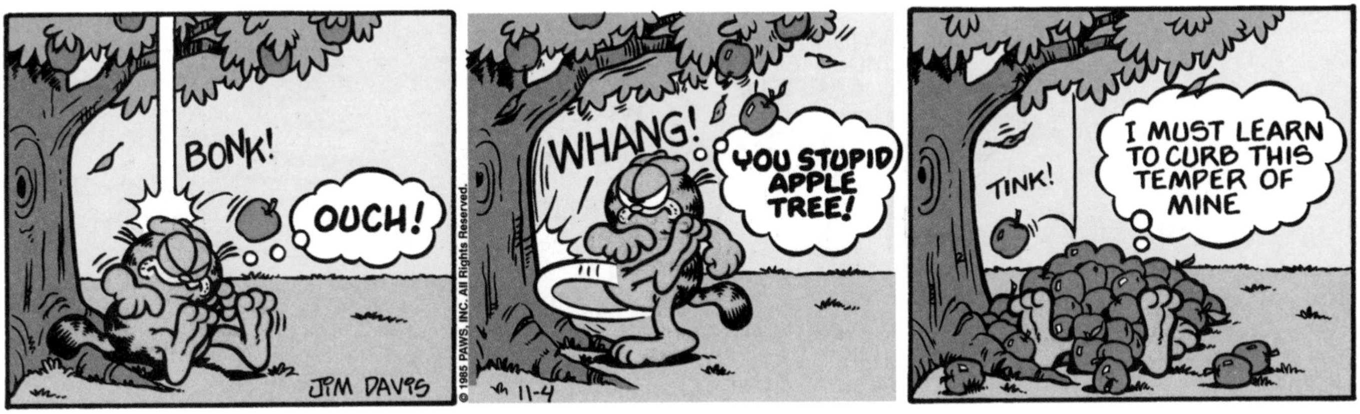
BONK!
OUCH!
JIM DAVIS
© 1985 PAWS, INC. All Rights Reserved.
WHANG!
YOU STUPID APPLE TREE!
11-4
TINK!
I MUST LEARN TO CURB THIS TEMPER OF MINE

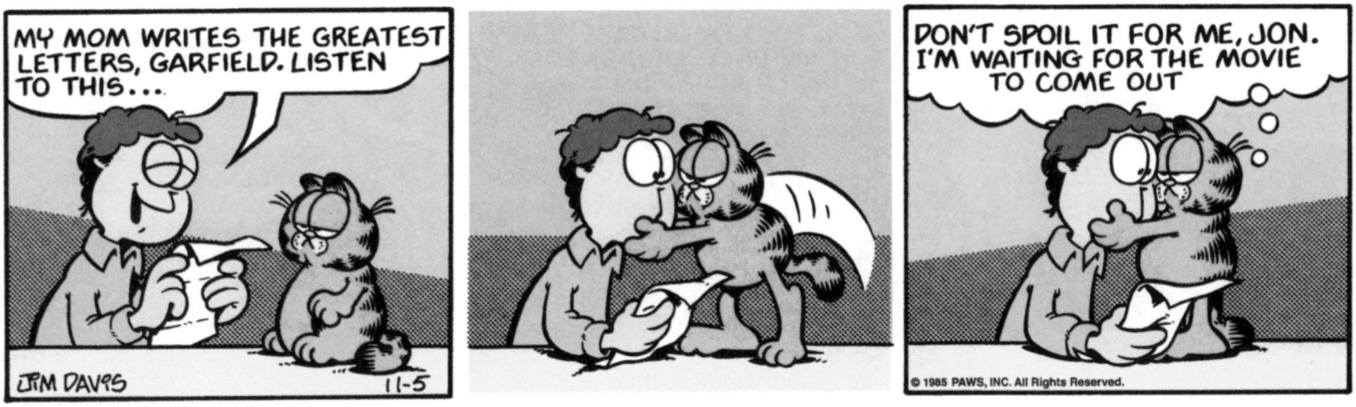
MY MOM WRITES THE GREATEST LETTERS, GARFIELD. LISTEN TO THIS...
JIM DAVIS
11-5
DON'T SPOIL IT FOR ME, JON. I'M WAITING FOR THE MOVIE TO COME OUT
© 1985 PAWS, INC. All Rights Reserved.

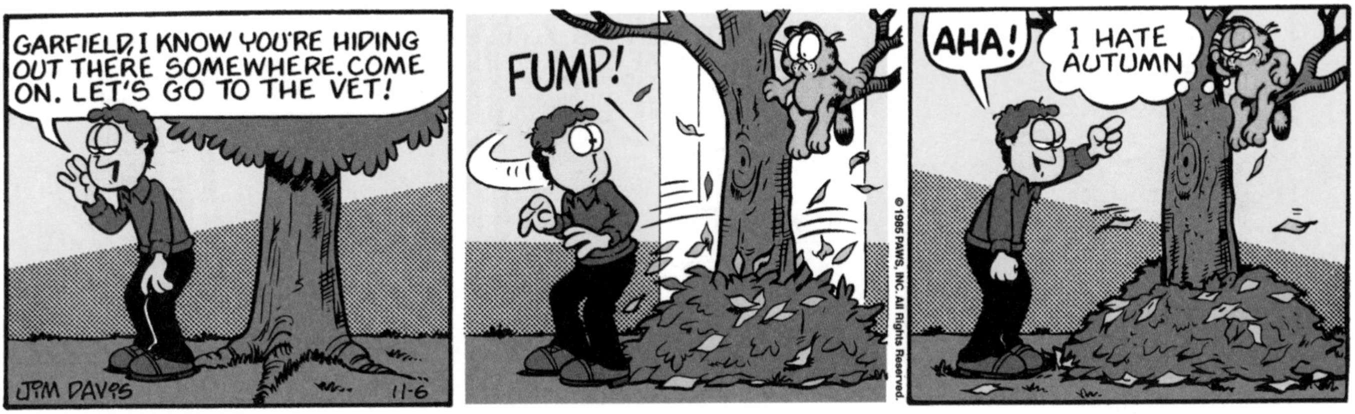
GARFIELD, I KNOW YOU'RE HIDING OUT THERE SOMEWHERE. COME ON. LET'S GO TO THE VET!
JIM DAVIS
11-6
FUMP!
© 1985 PAWS, INC. All Rights Reserved.
AHA!
I HATE AUTUMN

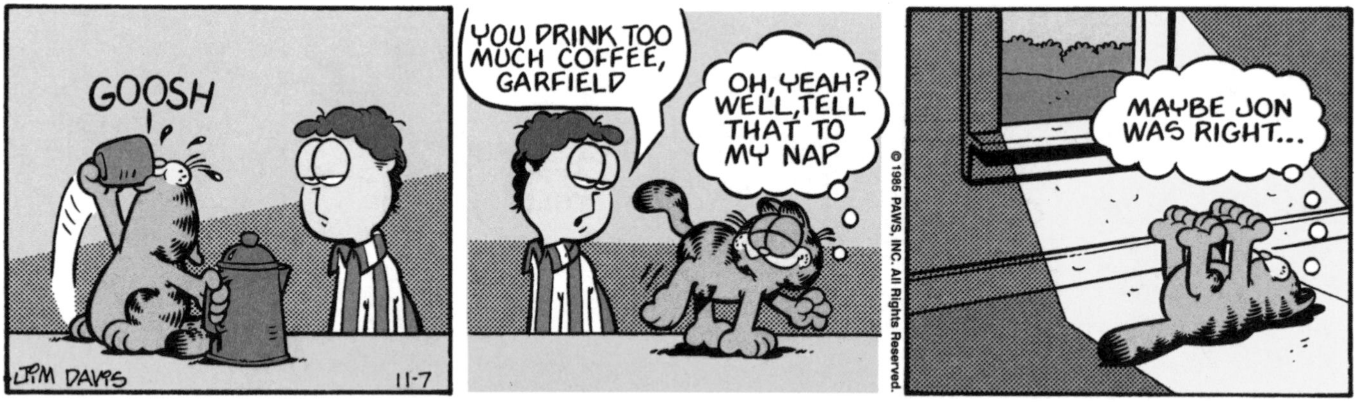
GOOSH
JIM DAVIS
11-7
YOU DRINK TOO MUCH COFFEE, GARFIELD
OH, YEAH? WELL, TELL THAT TO MY NAP
© 1985 PAWS, INC. All Rights Reserved.
MAYBE JON WAS RIGHT...

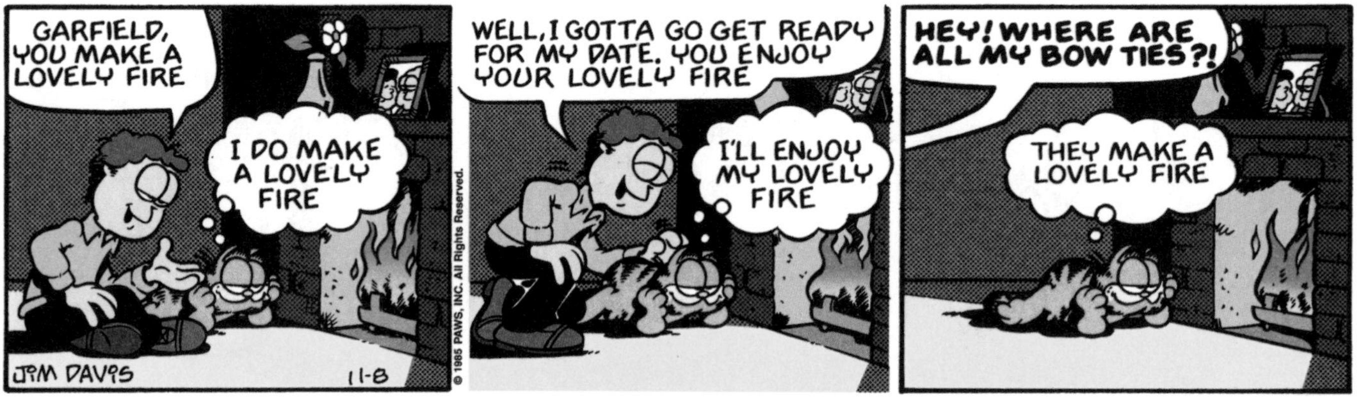
GARFIELD, YOU MAKE A LOVELY FIRE
I DO MAKE A LOVELY FIRE
JIM DAVIS
11-8
© 1985 PAWS, INC. All Rights Reserved.
WELL, I GOTTA GO GET READY FOR MY DATE. YOU ENJOY YOUR LOVELY FIRE
I'LL ENJOY MY LOVELY FIRE
HEY! WHERE ARE ALL MY BOW TIES?!
THEY MAKE A LOVELY FIRE

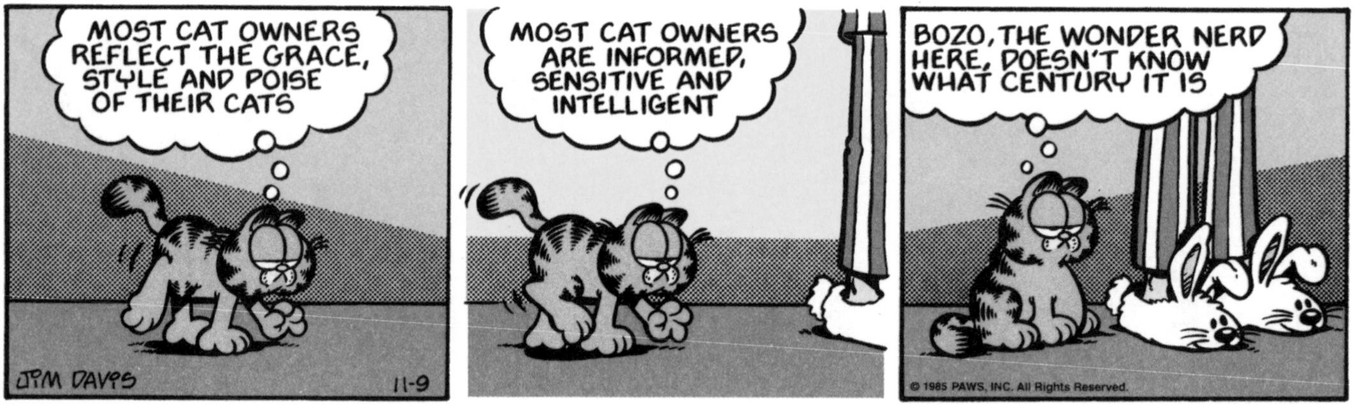
MOST CAT OWNERS REFLECT THE GRACE, STYLE AND POISE OF THEIR CATS
JIM DAVIS
11-9
MOST CAT OWNERS ARE INFORMED, SENSITIVE AND INTELLIGENT
BOZO, THE WONDER NERD HERE, DOESN'T KNOW WHAT CENTURY IT IS
© 1985 PAWS, INC. All Rights Reserved.

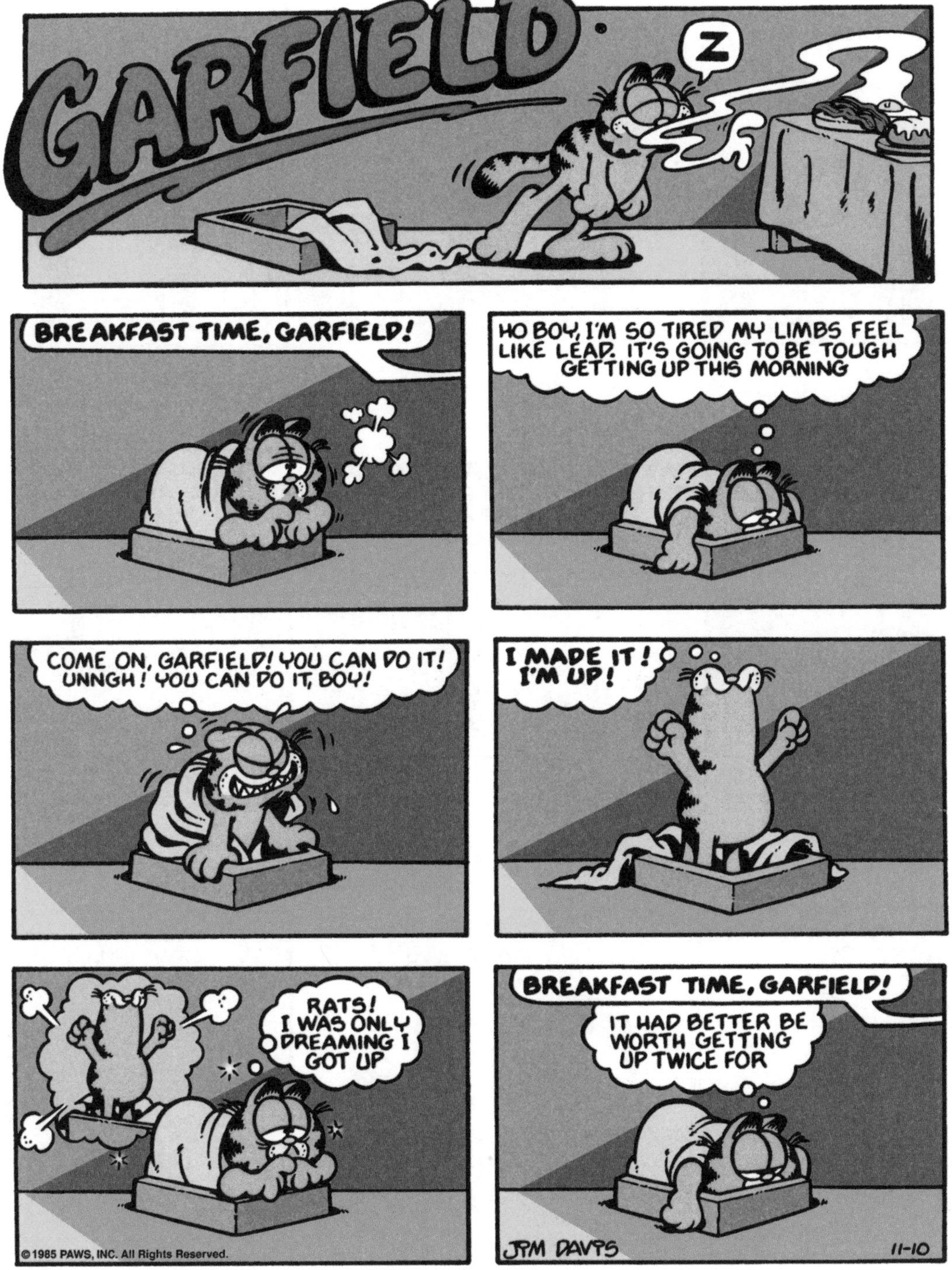
GARFIELD
Z
BREAKFAST TIME, GARFIELD!
HO BOY, I'M SO TIRED MY LIMBS FEEL LIKE LEAD. IT'S GOING TO BE TOUGH GETTING UP THIS MORNING
COME ON, GARFIELD! YOU CAN DO IT! UNNGH! YOU CAN DO IT, BOY!
I MADE IT! I'M UP!
RATS! I WAS ONLY DREAMING I GOT UP
BREAKFAST TIME, GARFIELD!
IT HAD BETTER BE WORTH GETTING UP TWICE FOR
© 1985 PAWS, INC. All Rights Reserved.
JIM DAVIS
11-10

OH, VERY WELL, GARFIELD, YOU MAY HAVE ONE BITE OF MY SPAGHETTI
© 1985 PAWS, INC. All Rights Reserved.
TWIRL TWIRL TWIRL
I DON'T GIVE THAT CAT ENOUGH CREDIT
JIM DAVIS 11-11

CAPTAIN! CAPTAIN! THERE'S A BLACK HOLE DEAD AHEAD!
11-12
JIM DAVIS
WE CAN'T TURN BACK! THE GRAVITATIONAL PULL IS TOO GREAT! ARRRRRRGH!
THEY JUST WENT WHERE NO MAN HAS GONE BEFORE
© 1985 PAWS, INC. All Rights Reserved.

WHICH DO YOU WANT, GARFIELD? THE LASAGNA OR THE BANANAS?
11-13
JIM DAVIS
© 1985 PAWS, INC. All Rights Reserved.
THE BANANAS?
WE'RE TALKING PLAY VALUE HERE

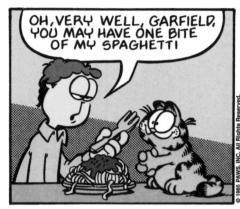

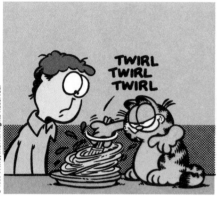

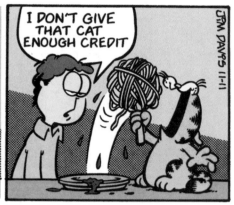

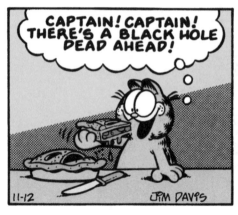

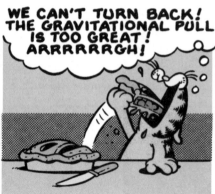

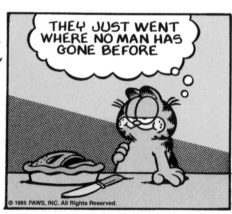

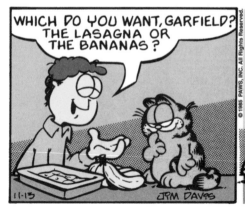

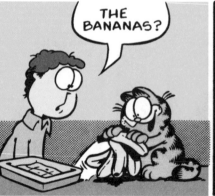

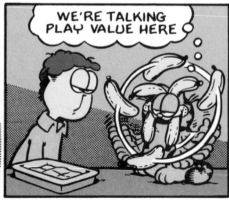

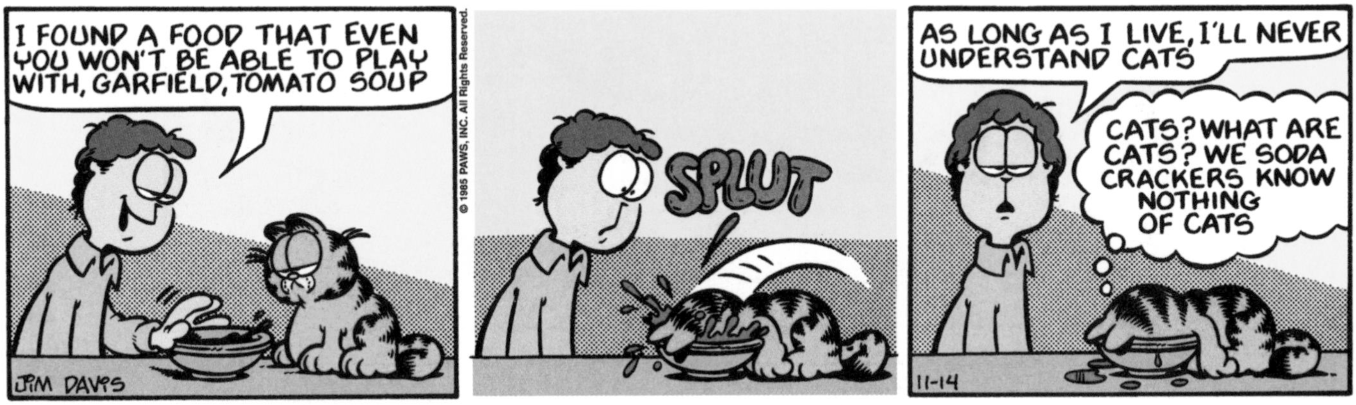
I FOUND A FOOD THAT EVEN YOU WON'T BE ABLE TO PLAY WITH, GARFIELD, TOMATO SOUP
JIM DAVIS
© 1985 PAWS, INC. All Rights Reserved.
SPLUT
AS LONG AS I LIVE, I'LL NEVER UNDERSTAND CATS
CATS? WHAT ARE CATS? WE SODA CRACKERS KNOW NOTHING OF CATS
11-14

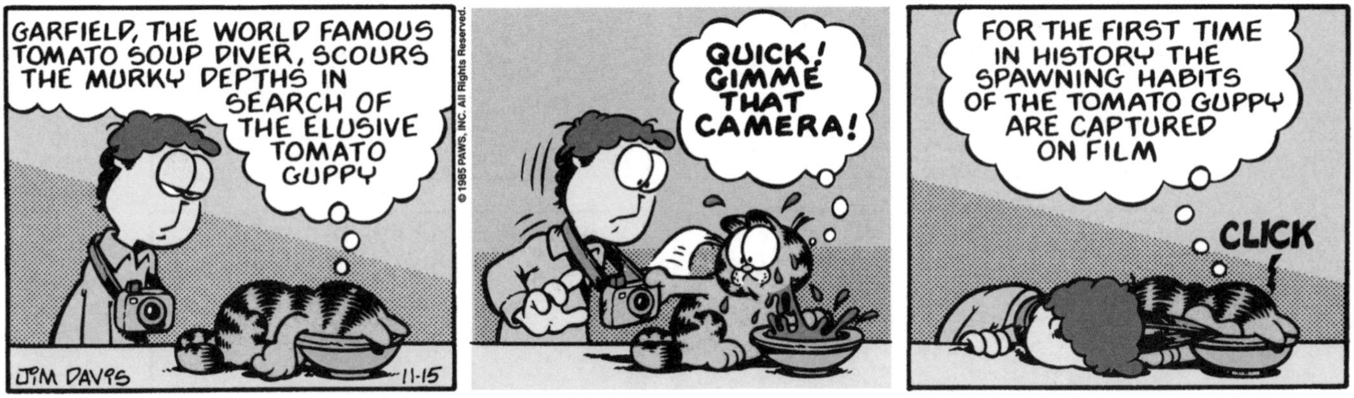
GARFIELD, THE WORLD FAMOUS TOMATO SOUP DIVER, SCOURS THE MURKY DEPTHS IN SEARCH OF THE ELUSIVE TOMATO GUPPY
JIM DAVIS
11-15
© 1985 PAWS, INC. All Rights Reserved.
QUICK! GIMME THAT CAMERA!
FOR THE FIRST TIME IN HISTORY THE SPAWNING HABITS OF THE TOMATO GUPPY ARE CAPTURED ON FILM
CLICK

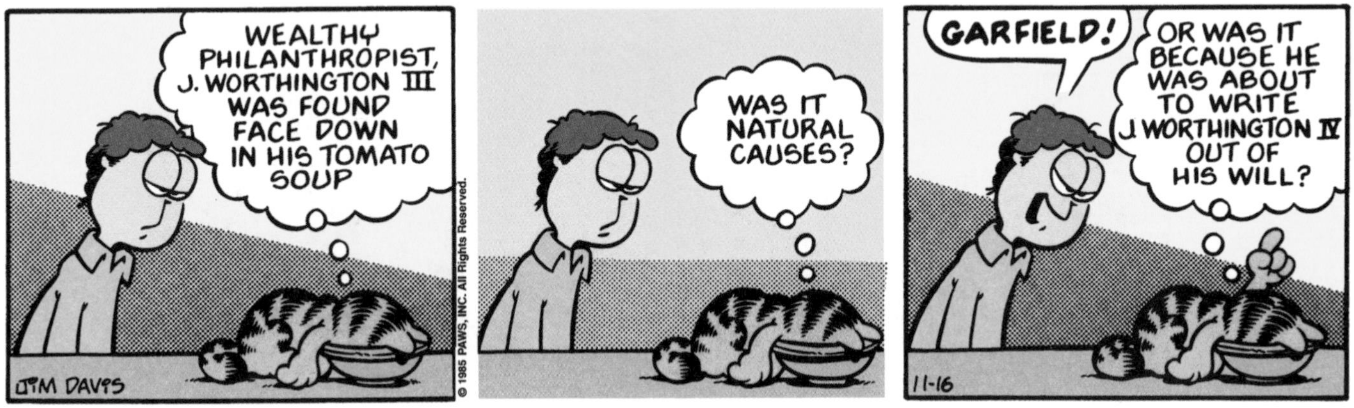
WEALTHY PHILANTHROPIST, J. WORTHINGTON III WAS FOUND FACE DOWN IN HIS TOMATO SOUP
JIM DAVIS
© 1985 PAWS, INC. All Rights Reserved.
WAS IT NATURAL CAUSES?
GARFIELD!
OR WAS IT BECAUSE HE WAS ABOUT TO WRITE J. WORTHINGTON IV OUT OF HIS WILL?
11-16

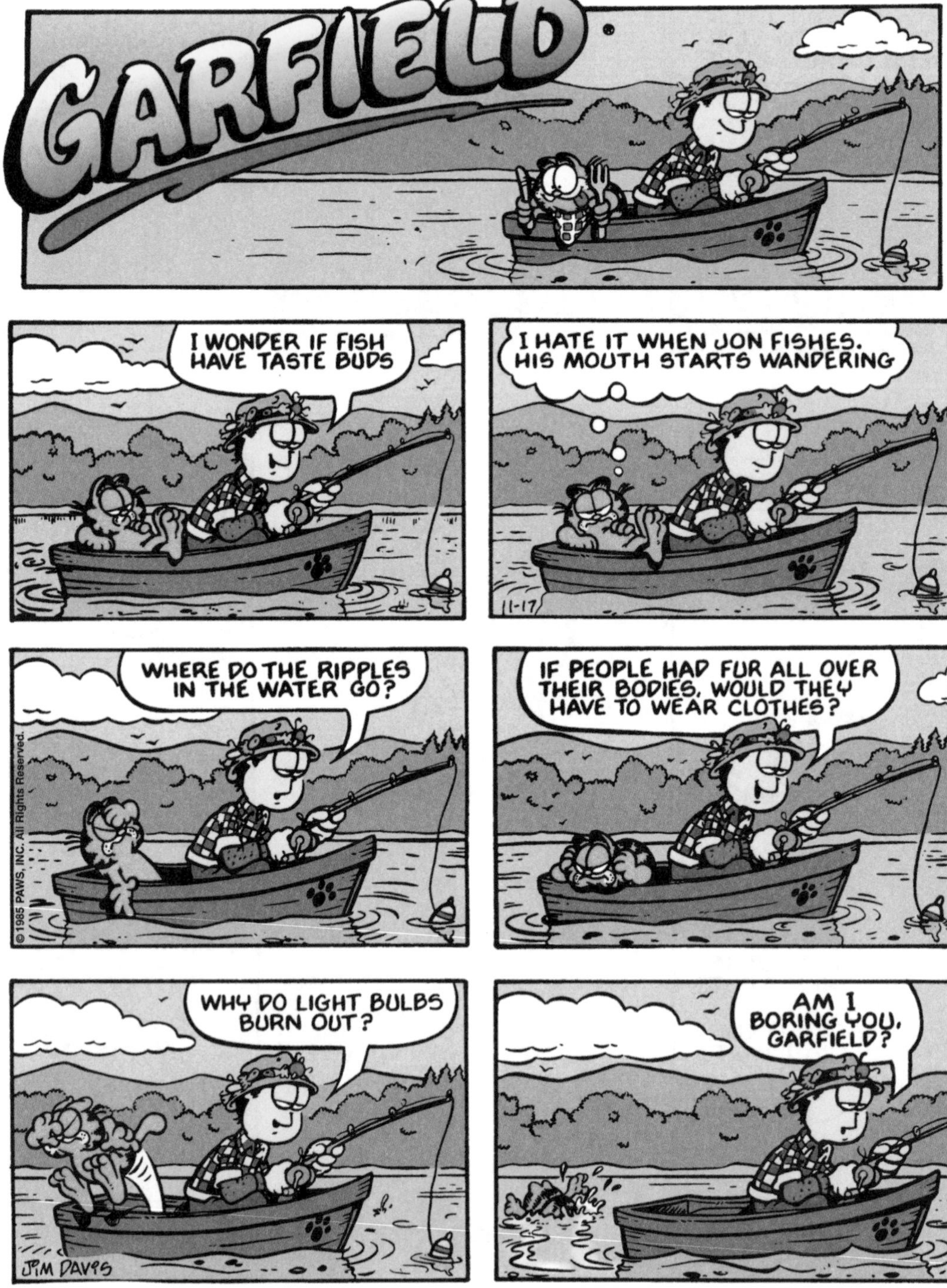
GARFIELD
I WONDER IF FISH HAVE TASTE BUDS
I HATE IT WHEN JON FISHES. HIS MOUTH STARTS WANDERING
11-17
WHERE DO THE RIPPLES IN THE WATER GO?
© 1985 PAWS, INC. All Rights Reserved.
IF PEOPLE HAD FUR ALL OVER THEIR BODIES, WOULD THEY HAVE TO WEAR CLOTHES?
WHY DO LIGHT BULBS BURN OUT?
JIM DAVIS
AM I BORING YOU, GARFIELD?

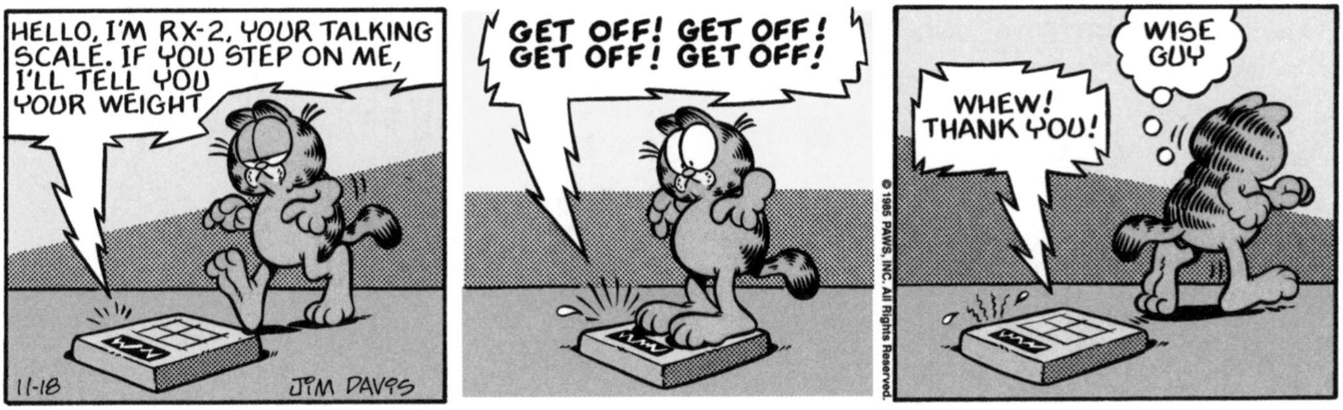
HELLO, I'M RX-2, YOUR TALKING SCALE. IF YOU STEP ON ME, I'LL TELL YOU YOUR WEIGHT
GET OFF! GET OFF! GET OFF! GET OFF!
WHEW! THANK YOU!
WISE GUY
11-18
JIM DAVIS
© 1985 PAWS, INC. All Rights Reserved.

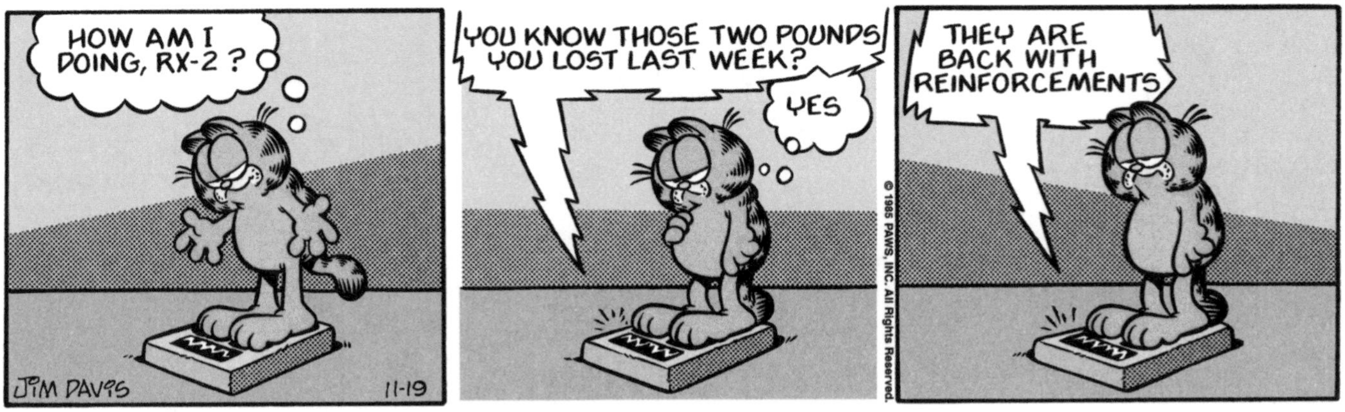
HOW AM I DOING, RX-2 ?
YOU KNOW THOSE TWO POUNDS YOU LOST LAST WEEK?
YES
THEY ARE BACK WITH REINFORCEMENTS
JIM DAVIS
11-19
© 1985 PAWS, INC. All Rights Reserved.

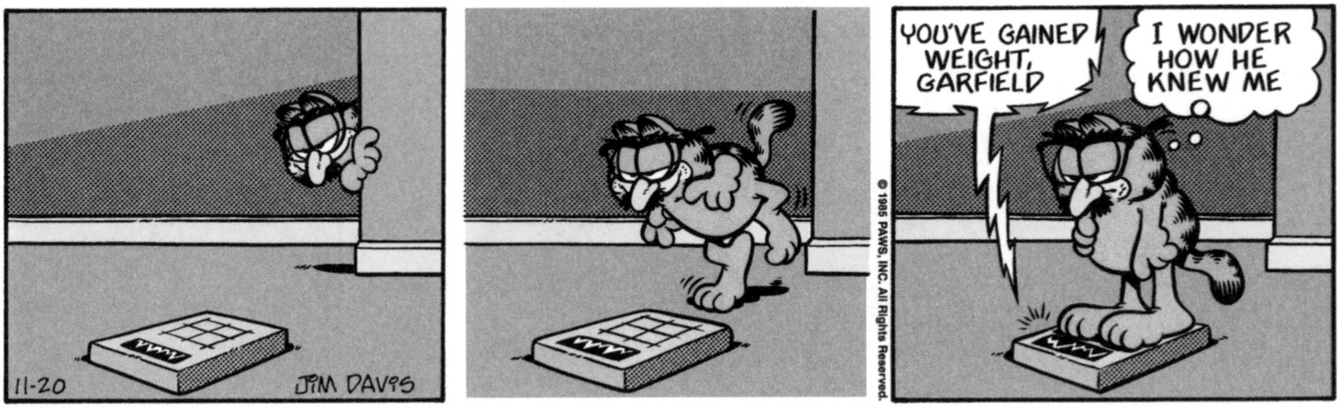
YOU'VE GAINED WEIGHT, GARFIELD
I WONDER HOW HE KNEW ME
11-20
JIM DAVIS
© 1985 PAWS, INC. All Rights Reserved.

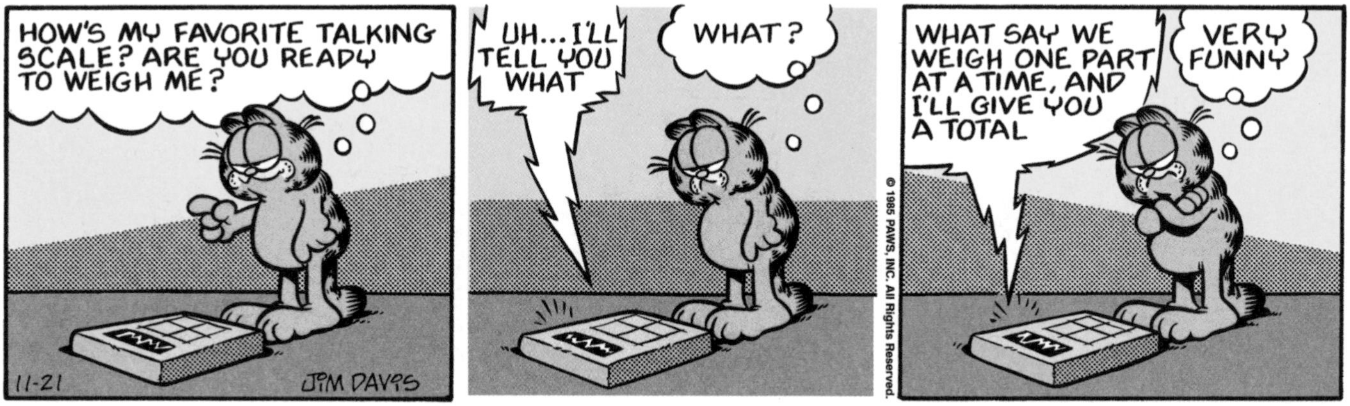
HOW'S MY FAVORITE TALKING SCALE? ARE YOU READY TO WEIGH ME?
11-21
JIM DAVIS
UH... I'LL TELL YOU WHAT
WHAT?
WHAT SAY WE WEIGH ONE PART AT A TIME, AND I'LL GIVE YOU A TOTAL
VERY FUNNY
© 1985 PAWS, INC. All Rights Reserved.

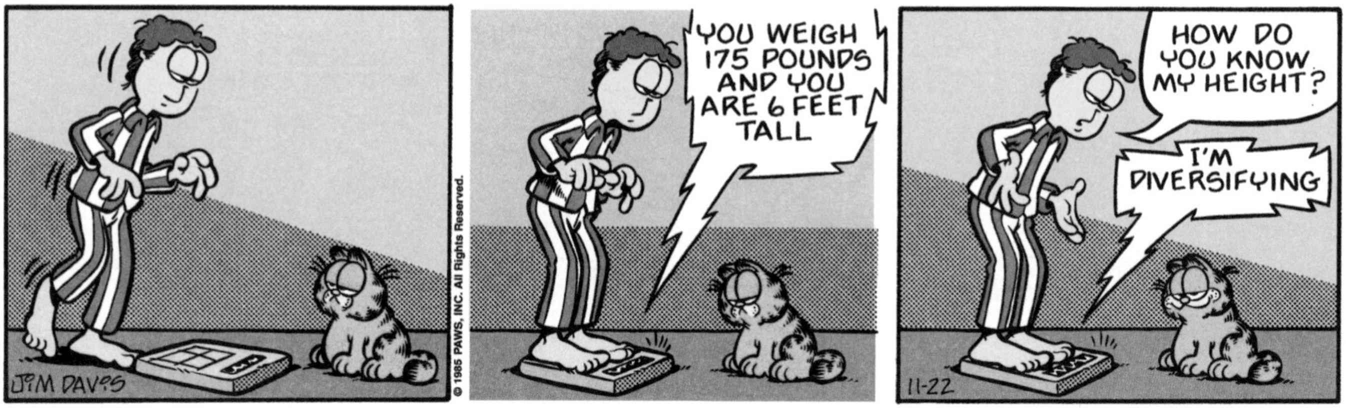
JIM DAVIS
© 1985 PAWS, INC. All Rights Reserved.
YOU WEIGH 175 POUNDS AND YOU ARE 6 FEET TALL
HOW DO YOU KNOW MY HEIGHT?
I'M DIVERSIFYING
11-22

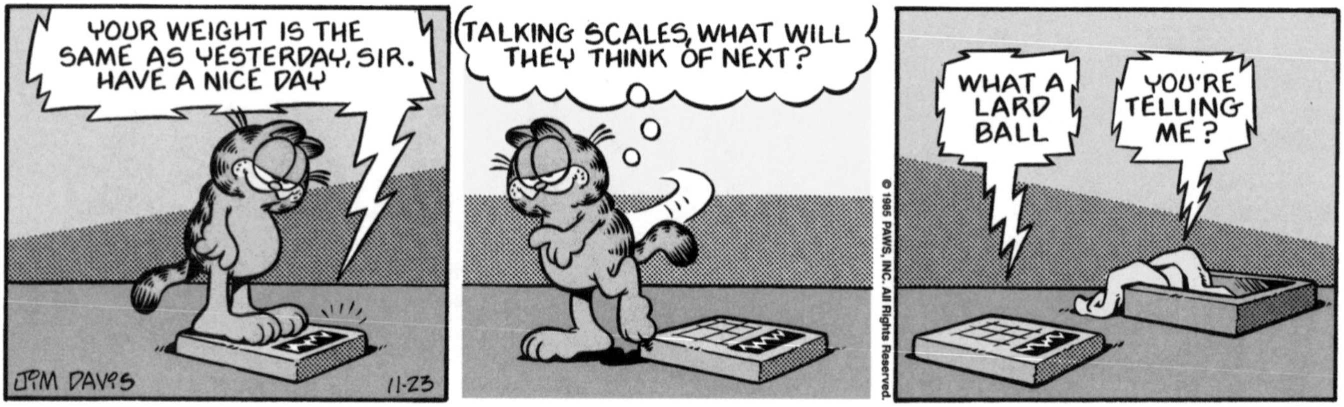
YOUR WEIGHT IS THE SAME AS YESTERDAY, SIR. HAVE A NICE DAY
JIM DAVIS
11-23
TALKING SCALES, WHAT WILL THEY THINK OF NEXT?
WHAT A LARD BALL
YOU'RE TELLING ME?
© 1985 PAWS, INC. All Rights Reserved.

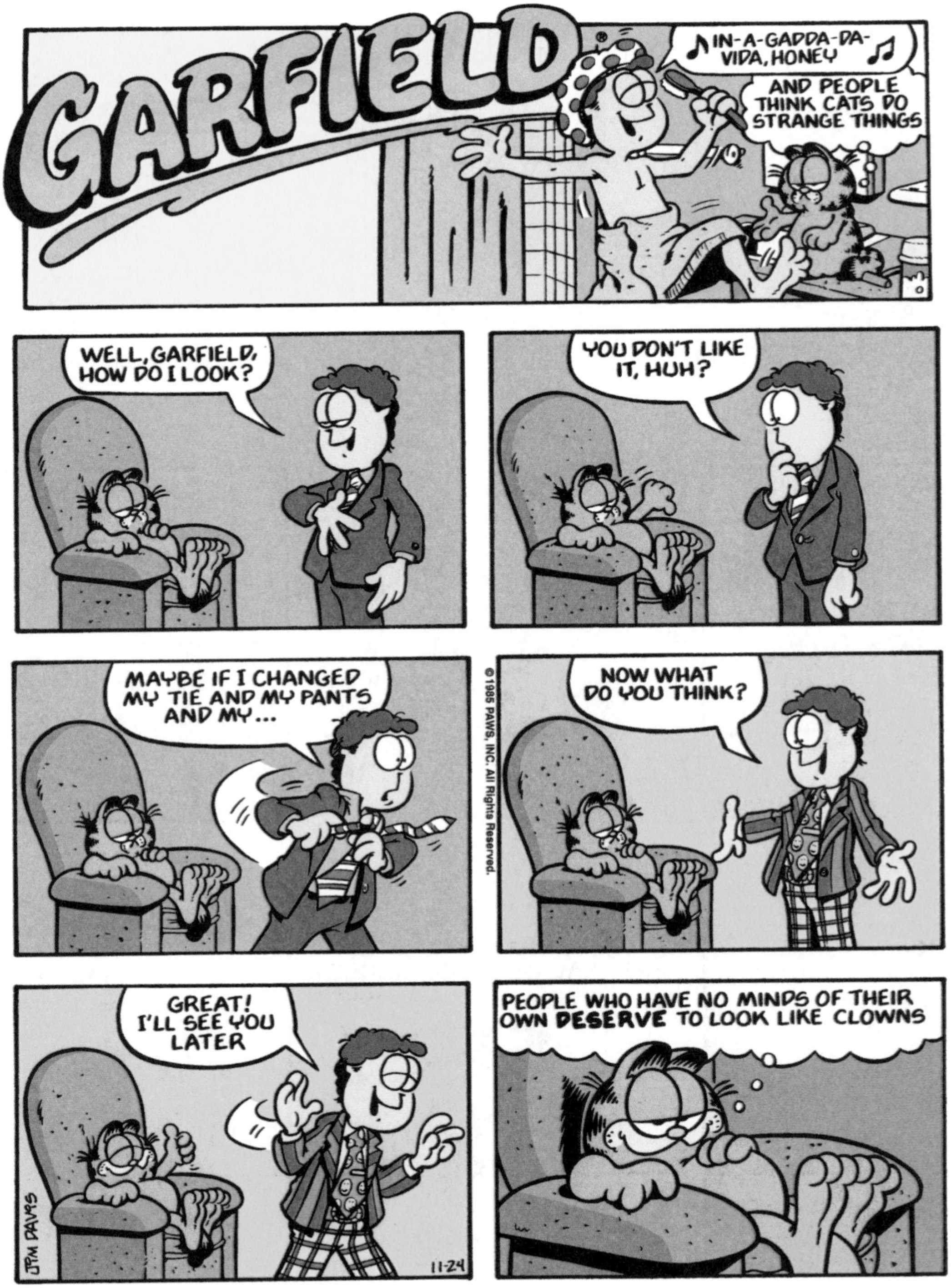
GARFIELD®
♪ IN-A-GADDA-DA-VIDA, HONEY ♫
AND PEOPLE THINK CATS DO STRANGE THINGS
WELL, GARFIELD, HOW DO I LOOK?
YOU DON'T LIKE IT, HUH?
MAYBE IF I CHANGED MY TIE AND MY PANTS AND MY...
NOW WHAT DO YOU THINK?
GREAT! I'LL SEE YOU LATER
PEOPLE WHO HAVE NO MINDS OF THEIR OWN **DESERVE** TO LOOK LIKE CLOWNS
JIM DAVIS
11-24

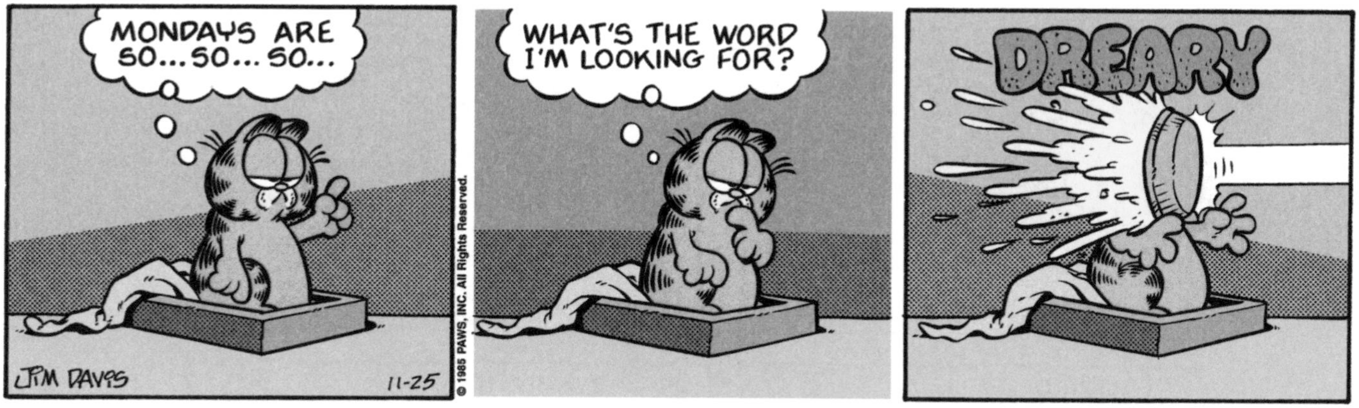
MONDAYS ARE SO... SO... SO...
WHAT'S THE WORD I'M LOOKING FOR?
DREARY
JIM DAVIS
11-25
© 1985 PAWS, INC. All Rights Reserved.

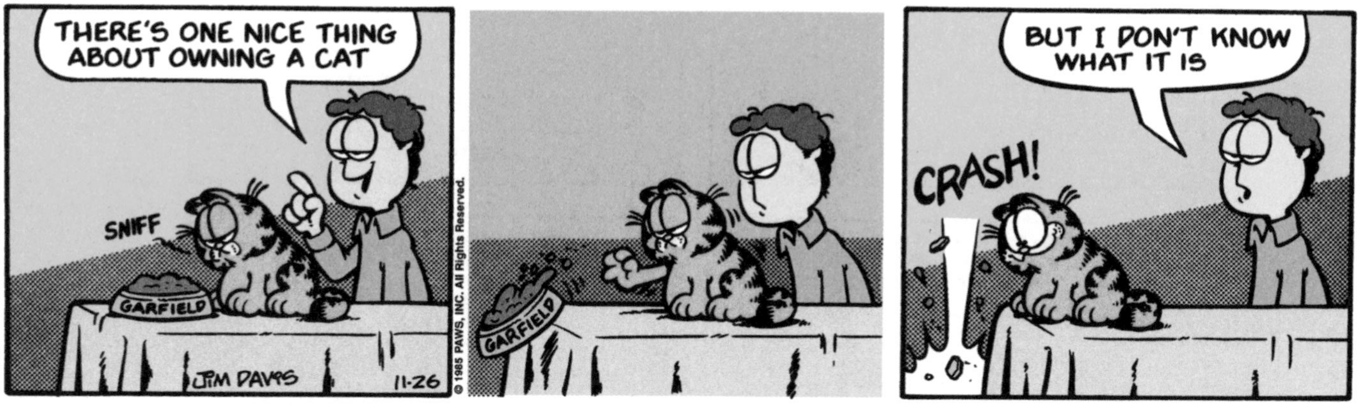
THERE'S ONE NICE THING ABOUT OWNING A CAT
SNIFF
GARFIELD
BUT I DON'T KNOW WHAT IT IS
CRASH!
JIM DAVIS
11-26
© 1985 PAWS, INC. All Rights Reserved.

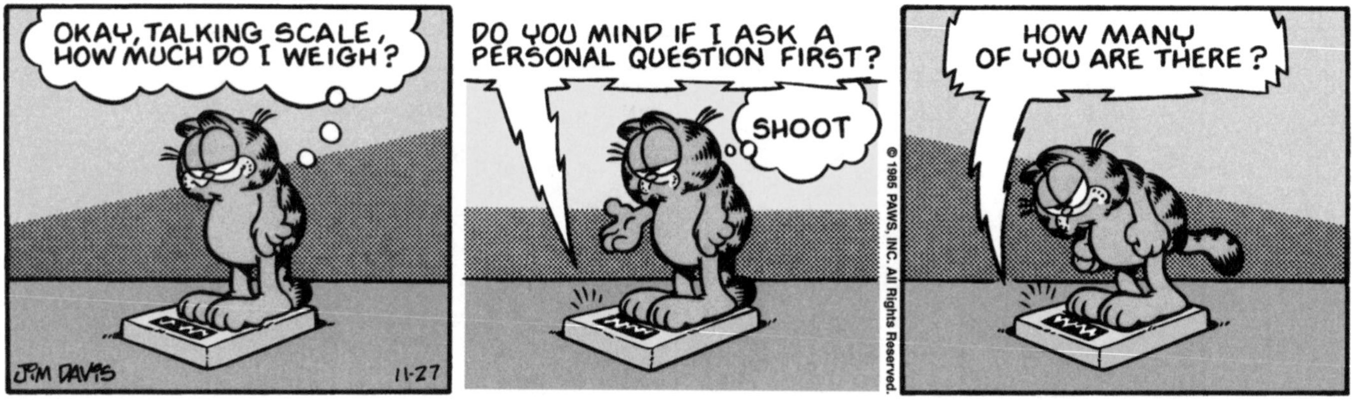
OKAY, TALKING SCALE, HOW MUCH DO I WEIGH?
DO YOU MIND IF I ASK A PERSONAL QUESTION FIRST?
SHOOT
HOW MANY OF YOU ARE THERE?
JIM DAVIS
11-27
© 1985 PAWS, INC. All Rights Reserved.

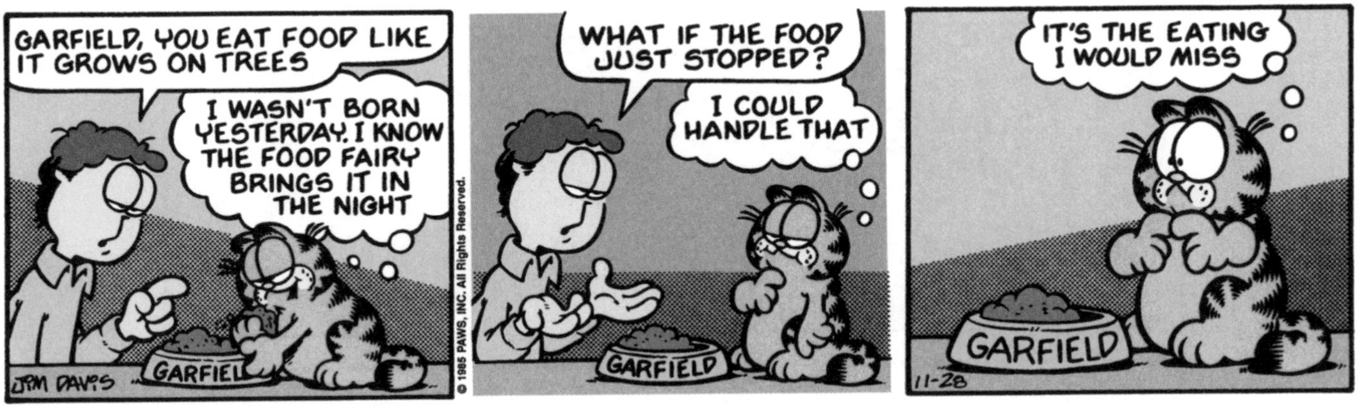
GARFIELD, YOU EAT FOOD LIKE IT GROWS ON TREES
I WASN'T BORN YESTERDAY. I KNOW THE FOOD FAIRY BRINGS IT IN THE NIGHT
JIM DAVIS
GARFIEL
© 1985 PAWS, INC. All Rights Reserved.
WHAT IF THE FOOD JUST STOPPED?
I COULD HANDLE THAT
GARFIELD
IT'S THE EATING I WOULD MISS
GARFIELD
11-28

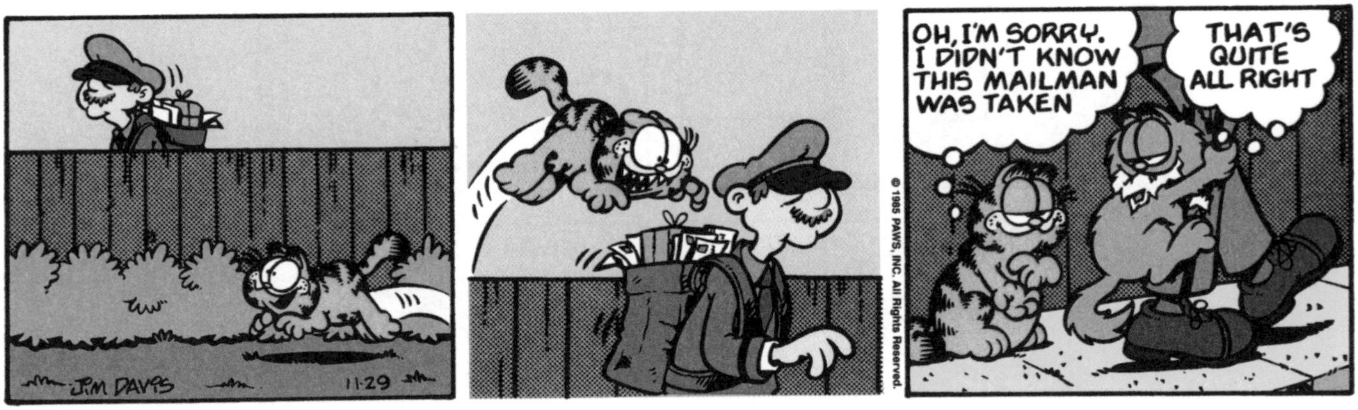
JIM DAVIS
11-29
OH, I'M SORRY. I DIDN'T KNOW THIS MAILMAN WAS TAKEN
THAT'S QUITE ALL RIGHT
© 1985 PAWS, INC. All Rights Reserved.

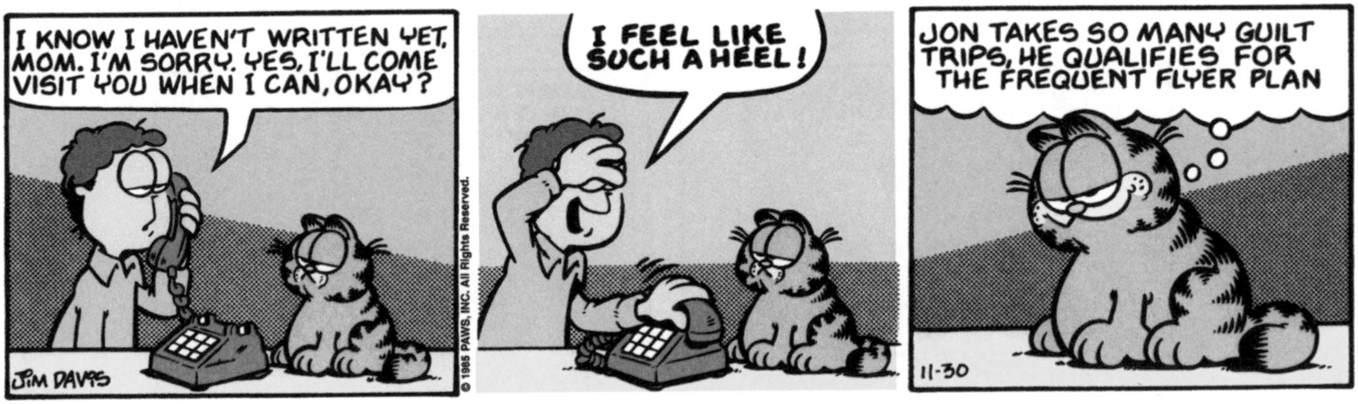
I KNOW I HAVEN'T WRITTEN YET, MOM. I'M SORRY. YES, I'LL COME VISIT YOU WHEN I CAN, OKAY?
JIM DAVIS
© 1985 PAWS, INC. All Rights Reserved.
I FEEL LIKE SUCH A HEEL!
JON TAKES SO MANY GUILT TRIPS, HE QUALIFIES FOR THE FREQUENT FLYER PLAN
11-30

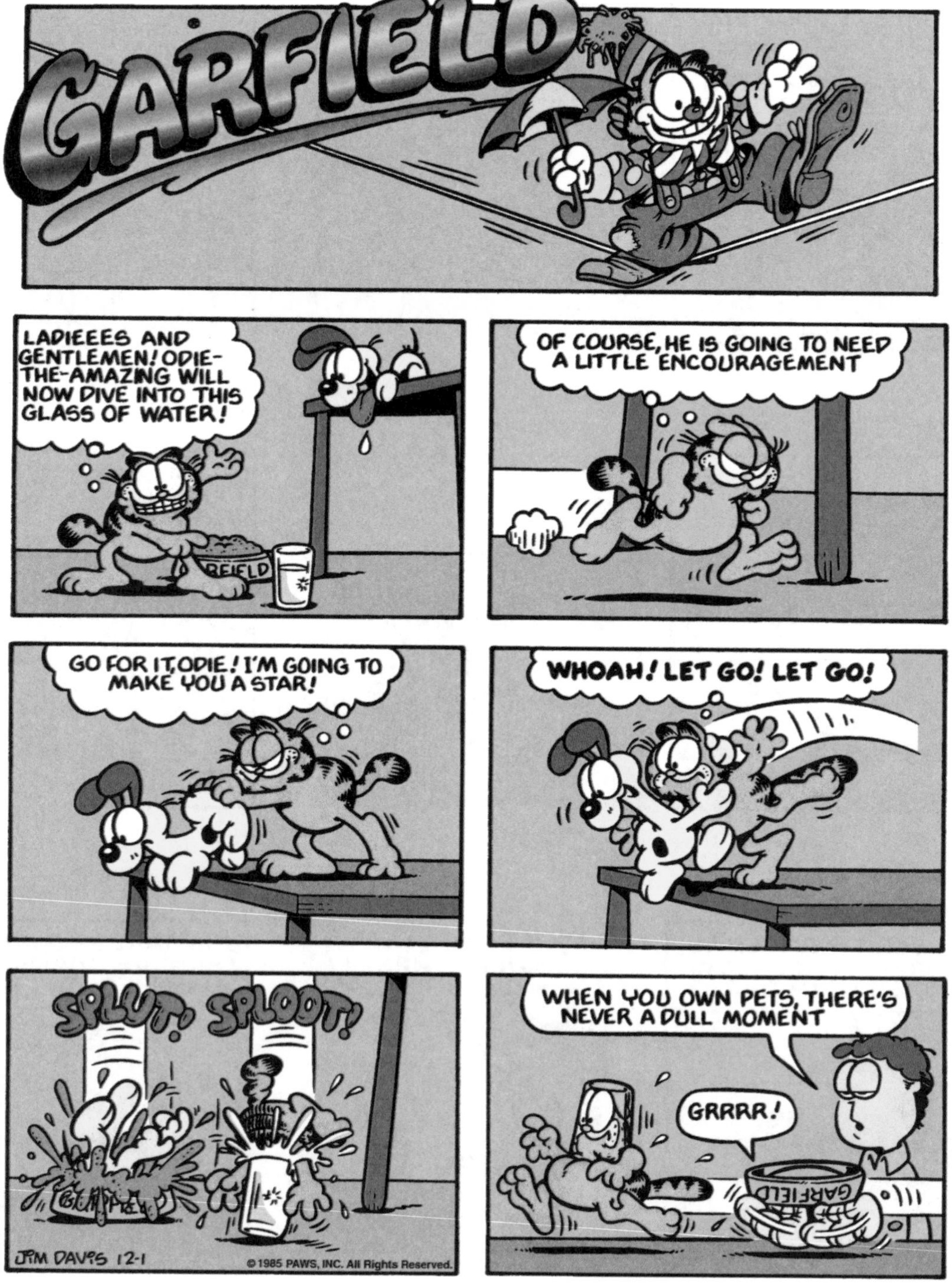
GARFIELD
LADIEEES AND GENTLEMEN! ODIE-THE-AMAZING WILL NOW DIVE INTO THIS GLASS OF WATER!
OF COURSE, HE IS GOING TO NEED A LITTLE ENCOURAGEMENT
GO FOR IT, ODIE! I'M GOING TO MAKE YOU A STAR!
WHOAH! LET GO! LET GO!
SPLUT! SPLOOT!
JIM DAVIS 12-1
© 1985 PAWS, INC. All Rights Reserved.
WHEN YOU OWN PETS, THERE'S NEVER A DULL MOMENT
GRRRR!
GARFIELD

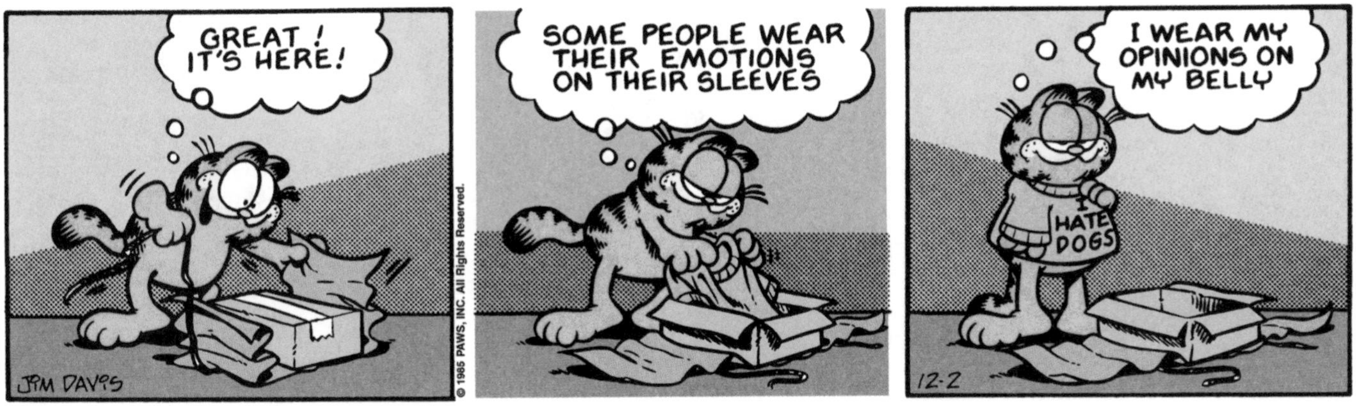
GREAT! IT'S HERE!
JIM DAVIS
© 1985 PAWS, INC. All Rights Reserved.
SOME PEOPLE WEAR THEIR EMOTIONS ON THEIR SLEEVES
I WEAR MY OPINIONS ON MY BELLY
I HATE DOGS
12-2

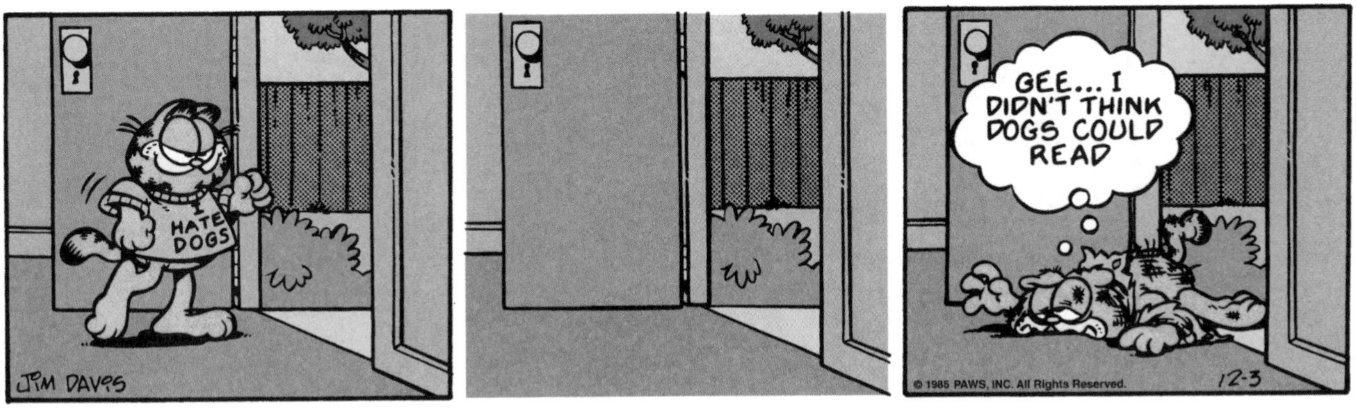
I HATE DOGS
JIM DAVIS
GEE... I DIDN'T THINK DOGS COULD READ
© 1985 PAWS, INC. All Rights Reserved.
12-3

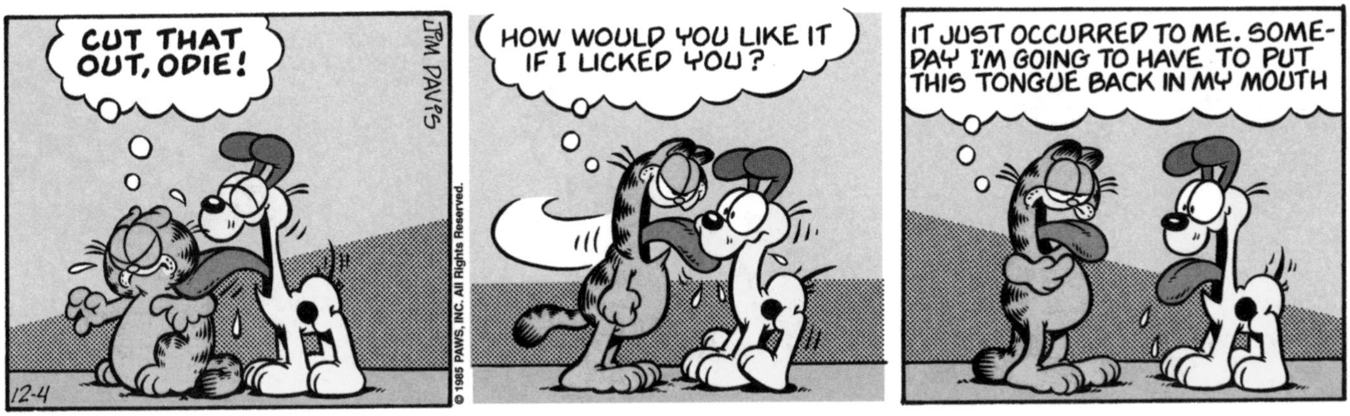
CUT THAT OUT, ODIE!
JIM DAVIS
12-4
© 1985 PAWS, INC. All Rights Reserved.
HOW WOULD YOU LIKE IT IF I LICKED YOU?
IT JUST OCCURRED TO ME. SOMEDAY I'M GOING TO HAVE TO PUT THIS TONGUE BACK IN MY MOUTH

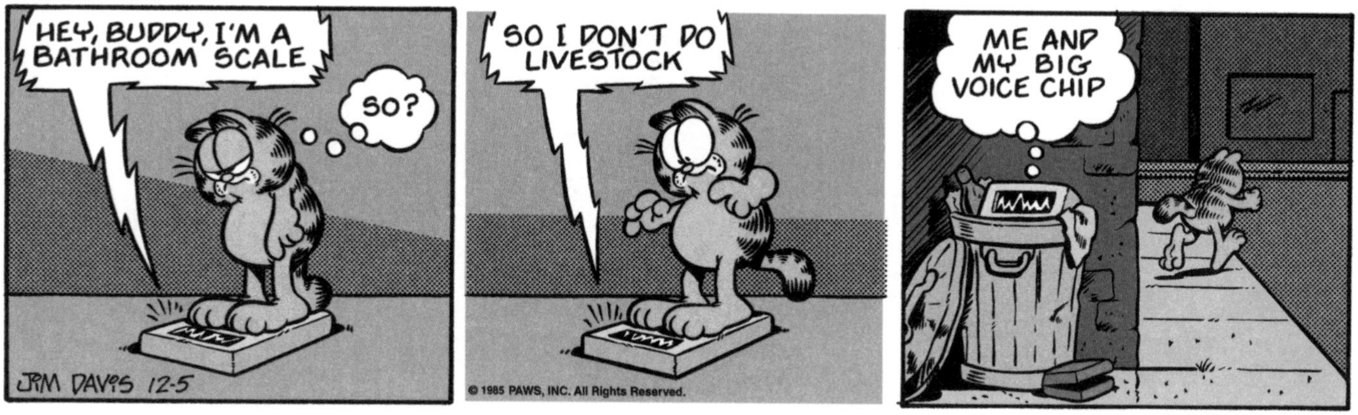
HEY, BUDDY, I'M A BATHROOM SCALE
SO?
JIM DAVIS 12-5
SO I DON'T DO LIVESTOCK
© 1985 PAWS, INC. All Rights Reserved.
ME AND MY BIG VOICE CHIP

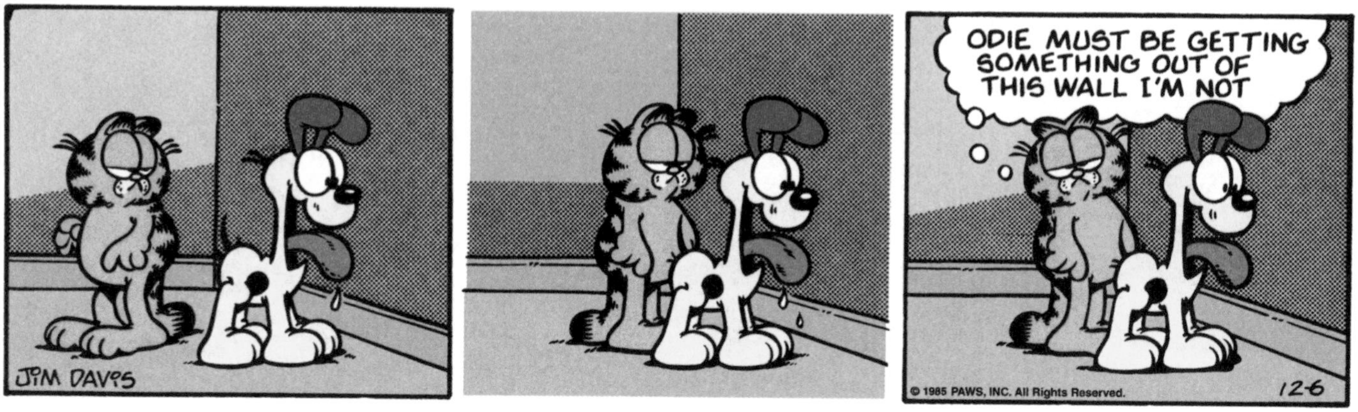
JIM DAVIS
ODIE MUST BE GETTING SOMETHING OUT OF THIS WALL I'M NOT
© 1985 PAWS, INC. All Rights Reserved.
12-6

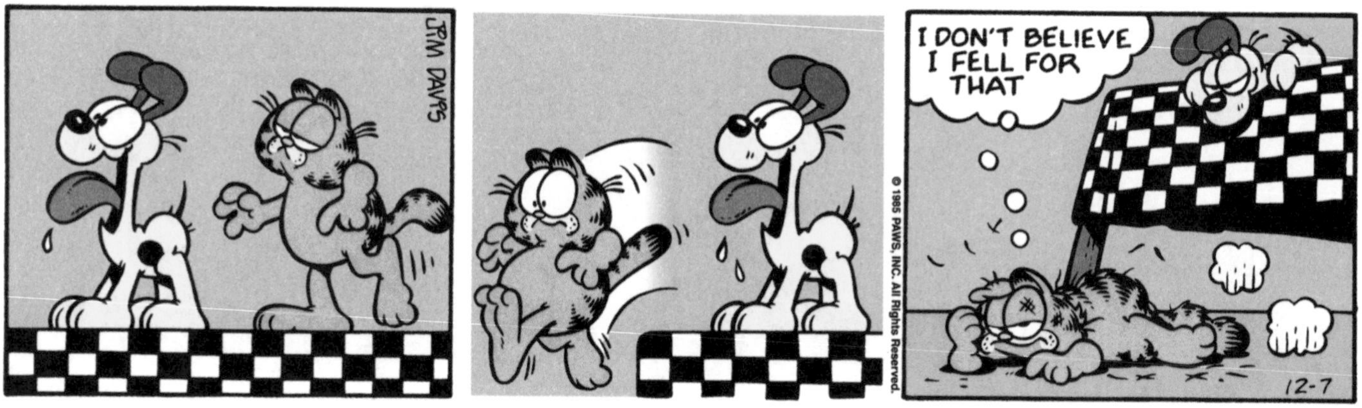
JIM DAVIS
© 1985 PAWS, INC. All Rights Reserved.
I DON'T BELIEVE I FELL FOR THAT
12-7

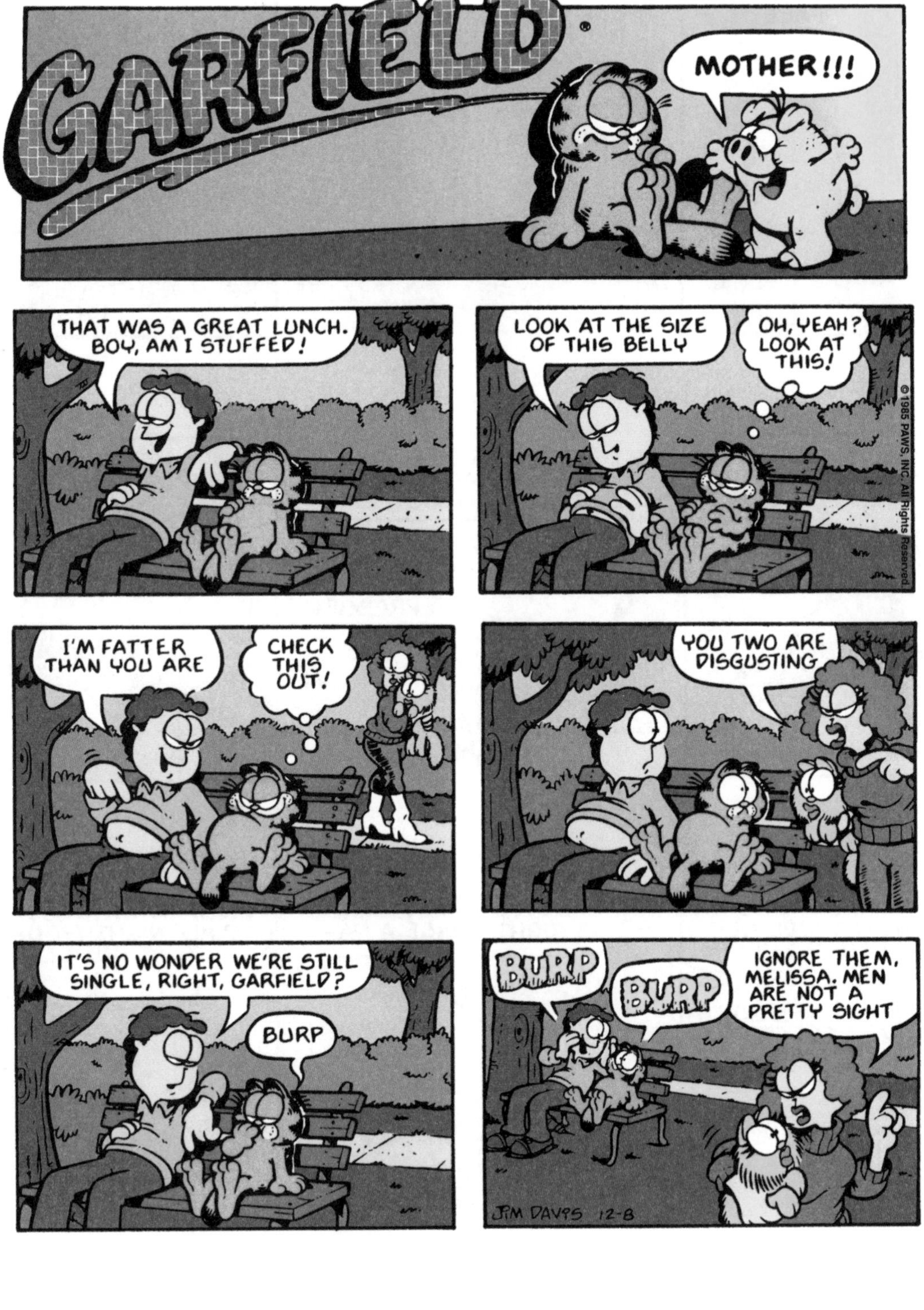

GARFIELD®
MOTHER!!!
THAT WAS A GREAT LUNCH. BOY, AM I STUFFED!
LOOK AT THE SIZE OF THIS BELLY
OH, YEAH? LOOK AT THIS!
© 1985 PAWS, INC. All Rights Reserved.
I'M FATTER THAN YOU ARE
CHECK THIS OUT!
YOU TWO ARE DISGUSTING
IT'S NO WONDER WE'RE STILL SINGLE, RIGHT, GARFIELD?
BURP
BURP
BURP
IGNORE THEM, MELISSA. MEN ARE NOT A PRETTY SIGHT
JIM DAVIS 12-8

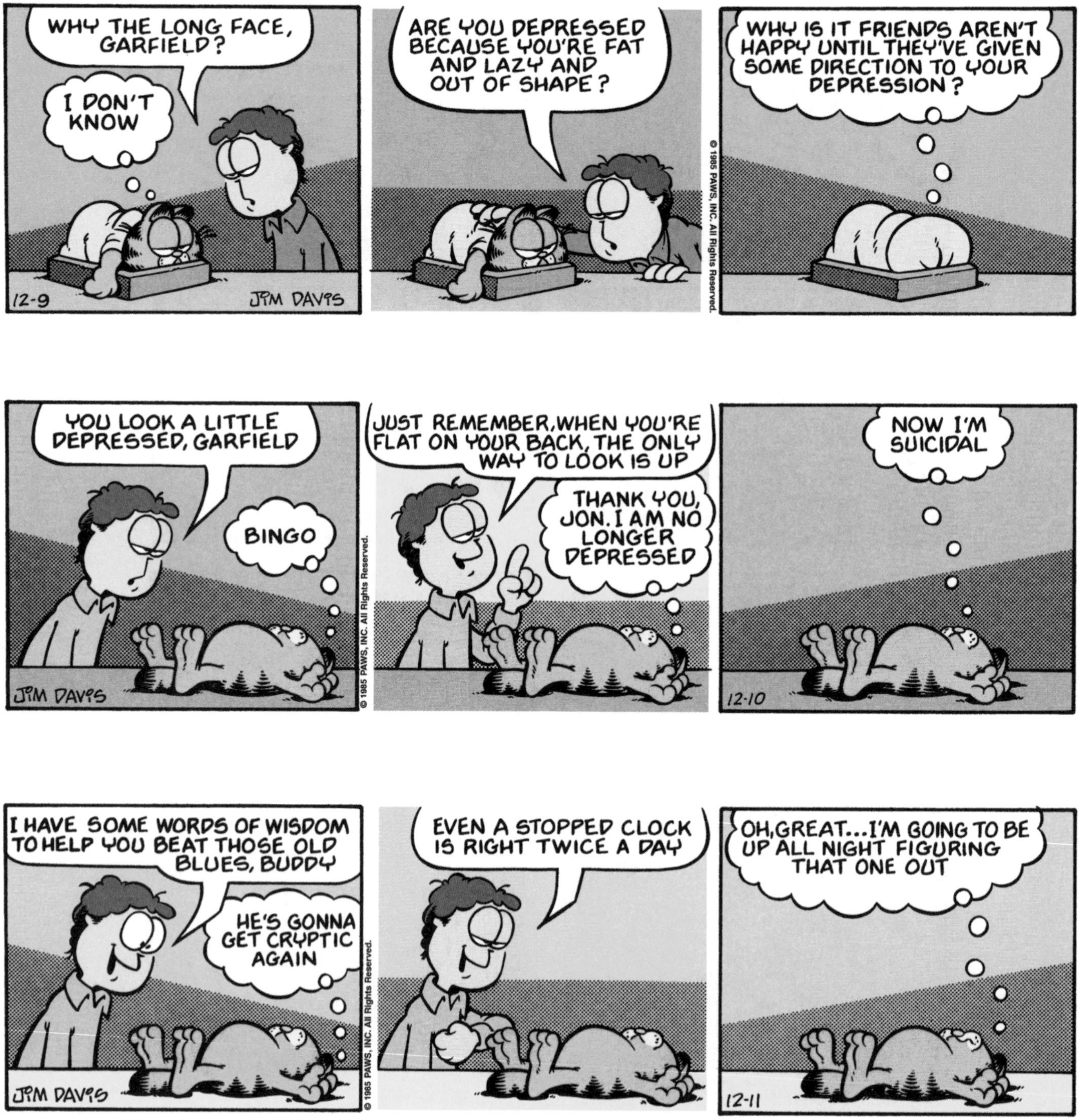
WHY THE LONG FACE, GARFIELD?
I DON'T KNOW
12-9
JIM DAVIS
ARE YOU DEPRESSED BECAUSE YOU'RE FAT AND LAZY AND OUT OF SHAPE?
© 1985 PAWS, INC. All Rights Reserved.
WHY IS IT FRIENDS AREN'T HAPPY UNTIL THEY'VE GIVEN SOME DIRECTION TO YOUR DEPRESSION?
YOU LOOK A LITTLE DEPRESSED, GARFIELD
BINGO
JIM DAVIS
© 1985 PAWS, INC. All Rights Reserved.
JUST REMEMBER, WHEN YOU'RE FLAT ON YOUR BACK, THE ONLY WAY TO LOOK IS UP
THANK YOU, JON. I AM NO LONGER DEPRESSED
NOW I'M SUICIDAL
12-10
I HAVE SOME WORDS OF WISDOM TO HELP YOU BEAT THOSE OLD BLUES, BUDDY
HE'S GONNA GET CRYPTIC AGAIN
JIM DAVIS
© 1985 PAWS, INC. All Rights Reserved.
EVEN A STOPPED CLOCK IS RIGHT TWICE A DAY
OH, GREAT... I'M GOING TO BE UP ALL NIGHT FIGURING THAT ONE OUT
12-11

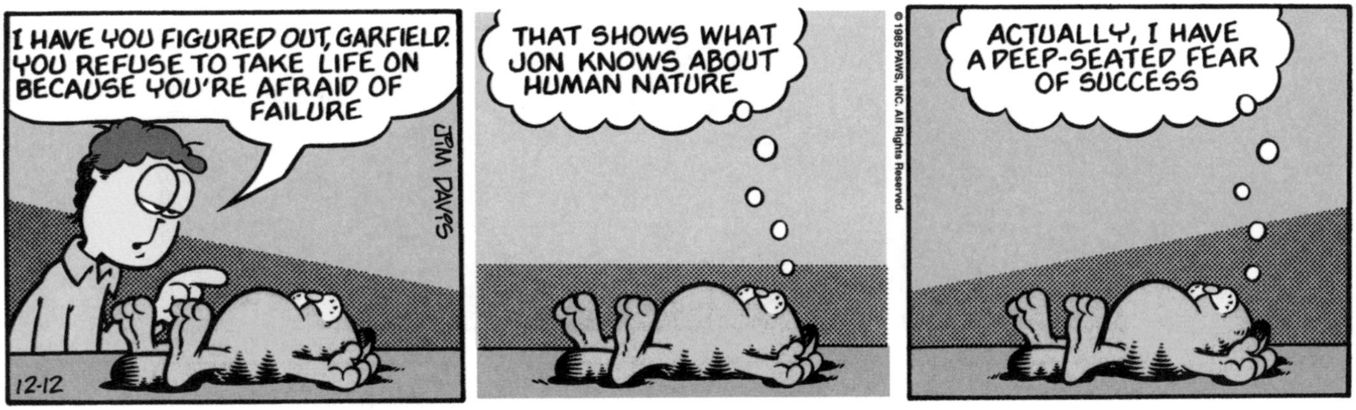
I HAVE YOU FIGURED OUT, GARFIELD. YOU REFUSE TO TAKE LIFE ON BECAUSE YOU'RE AFRAID OF FAILURE
JIM DAVIS
12-12
THAT SHOWS WHAT JON KNOWS ABOUT HUMAN NATURE
© 1985 PAWS, INC. All Rights Reserved.
ACTUALLY, I HAVE A DEEP-SEATED FEAR OF SUCCESS

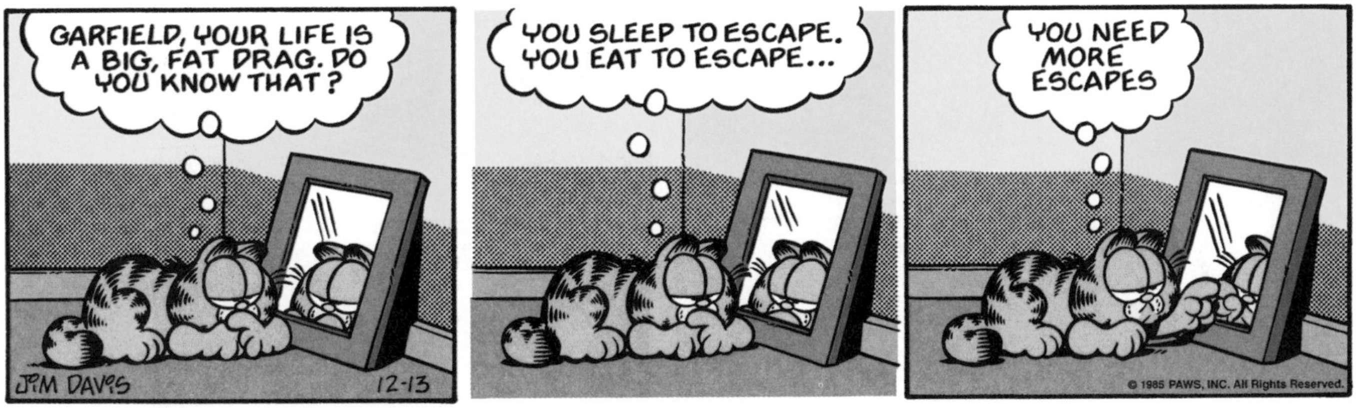
GARFIELD, YOUR LIFE IS A BIG, FAT DRAG. DO YOU KNOW THAT?
JIM DAVIS
12-13
YOU SLEEP TO ESCAPE. YOU EAT TO ESCAPE...
YOU NEED MORE ESCAPES
© 1985 PAWS, INC. All Rights Reserved.

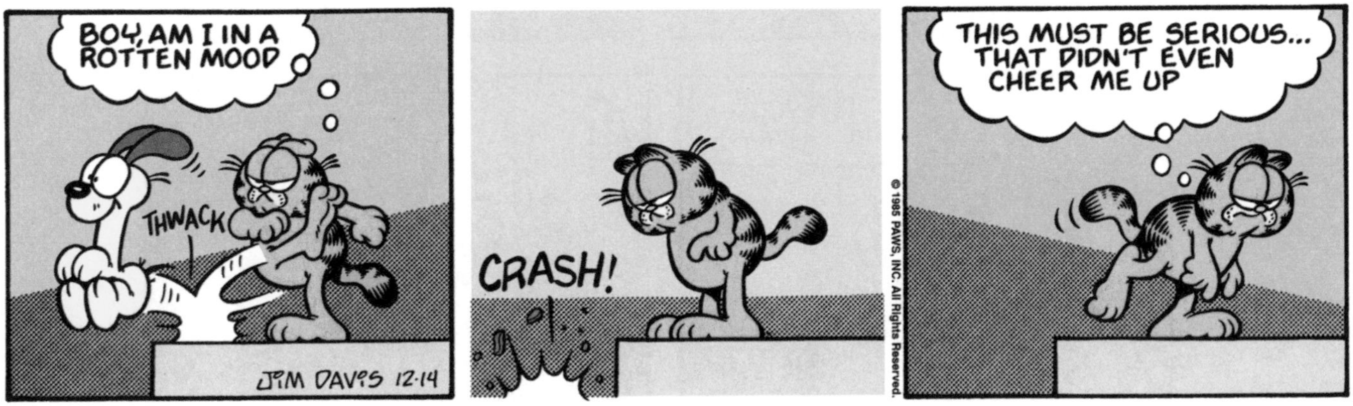
BOY, AM I IN A ROTTEN MOOD
THWACK
JIM DAVIS 12-14
CRASH!
© 1985 PAWS, INC. All Rights Reserved.
THIS MUST BE SERIOUS... THAT DIDN'T EVEN CHEER ME UP

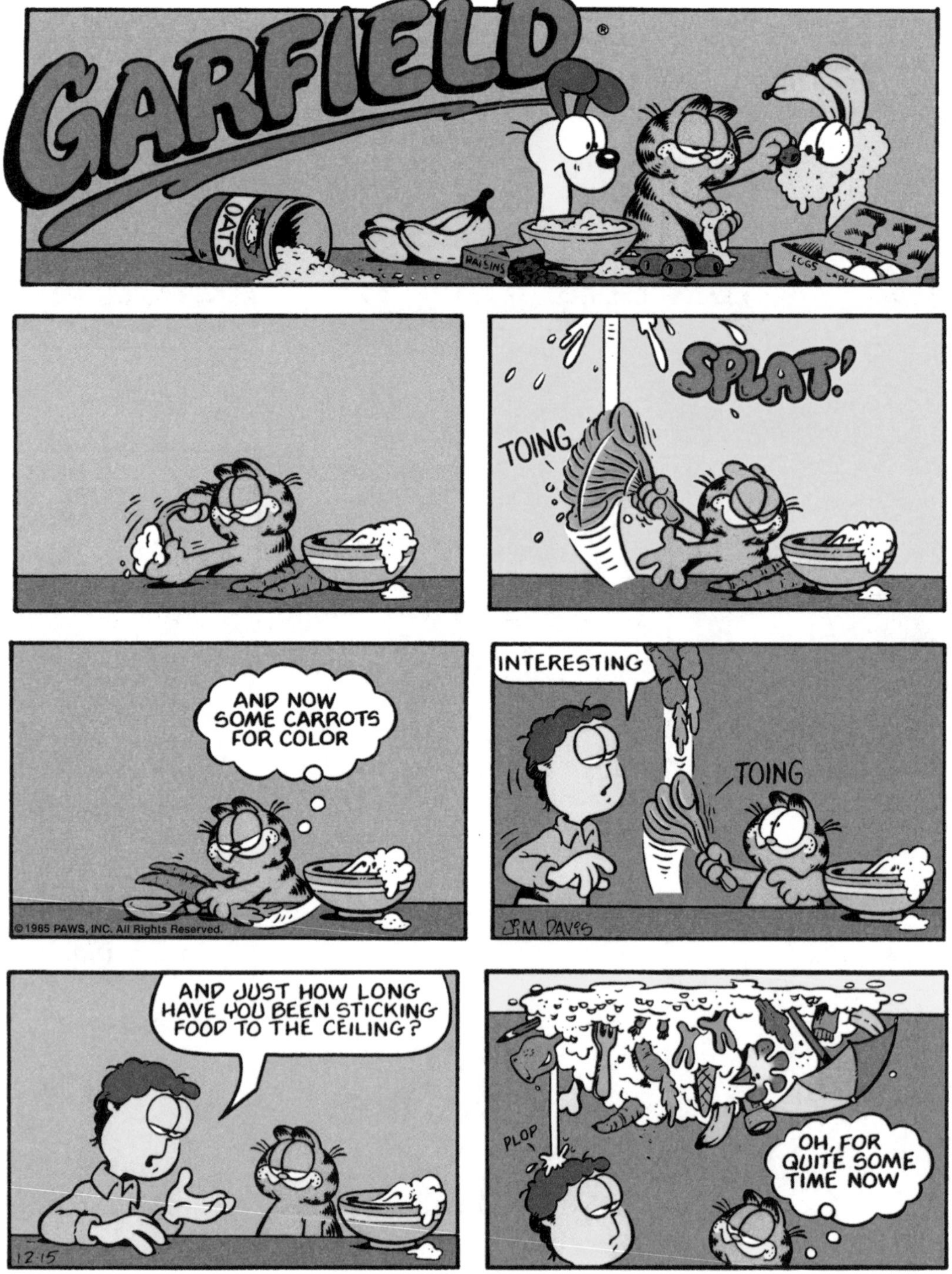
GARFIELD®
OATS
RAISINS
EGGS
SPLAT!
TOING
AND NOW SOME CARROTS FOR COLOR
© 1985 PAWS, INC. All Rights Reserved.
INTERESTING
TOING
JIM DAVIS
AND JUST HOW LONG HAVE YOU BEEN STICKING FOOD TO THE CEILING?
12-15
PLOP
OH, FOR QUITE SOME TIME NOW

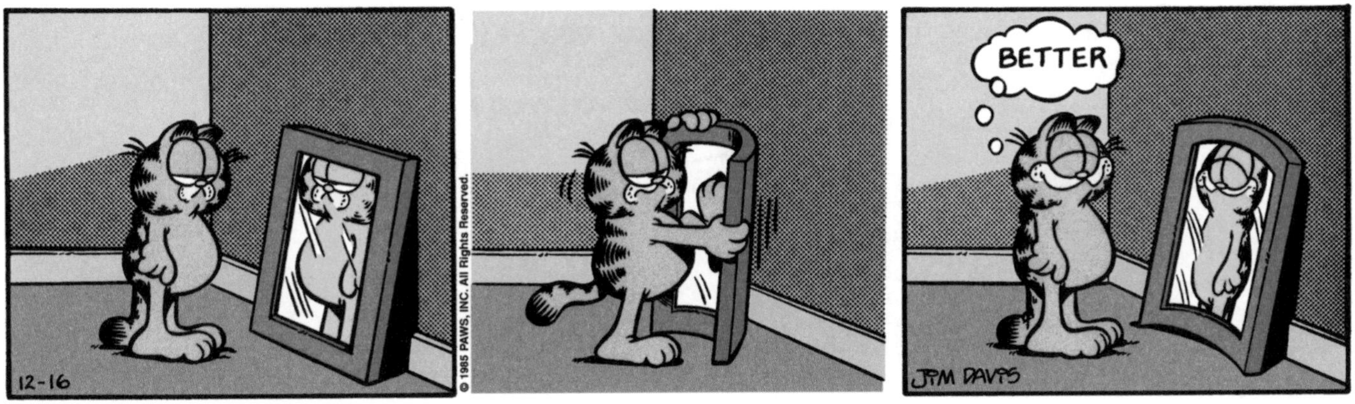
12-16
© 1985 PAWS, INC. All Rights Reserved.
BETTER
JIM DAVIS

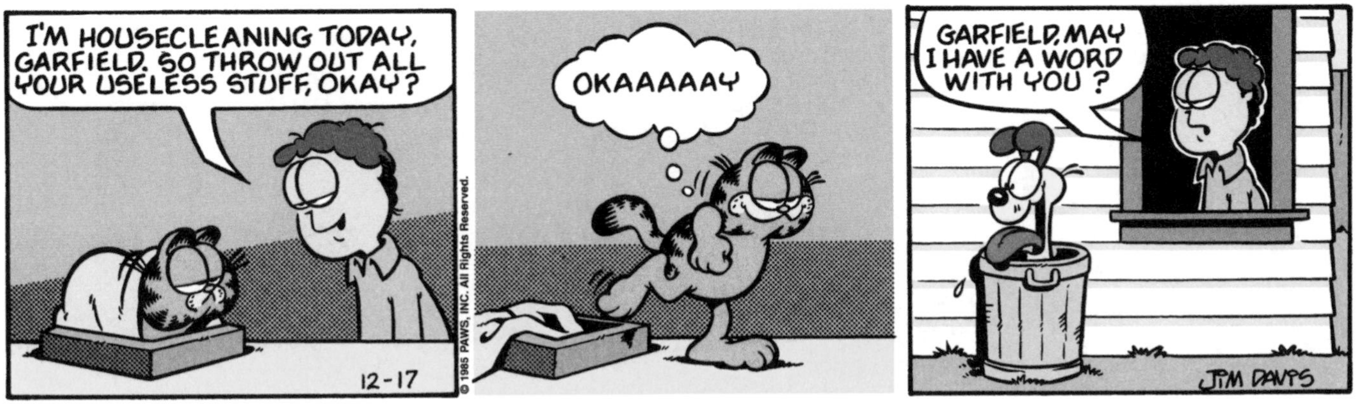
I'M HOUSECLEANING TODAY, GARFIELD. SO THROW OUT ALL YOUR USELESS STUFF, OKAY?
12-17
© 1985 PAWS, INC. All Rights Reserved.
OKAAAAAY
GARFIELD, MAY I HAVE A WORD WITH YOU?
JIM DAVIS

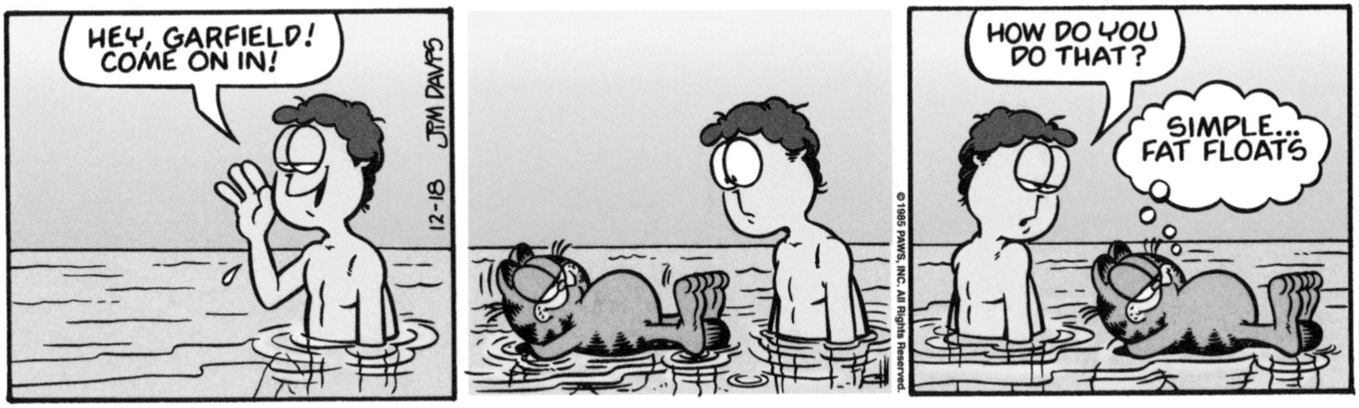
HEY, GARFIELD! COME ON IN!
JIM DAVIS
12-18
© 1985 PAWS, INC. All Rights Reserved.
HOW DO YOU DO THAT?
SIMPLE... FAT FLOATS

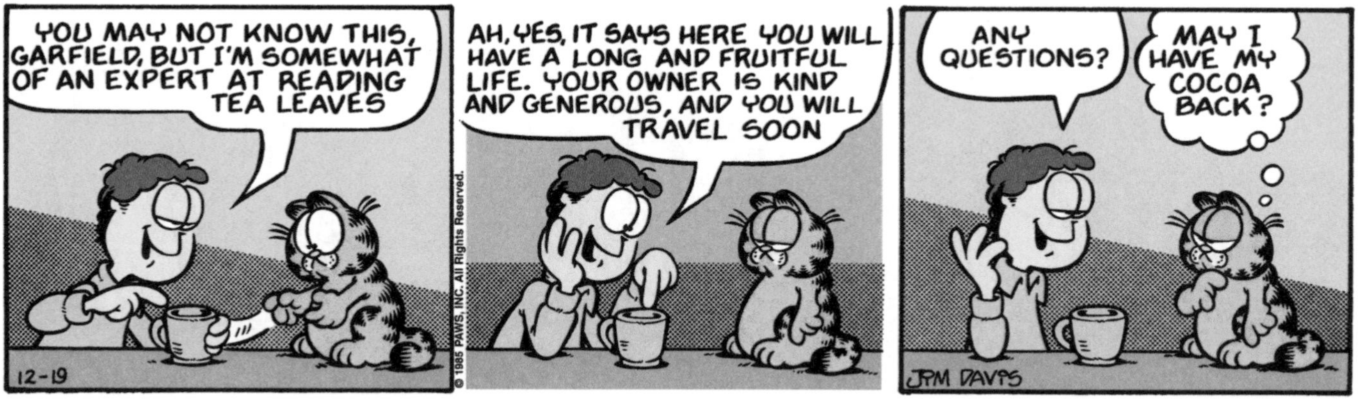
YOU MAY NOT KNOW THIS, GARFIELD, BUT I'M SOMEWHAT OF AN EXPERT AT READING TEA LEAVES
12-19
© 1985 PAWS, INC. All Rights Reserved.
AH, YES, IT SAYS HERE YOU WILL HAVE A LONG AND FRUITFUL LIFE. YOUR OWNER IS KIND AND GENEROUS, AND YOU WILL TRAVEL SOON
ANY QUESTIONS?
MAY I HAVE MY COCOA BACK?
JIM DAVIS

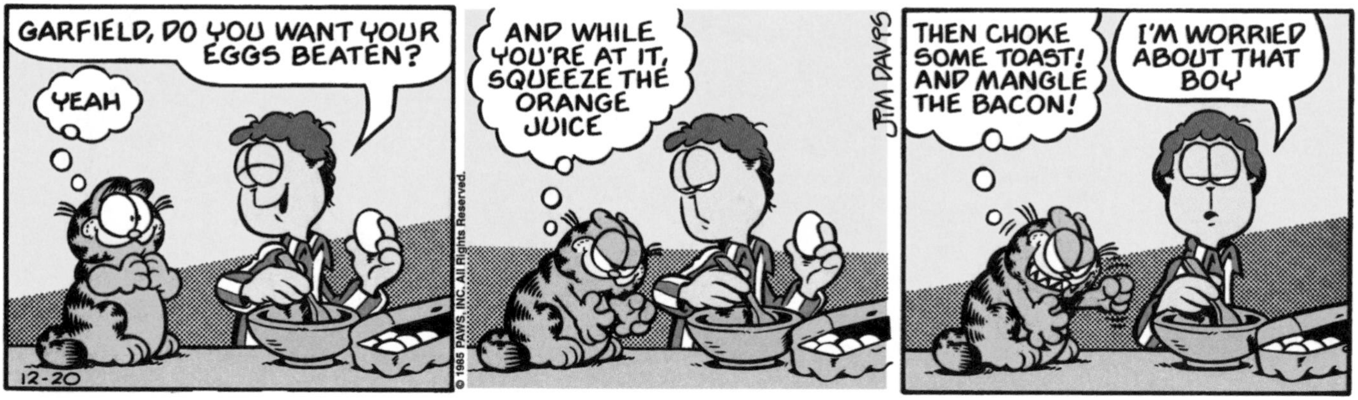
GARFIELD, DO YOU WANT YOUR EGGS BEATEN?
YEAH
12-20
© 1985 PAWS, INC. All Rights Reserved.
AND WHILE YOU'RE AT IT, SQUEEZE THE ORANGE JUICE
JIM DAVIS
THEN CHOKE SOME TOAST! AND MANGLE THE BACON!
I'M WORRIED ABOUT THAT BOY

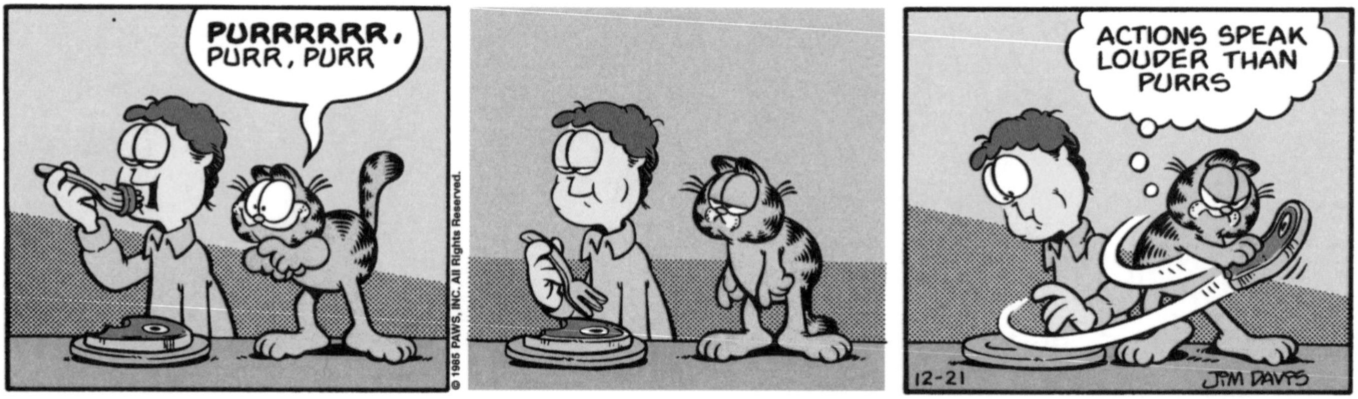
PURRRRRR, PURR, PURR
© 1985 PAWS, INC. All Rights Reserved.
ACTIONS SPEAK LOUDER THAN PURRS
12-21
JIM DAVIS

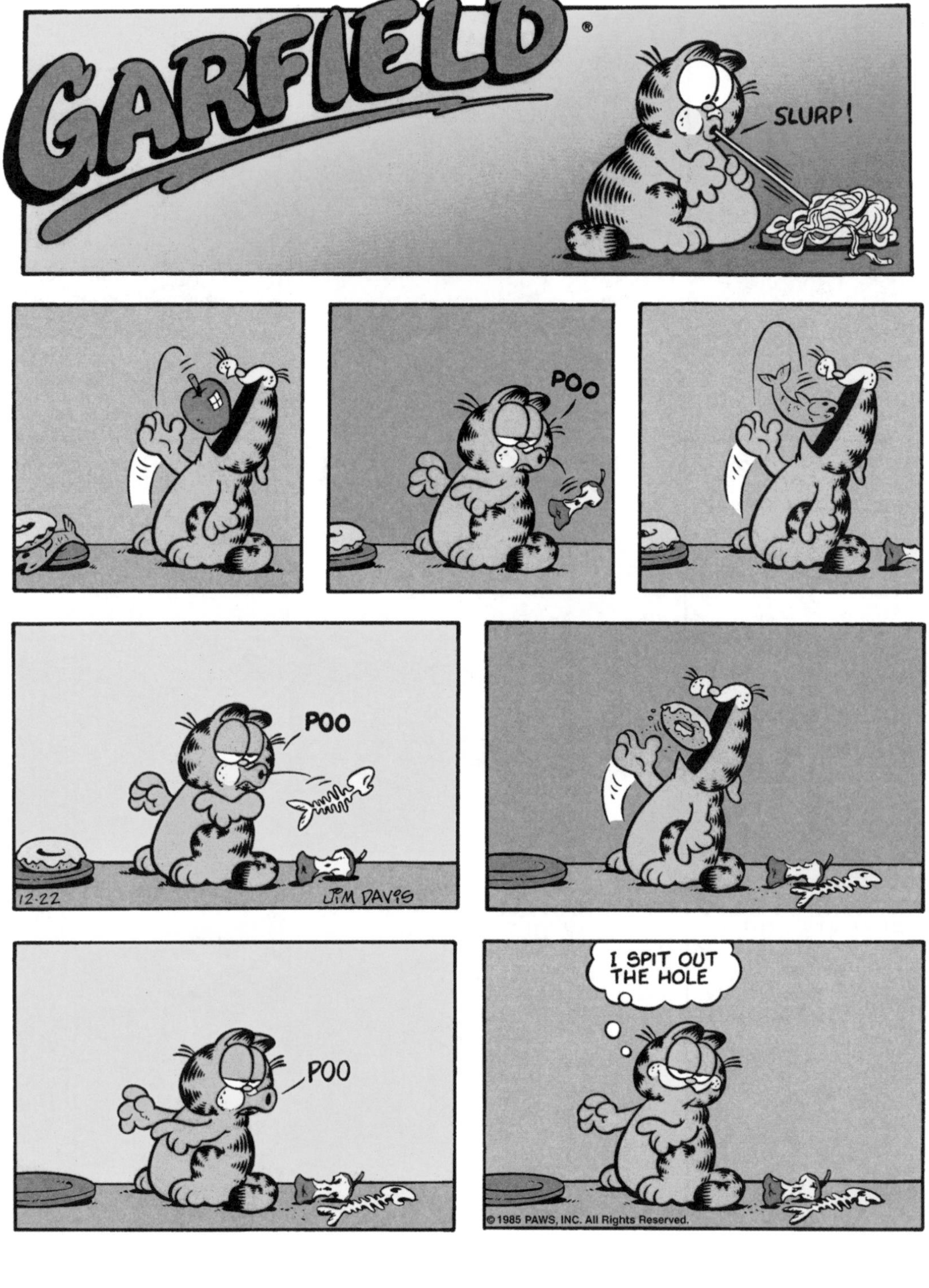
GARFIELD®
SLURP!
POO
POO
POO
I SPIT OUT THE HOLE
12-22
JIM DAVIS
© 1985 PAWS, INC. All Rights Reserved.

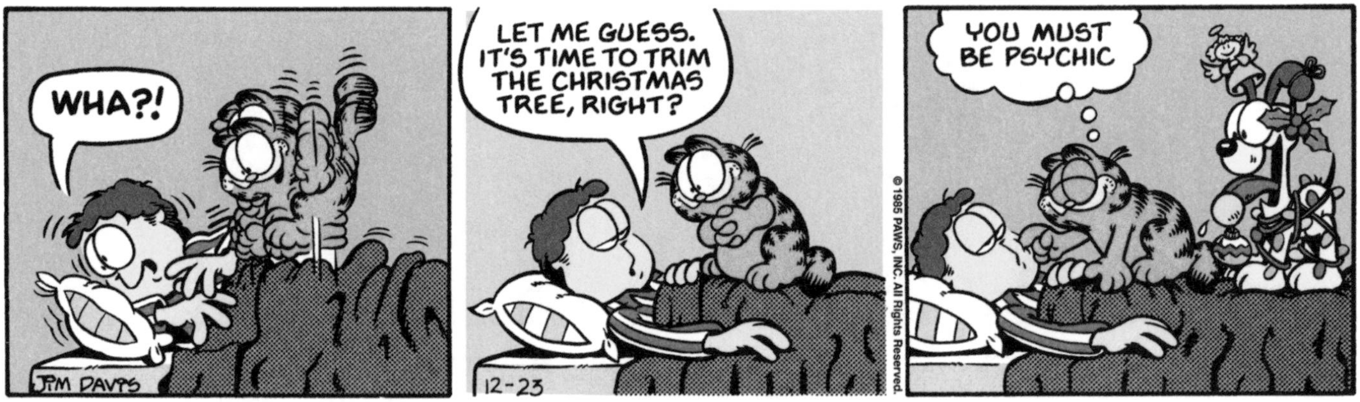
WHA?!
JIM DAVIS
LET ME GUESS. IT'S TIME TO TRIM THE CHRISTMAS TREE, RIGHT?
12-23
© 1985 PAWS, INC. All Rights Reserved.
YOU MUST BE PSYCHIC

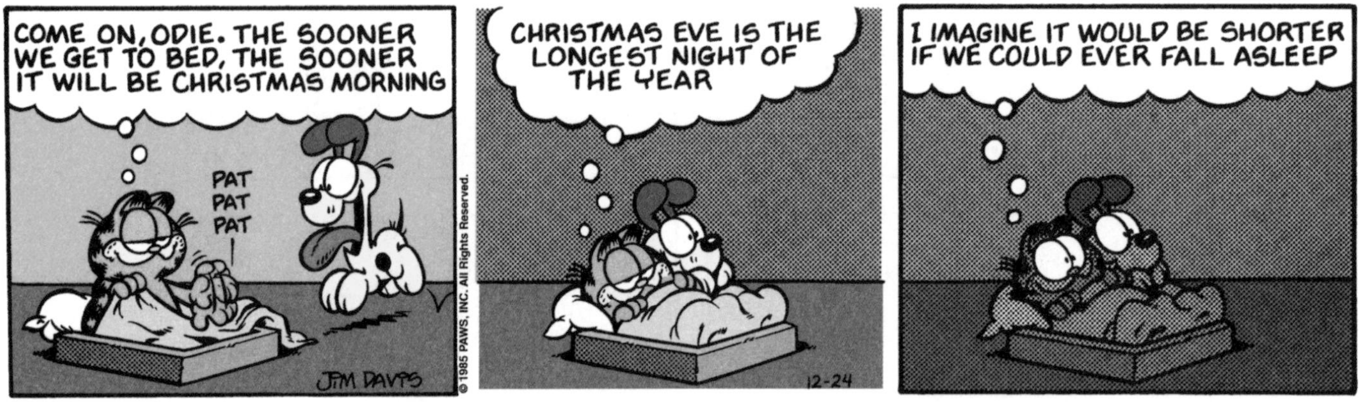
COME ON, ODIE. THE SOONER WE GET TO BED, THE SOONER IT WILL BE CHRISTMAS MORNING
PAT PAT PAT
JIM DAVIS
© 1985 PAWS, INC. All Rights Reserved.
CHRISTMAS EVE IS THE LONGEST NIGHT OF THE YEAR
12-24
I IMAGINE IT WOULD BE SHORTER IF WE COULD EVER FALL ASLEEP

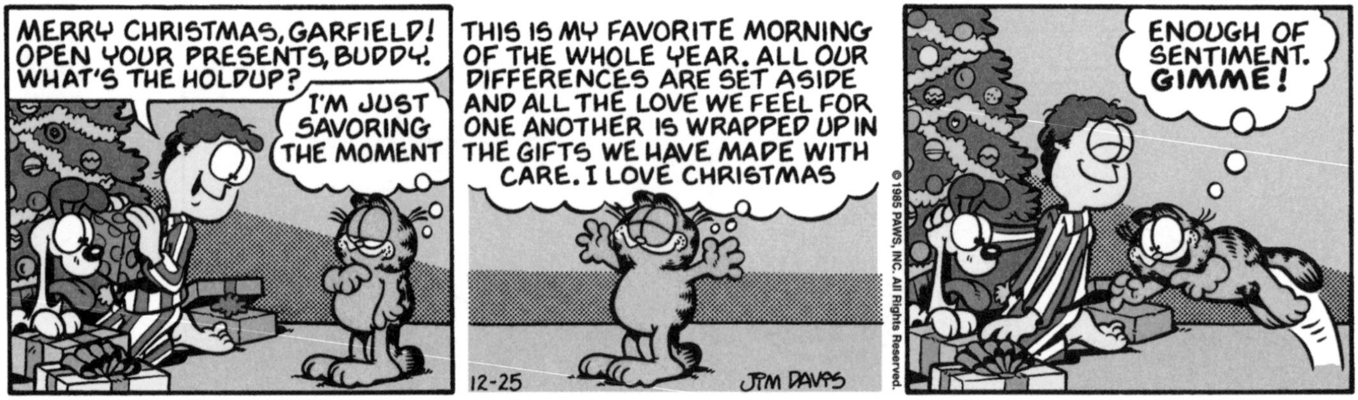
MERRY CHRISTMAS, GARFIELD! OPEN YOUR PRESENTS, BUDDY. WHAT'S THE HOLDUP?
I'M JUST SAVORING THE MOMENT
THIS IS MY FAVORITE MORNING OF THE WHOLE YEAR. ALL OUR DIFFERENCES ARE SET ASIDE AND ALL THE LOVE WE FEEL FOR ONE ANOTHER IS WRAPPED UP IN THE GIFTS WE HAVE MADE WITH CARE. I LOVE CHRISTMAS
12-25
JIM DAVIS
© 1985 PAWS, INC. All Rights Reserved.
ENOUGH OF SENTIMENT. GIMME!

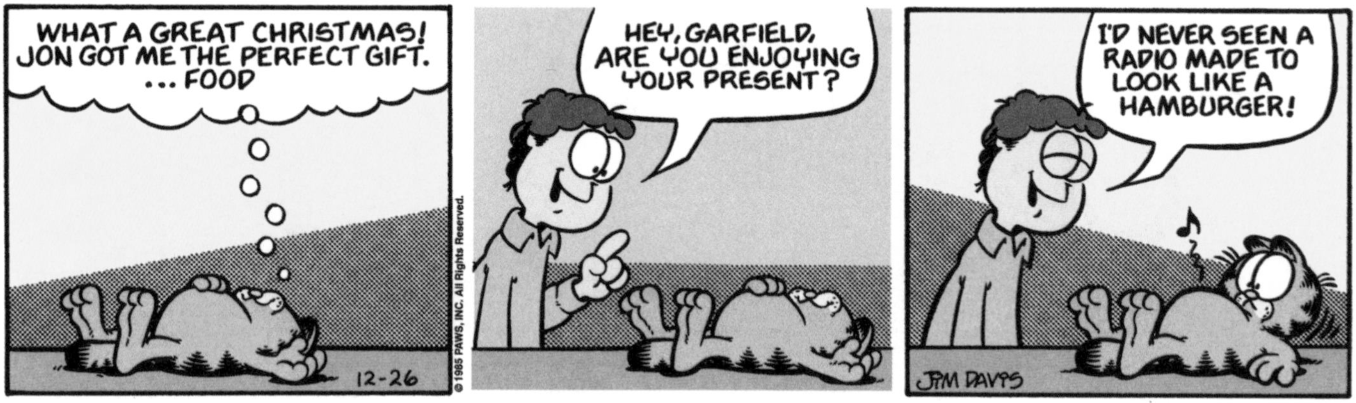
WHAT A GREAT CHRISTMAS! JON GOT ME THE PERFECT GIFT. ...FOOD
12-26
© 1985 PAWS, INC. All Rights Reserved.
HEY, GARFIELD, ARE YOU ENJOYING YOUR PRESENT?
I'D NEVER SEEN A RADIO MADE TO LOOK LIKE A HAMBURGER!
JIM DAVIS

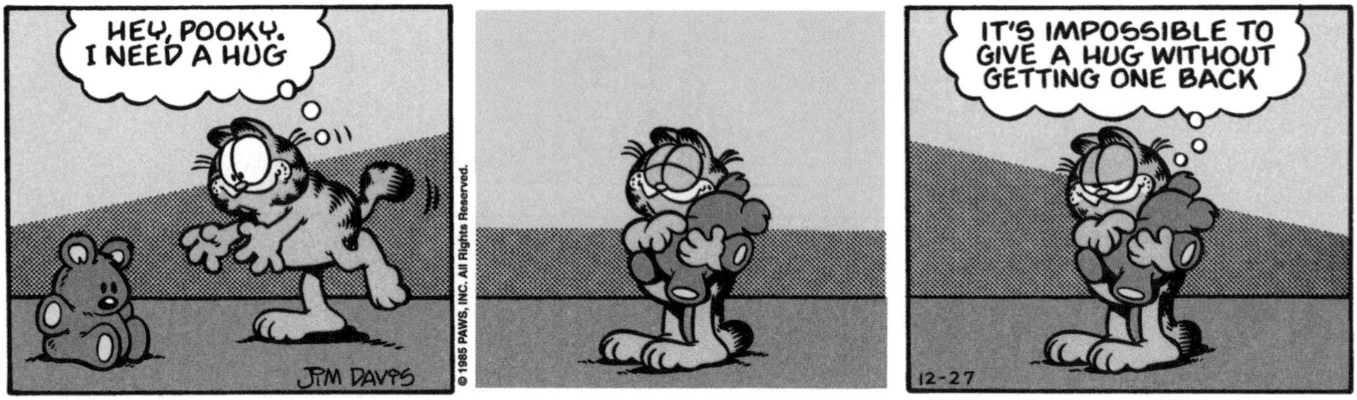
HEY, POOKY. I NEED A HUG
JIM DAVIS
© 1985 PAWS, INC. All Rights Reserved.
IT'S IMPOSSIBLE TO GIVE A HUG WITHOUT GETTING ONE BACK
12-27

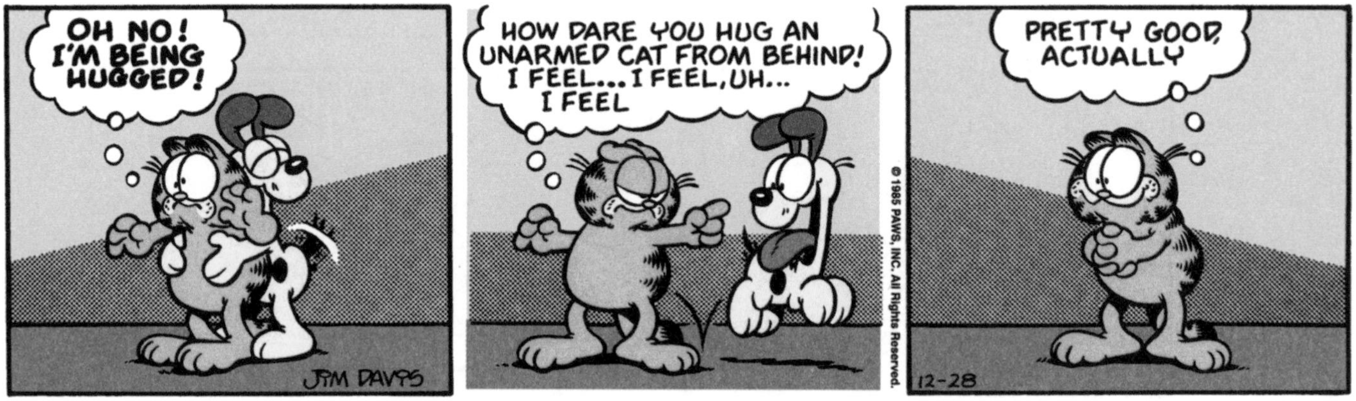
OH NO! I'M BEING HUGGED!
JIM DAVIS
HOW DARE YOU HUG AN UNARMED CAT FROM BEHIND! I FEEL... I FEEL, UH... I FEEL
© 1985 PAWS, INC. All Rights Reserved.
PRETTY GOOD, ACTUALLY
12-28

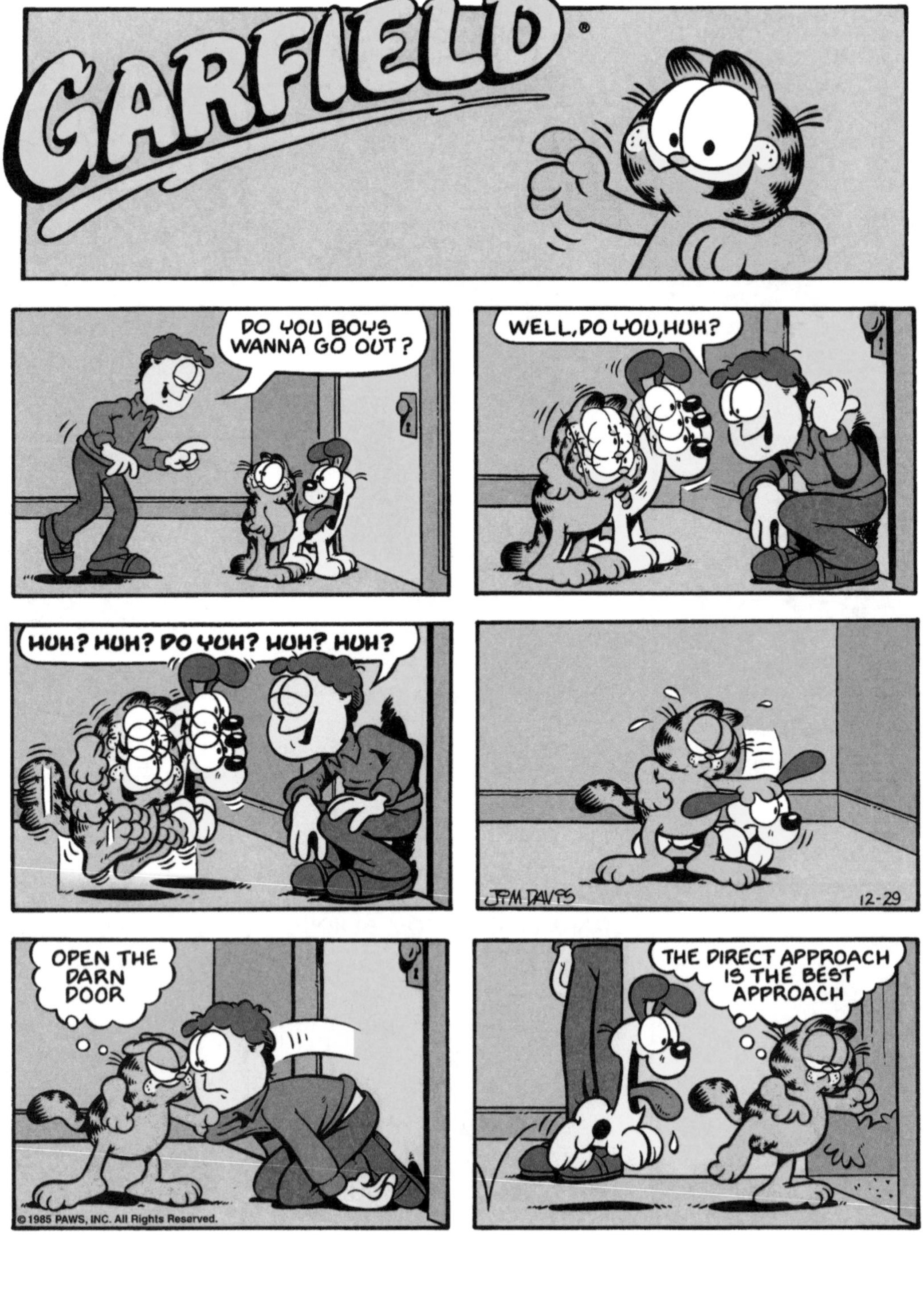
GARFIELD®
DO YOU BOYS WANNA GO OUT?
WELL, DO YOU, HUH?
HUH? HUH? DO YUH? HUH? HUH?
JIM DAVIS
12-29
OPEN THE DARN DOOR
THE DIRECT APPROACH IS THE BEST APPROACH
© 1985 PAWS, INC. All Rights Reserved.

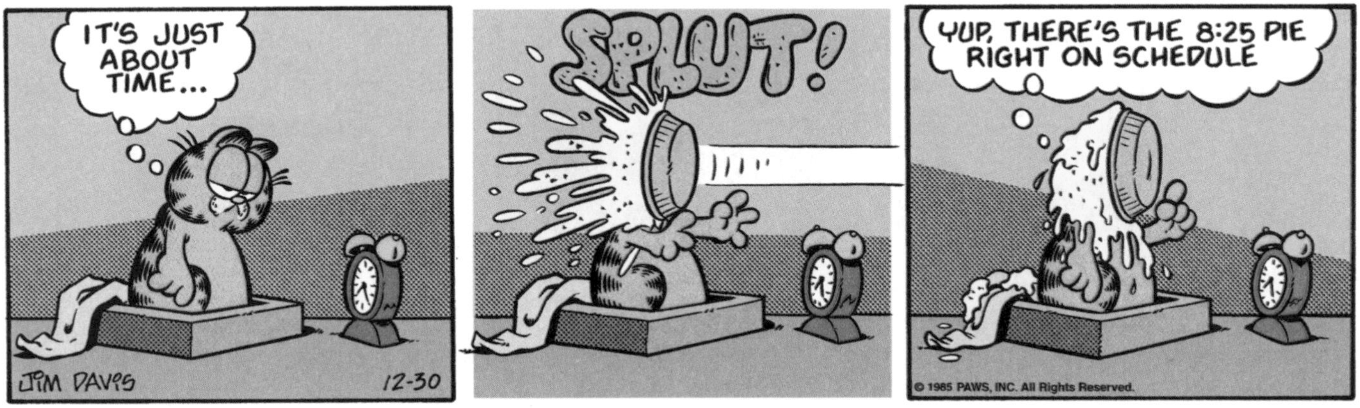
IT'S JUST ABOUT TIME...
SPLUT!
YUP, THERE'S THE 8:25 PIE RIGHT ON SCHEDULE
JIM DAVIS
12-30
© 1985 PAWS, INC. All Rights Reserved.

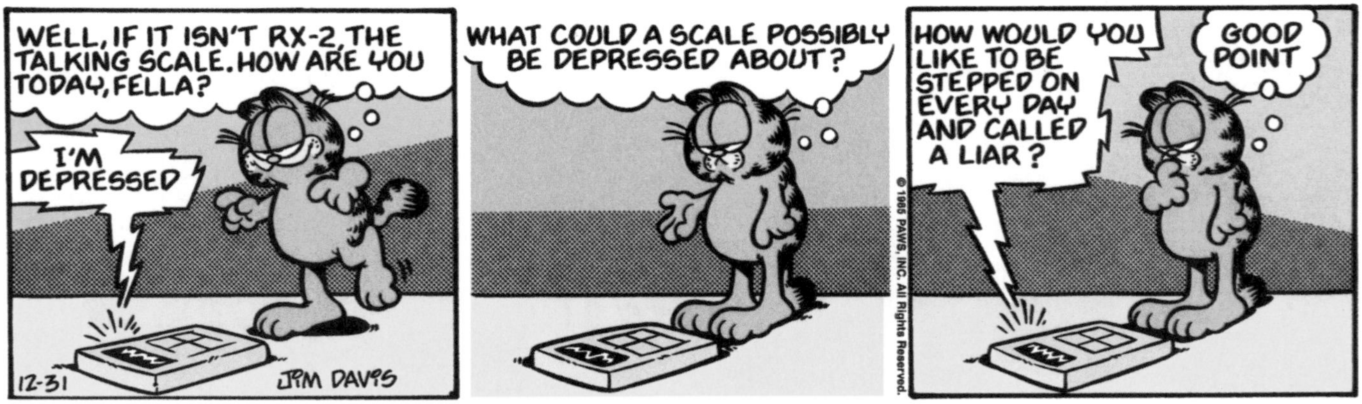
WELL, IF IT ISN'T RX-2, THE TALKING SCALE. HOW ARE YOU TODAY, FELLA?
I'M DEPRESSED
WHAT COULD A SCALE POSSIBLY BE DEPRESSED ABOUT?
HOW WOULD YOU LIKE TO BE STEPPED ON EVERY DAY AND CALLED A LIAR?
GOOD POINT
12-31
JIM DAVIS
© 1985 PAWS, INC. All Rights Reserved.

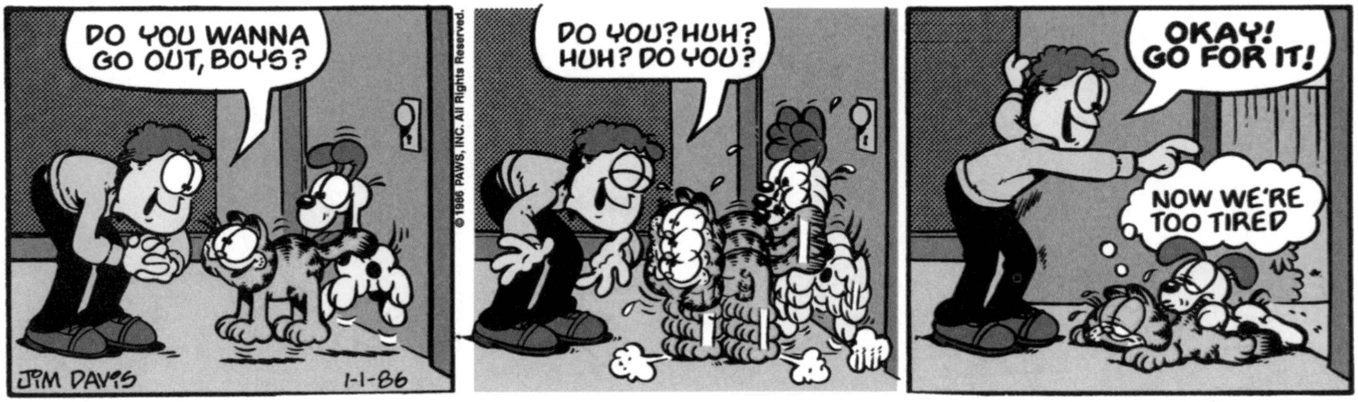
DO YOU WANNA GO OUT, BOYS?
DO YOU? HUH? HUH? DO YOU?
OKAY! GO FOR IT!
NOW WE'RE TOO TIRED
JIM DAVIS
1-1-86
© 1986 PAWS, INC. All Rights Reserved.

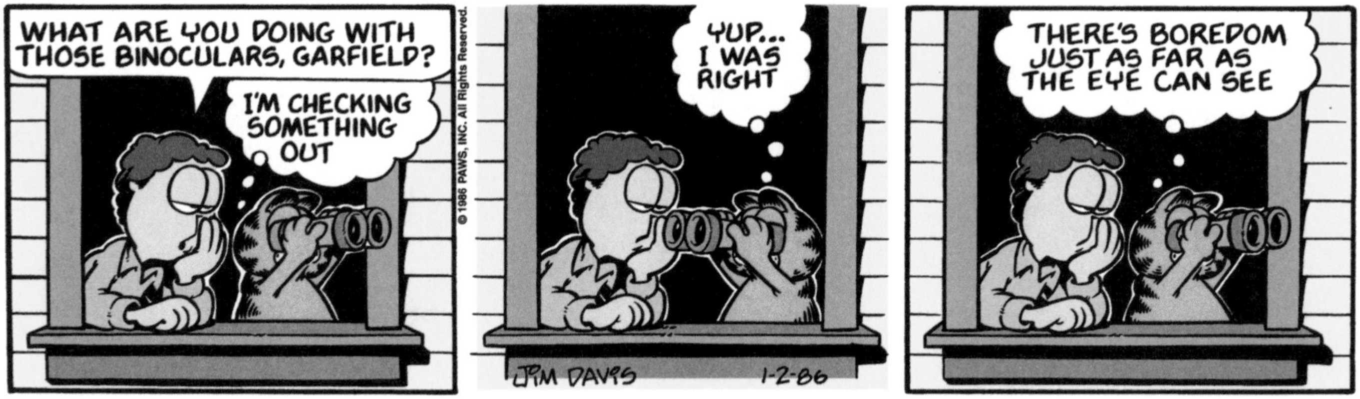
WHAT ARE YOU DOING WITH THOSE BINOCULARS, GARFIELD?
I'M CHECKING SOMETHING OUT
© 1986 PAWS, INC. All Rights Reserved.
YUP... I WAS RIGHT
JIM DAVIS 1-2-86
THERE'S BOREDOM JUST AS FAR AS THE EYE CAN SEE

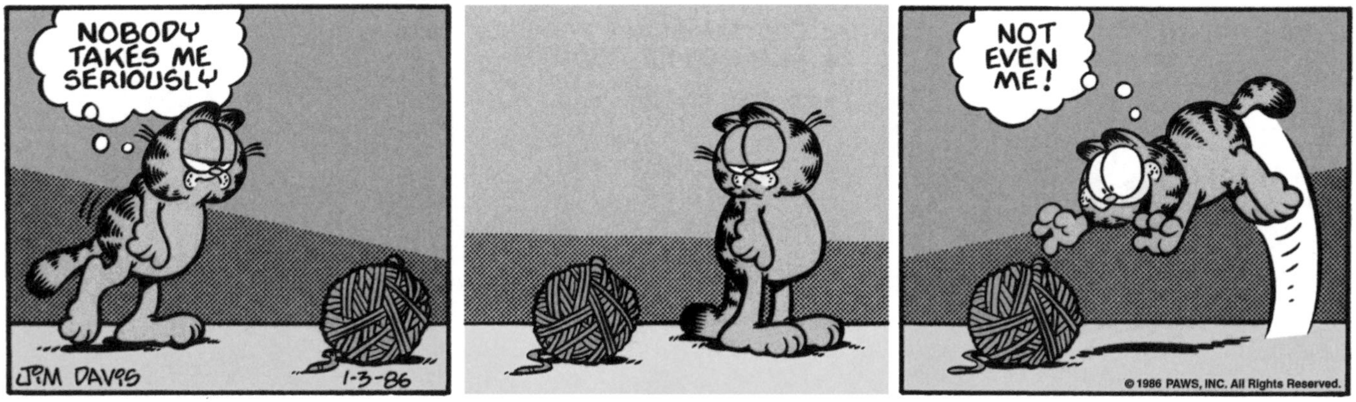
NOBODY TAKES ME SERIOUSLY
JIM DAVIS 1-3-86
NOT EVEN ME!
© 1986 PAWS, INC. All Rights Reserved.

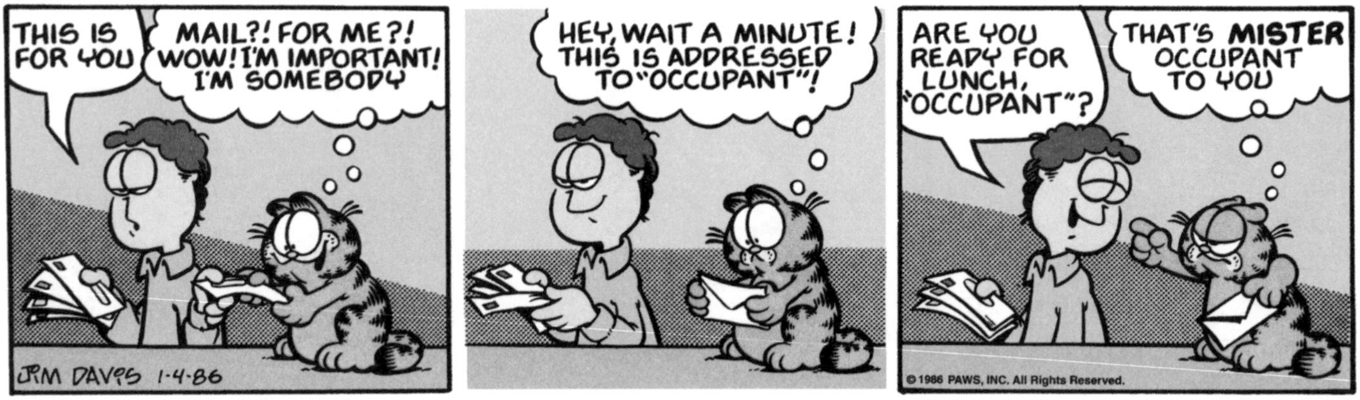
THIS IS FOR YOU
MAIL?! FOR ME?! WOW! I'M IMPORTANT! I'M SOMEBODY
JIM DAVIS 1-4-86
HEY, WAIT A MINUTE! THIS IS ADDRESSED TO "OCCUPANT"!
ARE YOU READY FOR LUNCH, "OCCUPANT"?
THAT'S **MISTER** OCCUPANT TO YOU
© 1986 PAWS, INC. All Rights Reserved.

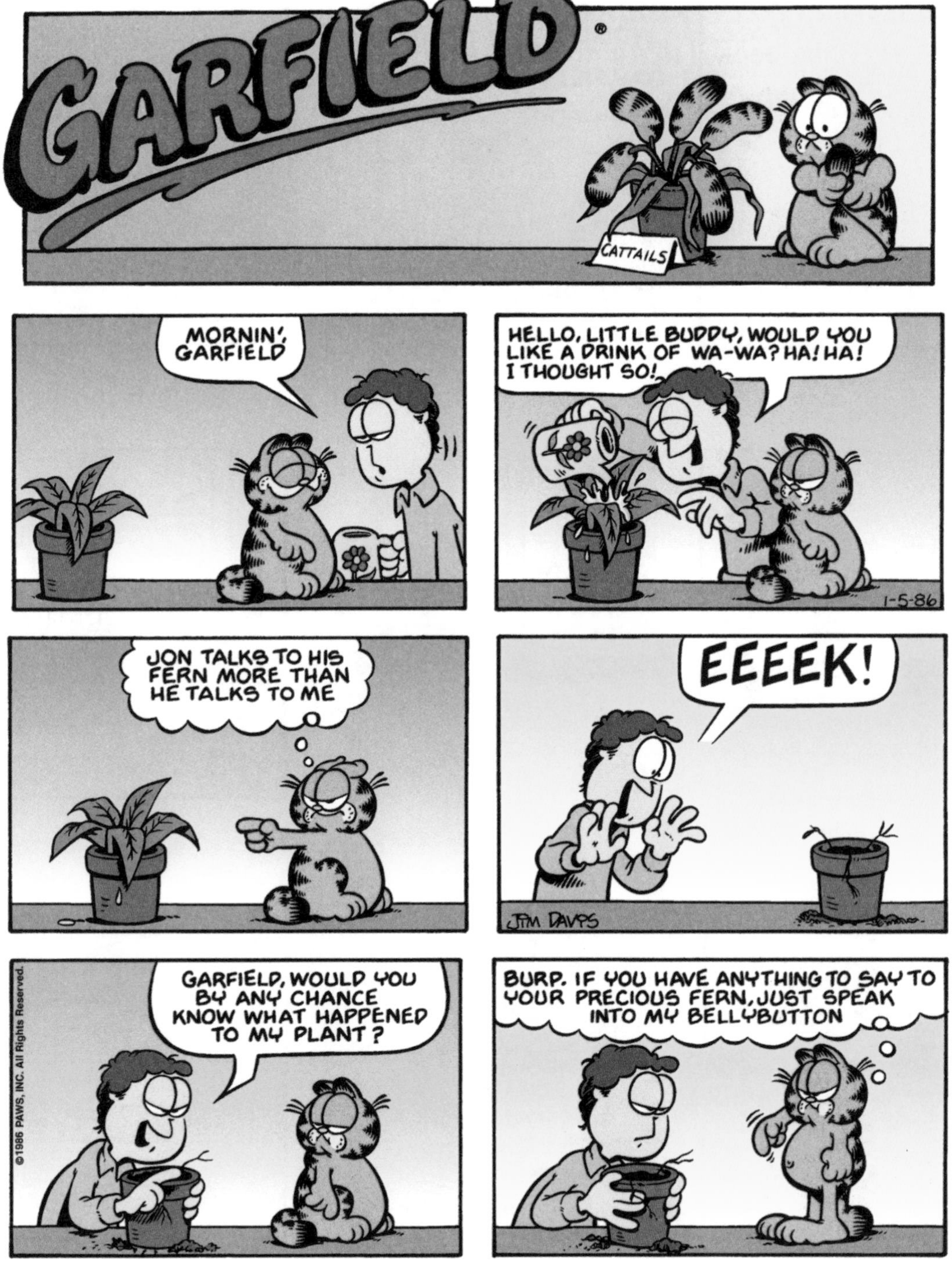
GARFIELD®
CATTAILS
MORNIN', GARFIELD
HELLO, LITTLE BUDDY, WOULD YOU LIKE A DRINK OF WA-WA? HA! HA! I THOUGHT SO!
1-5-86
JON TALKS TO HIS FERN MORE THAN HE TALKS TO ME
EEEEK!
JIM DAVIS
GARFIELD, WOULD YOU BY ANY CHANCE KNOW WHAT HAPPENED TO MY PLANT?
BURP. IF YOU HAVE ANYTHING TO SAY TO YOUR PRECIOUS FERN, JUST SPEAK INTO MY BELLYBUTTON

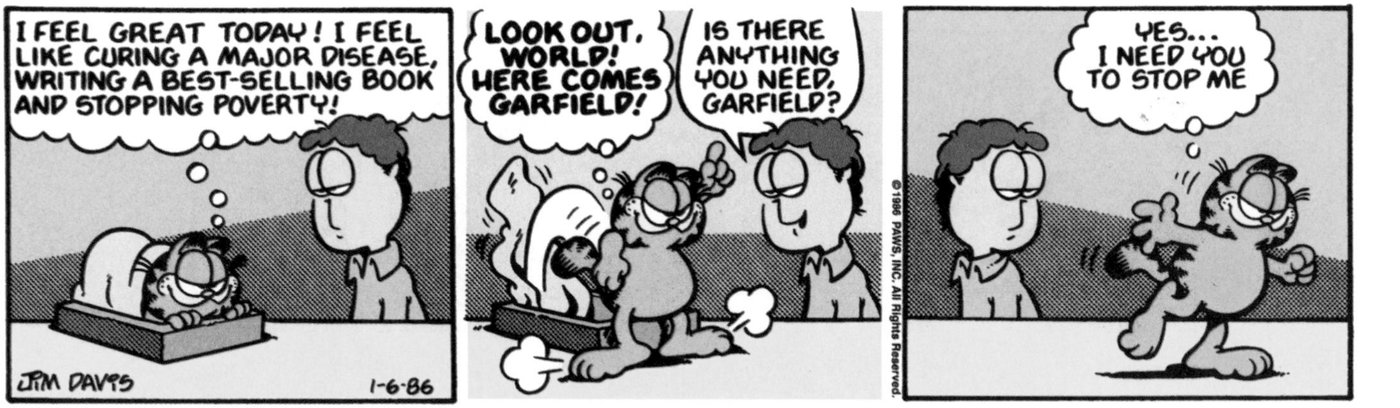
I FEEL GREAT TODAY! I FEEL LIKE CURING A MAJOR DISEASE, WRITING A BEST-SELLING BOOK AND STOPPING POVERTY!
JIM DAVIS
1-6-86
LOOK OUT, WORLD! HERE COMES GARFIELD!
IS THERE ANYTHING YOU NEED, GARFIELD?
©1986 PAWS, INC. All Rights Reserved.
YES... I NEED YOU TO STOP ME

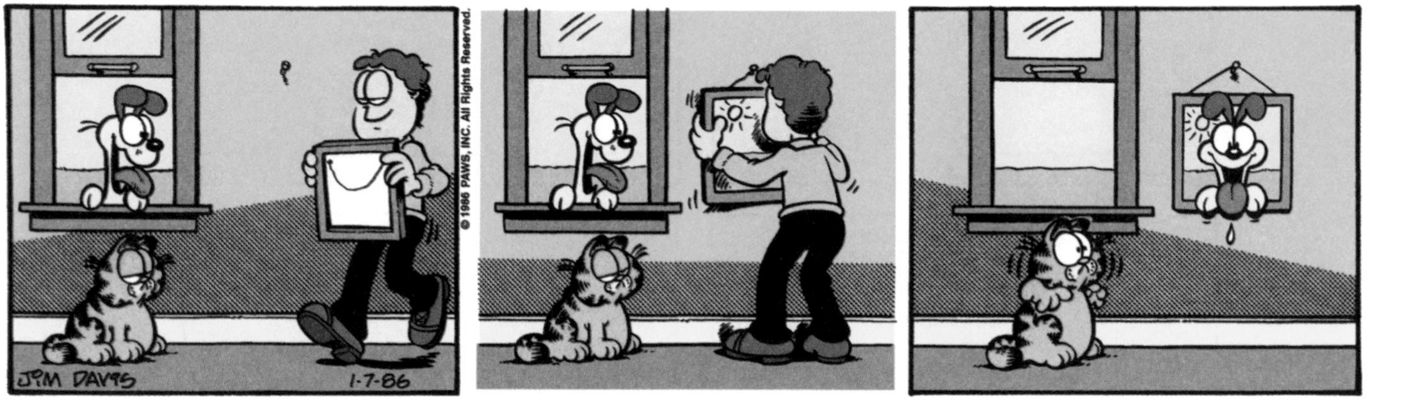
JIM DAVIS
1-7-86
©1986 PAWS, INC. All Rights Reserved.

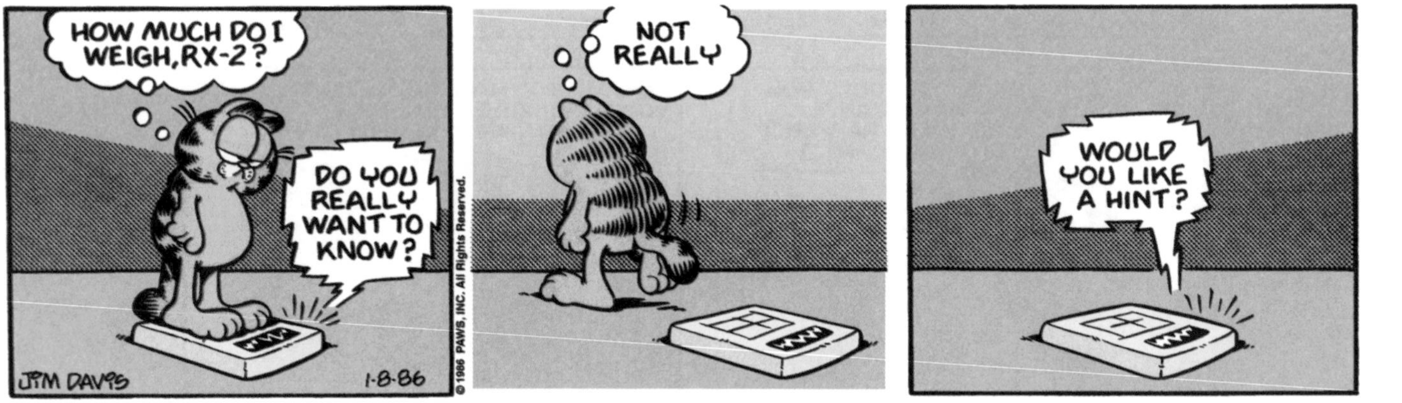
HOW MUCH DO I WEIGH, RX-2?
DO YOU REALLY WANT TO KNOW?
JIM DAVIS
1-8-86
©1986 PAWS, INC. All Rights Reserved.
NOT REALLY
WOULD YOU LIKE A HINT?

LET'S SEE HOW MUCH YOU KNOW ABOUT CATS
JIM DAVIS
© 1986 PAWS, INC. All Rights Reserved.
HERE ARE TWO PEOPLE WHO, FOR ALL PRACTICAL PURPOSES, APPEAR TO BE IDENTICAL
1-9-86
GUESS WHICH ONE IS ALLERGIC TO CATS

I WONDER IF THAT FLOOR IS COLD
1-10-86
JIM DAVIS
© 1986 PAWS, INC. All Rights Reserved.
YUP... IT'S COLD ALL RIGHT

I LOVE HANGING ON THE SCREEN DOOR. I CAN BE A FLY OR A MOUNTAIN CLIMBER...
ACME
WHAM! WHAM! WHAM!
1-11-86
© 1986 PAWS, INC. All Rights Reserved.
OR A DOOR KNOCKER
JIM DAVIS

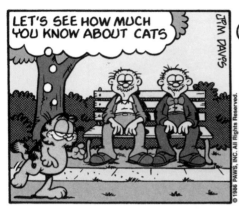

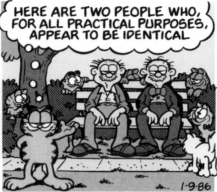

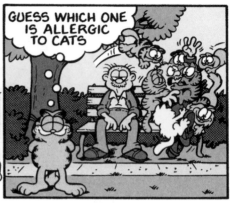

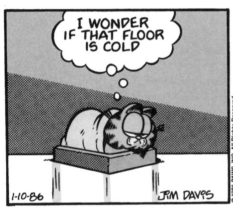

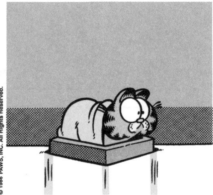

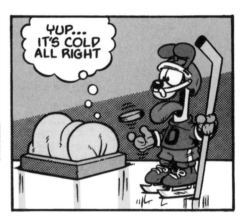

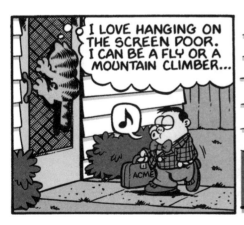

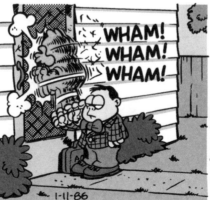

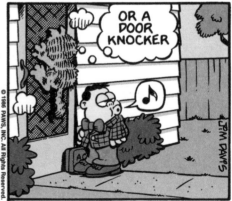

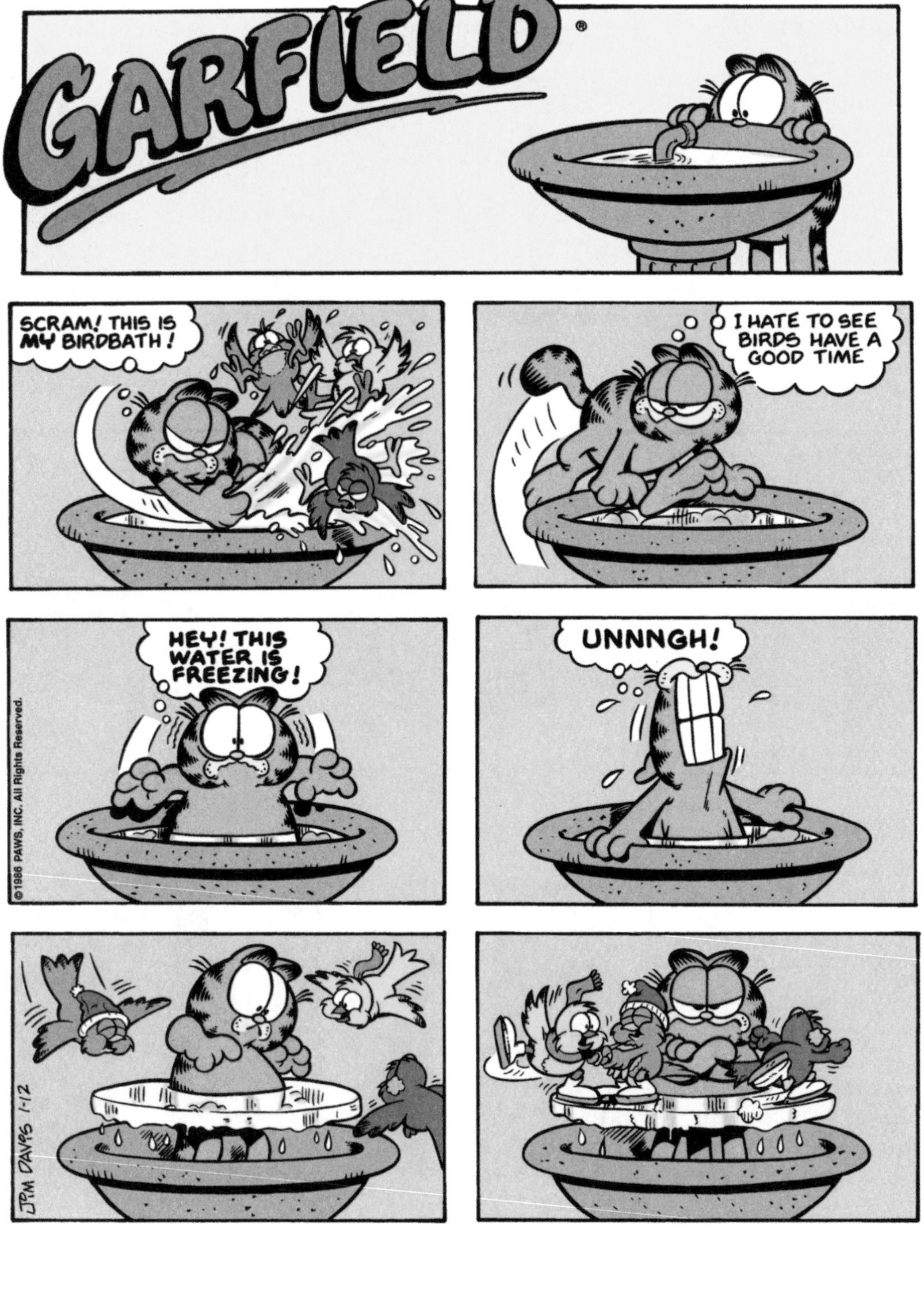
GARFIELD®
SCRAM! THIS IS MY BIRDBATH!
I HATE TO SEE BIRDS HAVE A GOOD TIME
HEY! THIS WATER IS FREEZING!
UNNNGH!
©1986 PAWS, INC. All Rights Reserved.
JPM DAVPS 1-12

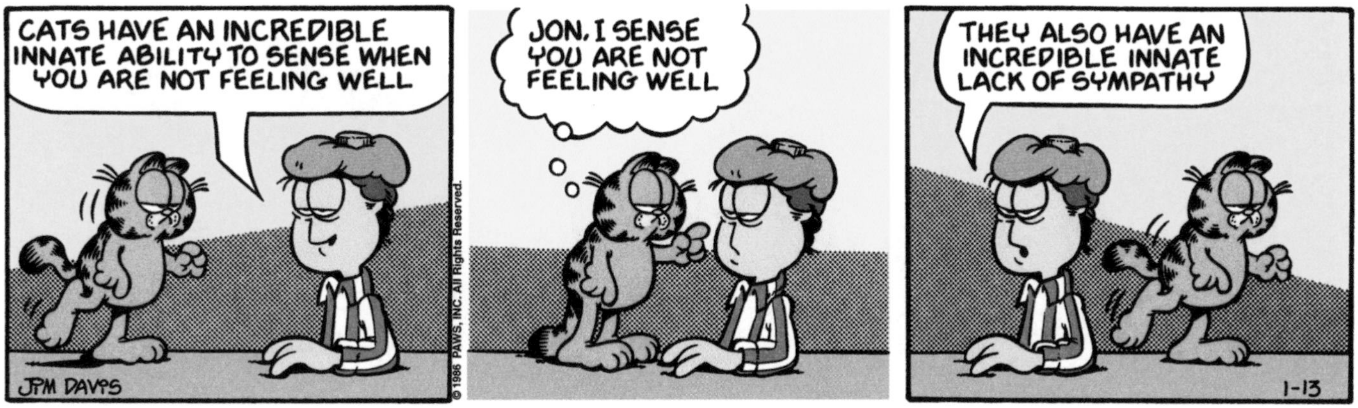
CATS HAVE AN INCREDIBLE INNATE ABILITY TO SENSE WHEN YOU ARE NOT FEELING WELL
JIM DAVIS
© 1986 PAWS, INC. All Rights Reserved.
JON, I SENSE YOU ARE NOT FEELING WELL
THEY ALSO HAVE AN INCREDIBLE INNATE LACK OF SYMPATHY
1-13

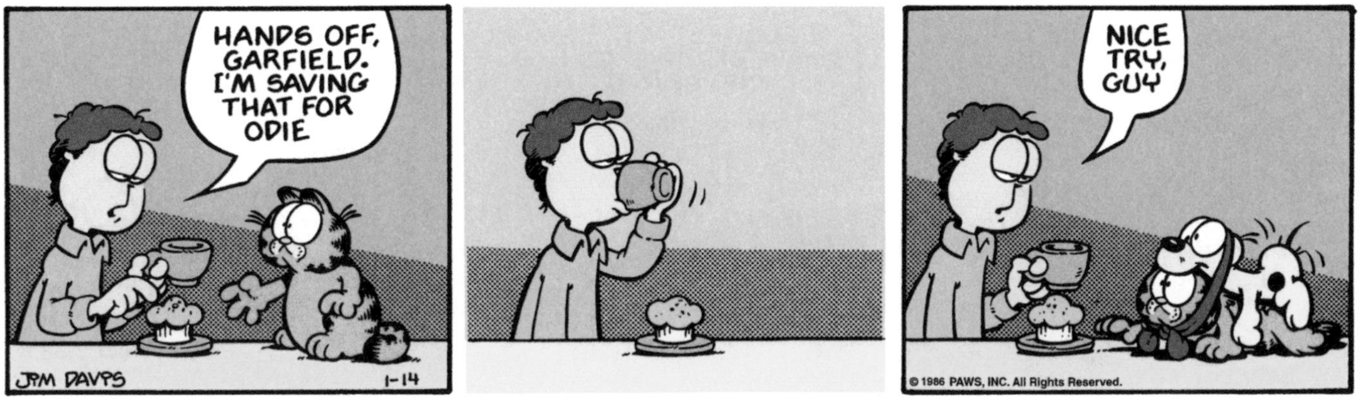
HANDS OFF, GARFIELD. I'M SAVING THAT FOR ODIE
JIM DAVIS
1-14
NICE TRY, GUY
© 1986 PAWS, INC. All Rights Reserved.

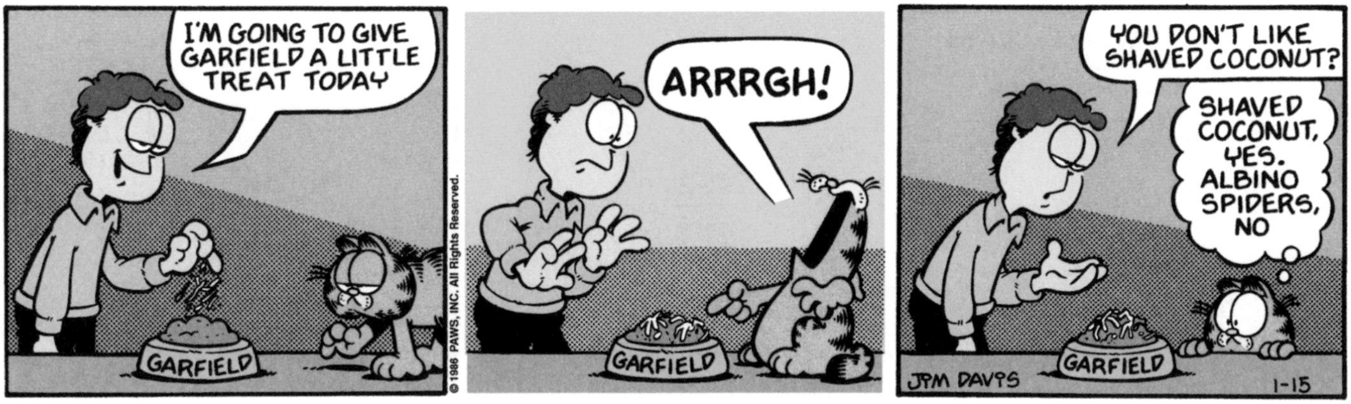
I'M GOING TO GIVE GARFIELD A LITTLE TREAT TODAY
GARFIELD
© 1986 PAWS, INC. All Rights Reserved.
ARRRGH!
GARFIELD
YOU DON'T LIKE SHAVED COCONUT?
SHAVED COCONUT, YES. ALBINO SPIDERS, NO
GARFIELD
JIM DAVIS
1-15

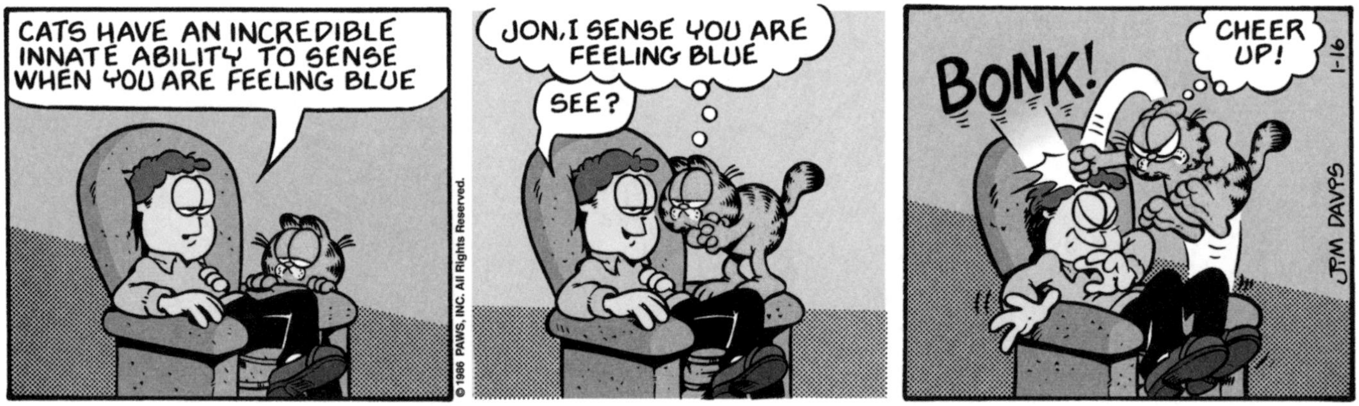
CATS HAVE AN INCREDIBLE INNATE ABILITY TO SENSE WHEN YOU ARE FEELING BLUE
JON, I SENSE YOU ARE FEELING BLUE
SEE?
BONK!
CHEER UP!
JIM DAVIS
1-16

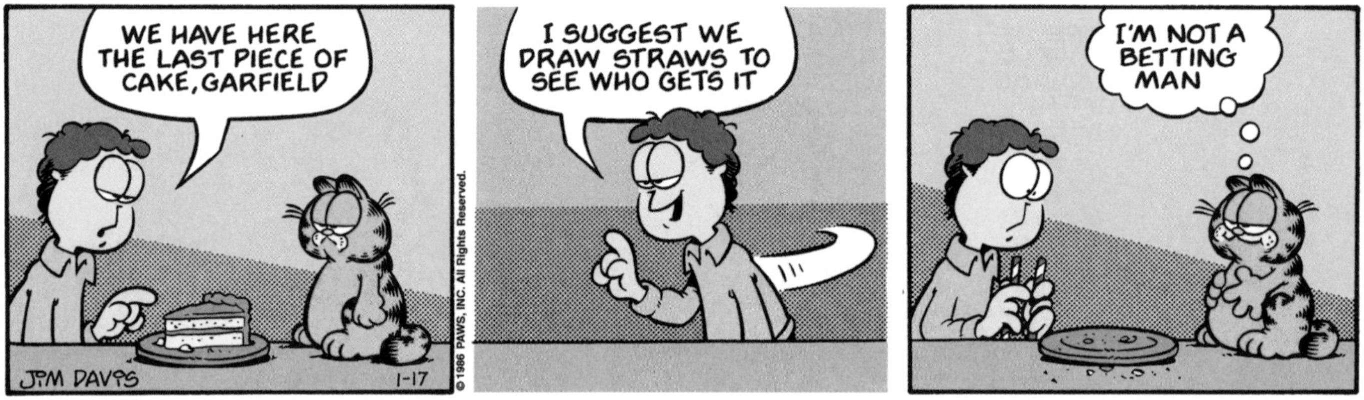
WE HAVE HERE THE LAST PIECE OF CAKE, GARFIELD
JIM DAVIS
1-17
I SUGGEST WE DRAW STRAWS TO SEE WHO GETS IT
I'M NOT A BETTING MAN

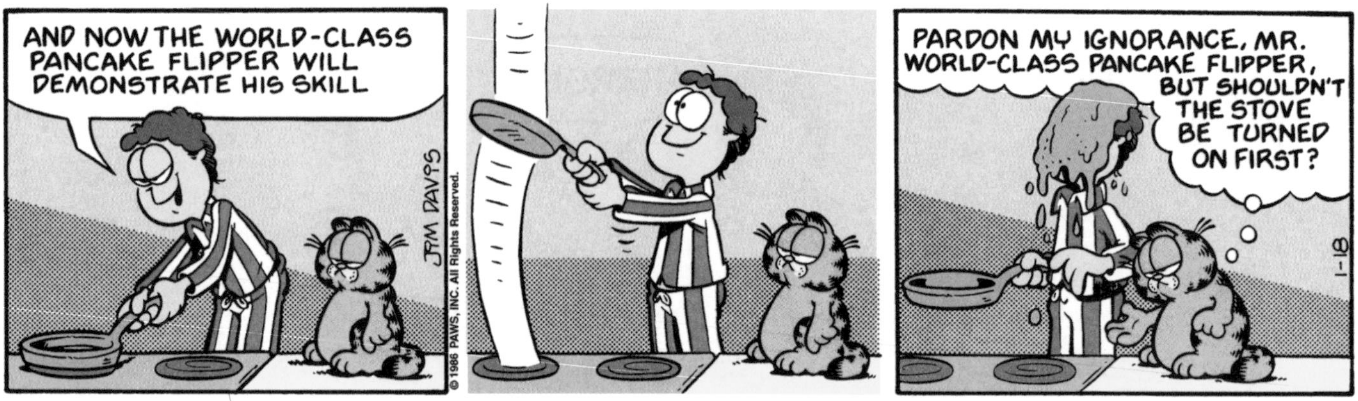
AND NOW THE WORLD-CLASS PANCAKE FLIPPER WILL DEMONSTRATE HIS SKILL
JIM DAVIS
PARDON MY IGNORANCE, MR. WORLD-CLASS PANCAKE FLIPPER, BUT SHOULDN'T THE STOVE BE TURNED ON FIRST?
1-18

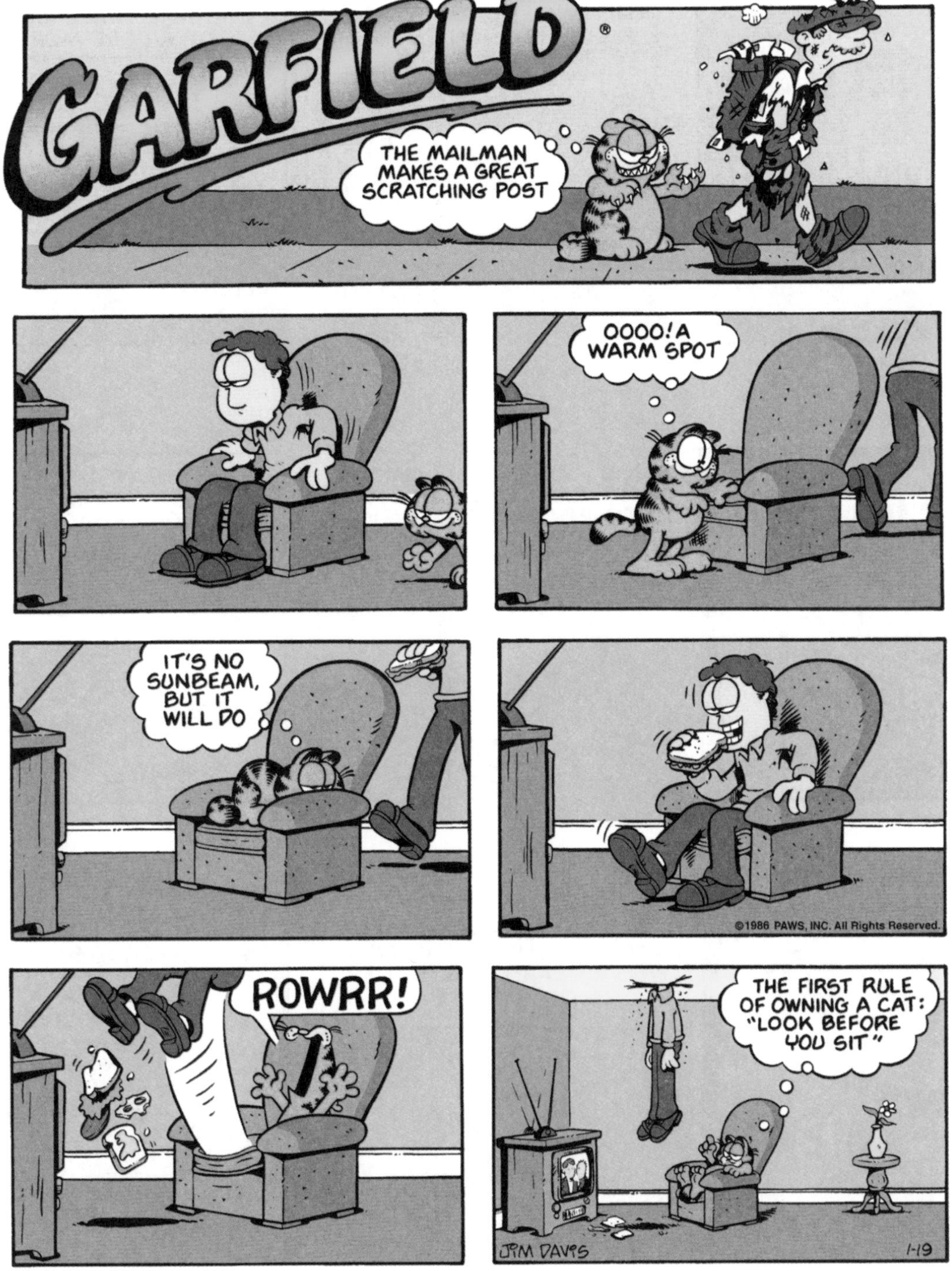
GARFIELD®
THE MAILMAN MAKES A GREAT SCRATCHING POST
OOOO! A WARM SPOT
IT'S NO SUNBEAM, BUT IT WILL DO
©1986 PAWS, INC. All Rights Reserved.
ROWRR!
THE FIRST RULE OF OWNING A CAT: "LOOK BEFORE YOU SIT"
JIM DAVIS
1-19

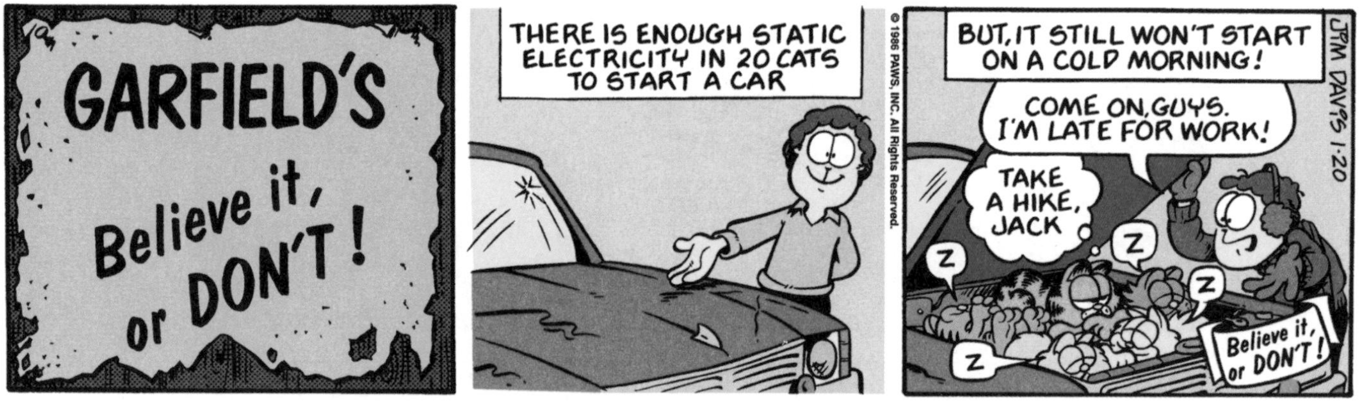
GARFIELD'S
Believe it, or DON'T!
THERE IS ENOUGH STATIC ELECTRICITY IN 20 CATS TO START A CAR
© 1986 PAWS, INC. All Rights Reserved.
BUT, IT STILL WON'T START ON A COLD MORNING!
COME ON, GUYS. I'M LATE FOR WORK!
TAKE A HIKE, JACK
Z
Z
Z
Z
Believe it, or DON'T!
JIM DAVIS 1-20

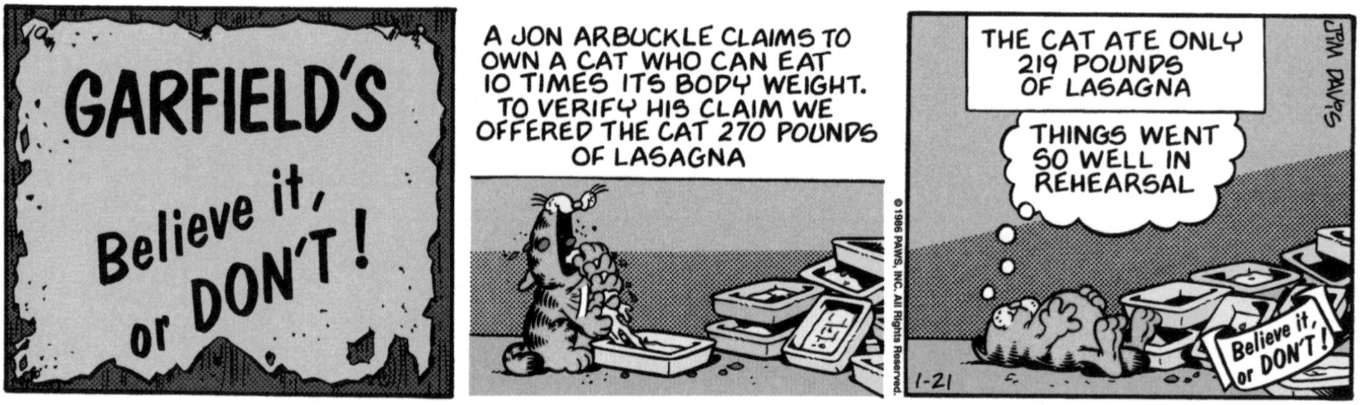
GARFIELD'S
Believe it, or DON'T!
A JON ARBUCKLE CLAIMS TO OWN A CAT WHO CAN EAT 10 TIMES ITS BODY WEIGHT. TO VERIFY HIS CLAIM WE OFFERED THE CAT 270 POUNDS OF LASAGNA
© 1986 PAWS, INC. All Rights Reserved.
THE CAT ATE ONLY 219 POUNDS OF LASAGNA
THINGS WENT SO WELL IN REHEARSAL
Believe it, or DON'T!
JIM DAVIS
1-21

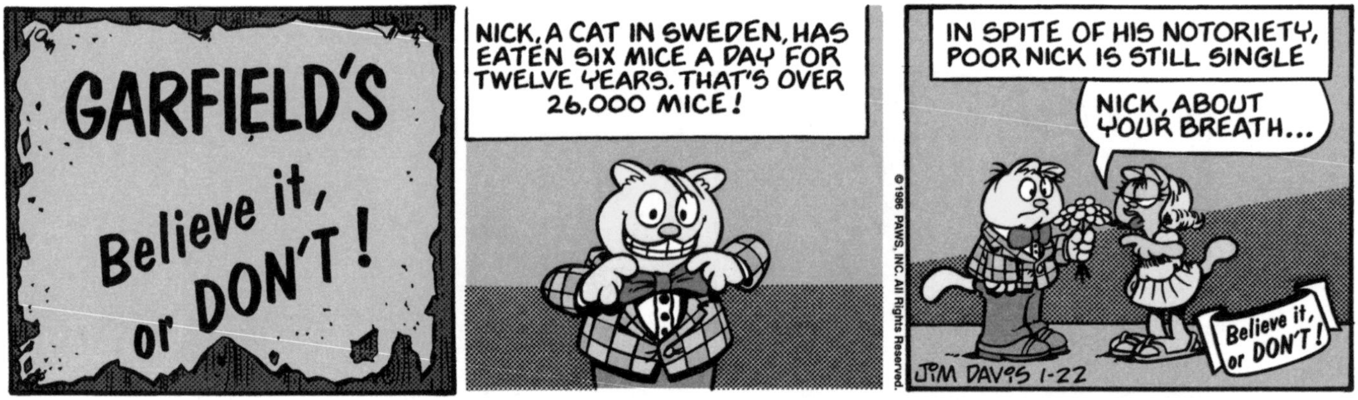
GARFIELD'S
Believe it, or DON'T!
NICK, A CAT IN SWEDEN, HAS EATEN SIX MICE A DAY FOR TWELVE YEARS. THAT'S OVER 26,000 MICE!
© 1986 PAWS, INC. All Rights Reserved.
IN SPITE OF HIS NOTORIETY, POOR NICK IS STILL SINGLE
NICK, ABOUT YOUR BREATH...
Believe it, or DON'T!
JIM DAVIS 1-22

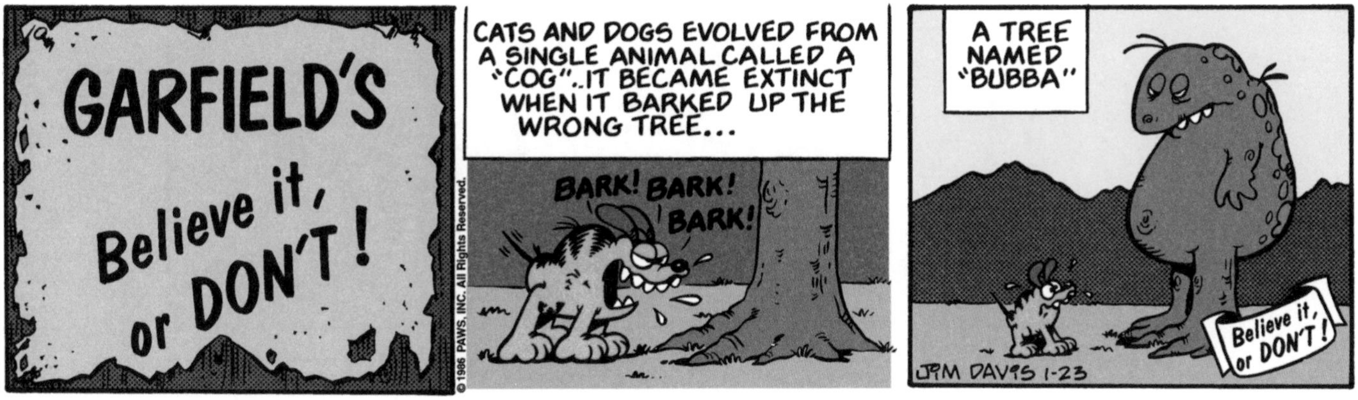
GARFIELD'S
Believe it, or DON'T!
CATS AND DOGS EVOLVED FROM A SINGLE ANIMAL CALLED A "COG". IT BECAME EXTINCT WHEN IT BARKED UP THE WRONG TREE...
BARK! BARK! BARK!
© 1986 PAWS, INC. All Rights Reserved.
A TREE NAMED "BUBBA"
Believe it, or DON'T!
JIM DAVIS 1-23

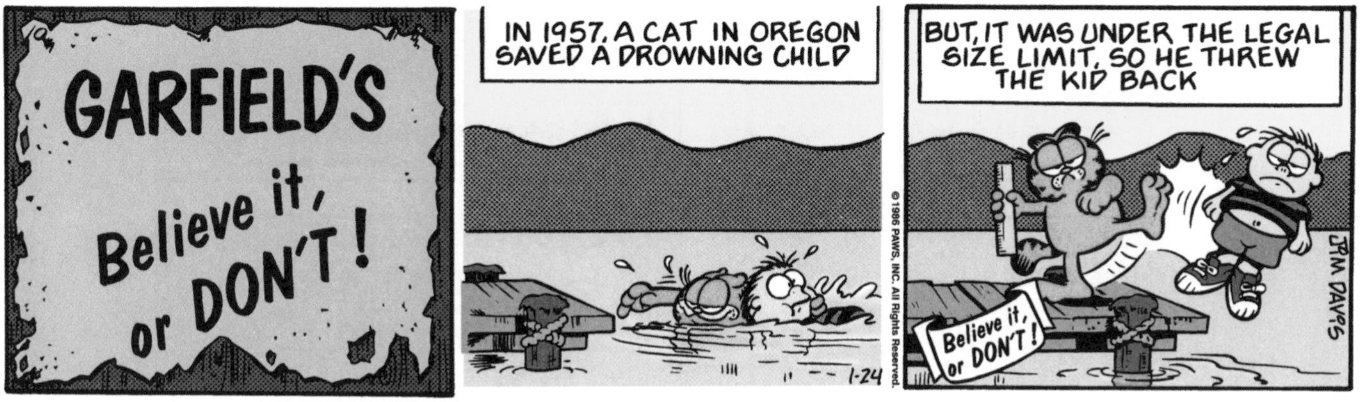
GARFIELD'S
Believe it, or DON'T!
IN 1957, A CAT IN OREGON SAVED A DROWNING CHILD
1-24
© 1986 PAWS, INC. All Rights Reserved.
BUT, IT WAS UNDER THE LEGAL SIZE LIMIT, SO HE THREW THE KID BACK
Believe it, or DON'T!
JIM DAVIS

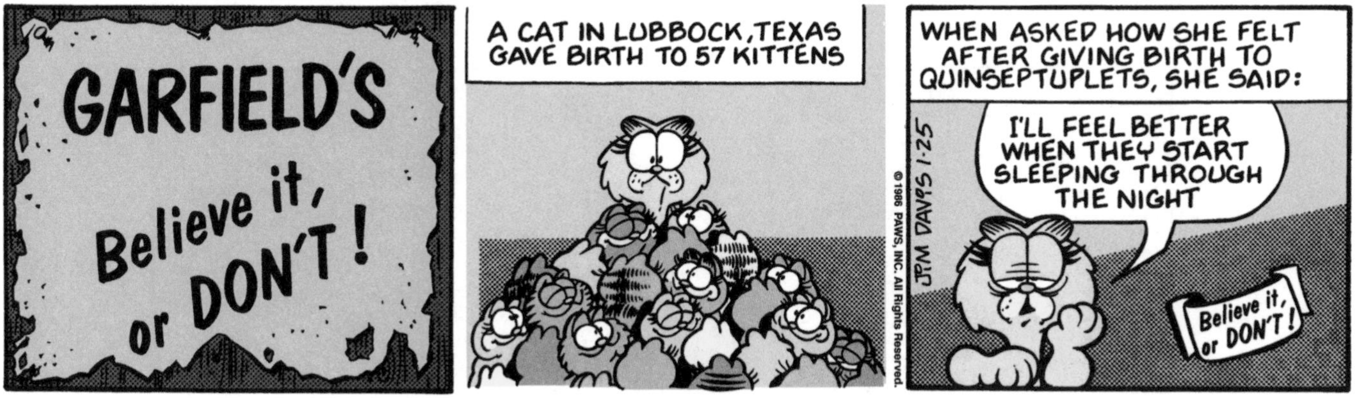
GARFIELD'S
Believe it, or DON'T!
A CAT IN LUBBOCK, TEXAS GAVE BIRTH TO 57 KITTENS
© 1986 PAWS, INC. All Rights Reserved.
JIM DAVIS 1-25
WHEN ASKED HOW SHE FELT AFTER GIVING BIRTH TO QUINSEPTUPLETS, SHE SAID:
I'LL FEEL BETTER WHEN THEY START SLEEPING THROUGH THE NIGHT
Believe it, or DON'T!

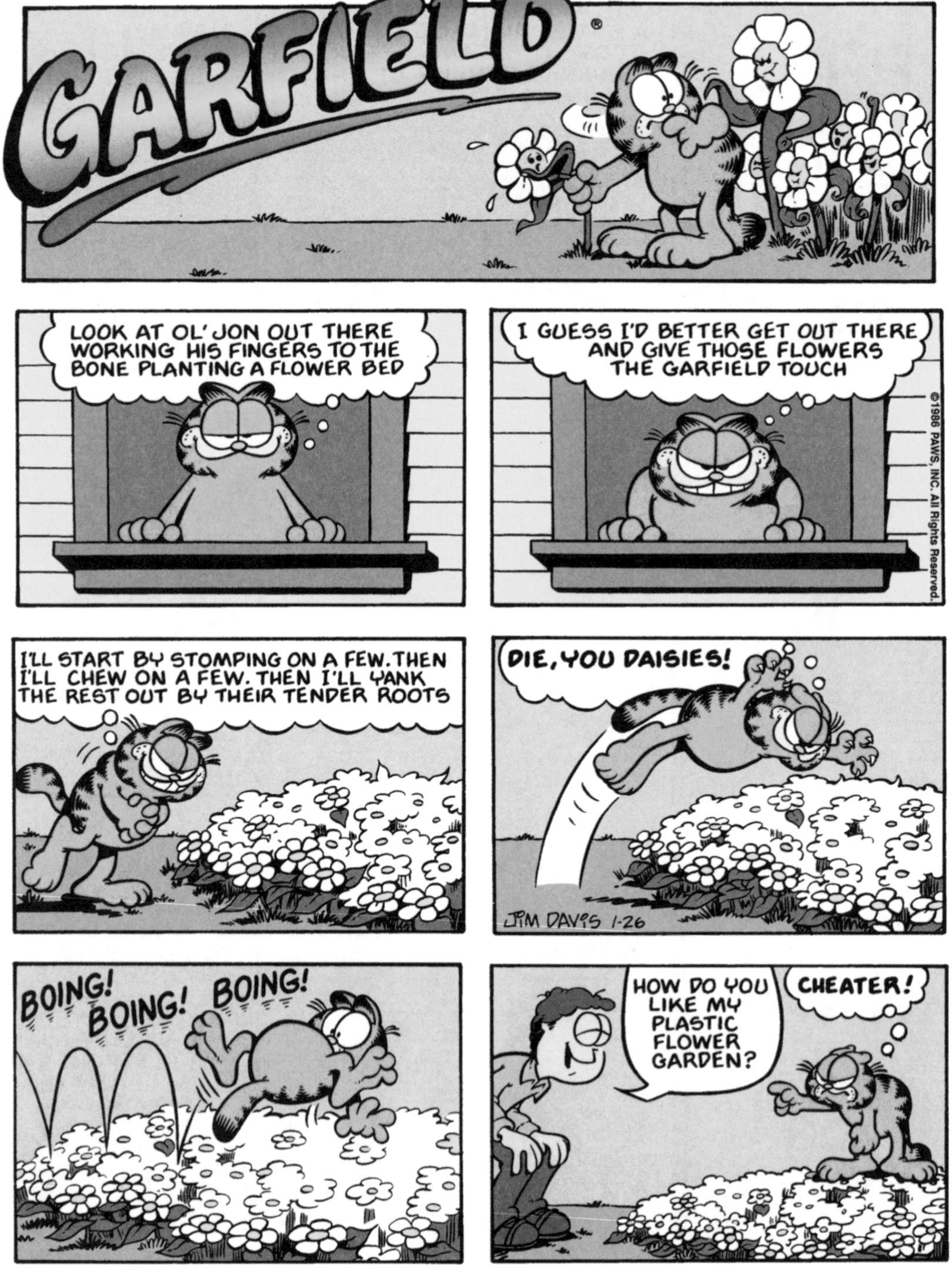

GARFIELD®
LOOK AT OL' JON OUT THERE WORKING HIS FINGERS TO THE BONE PLANTING A FLOWER BED
I GUESS I'D BETTER GET OUT THERE AND GIVE THOSE FLOWERS THE GARFIELD TOUCH
©1986 PAWS, INC. All Rights Reserved.
I'LL START BY STOMPING ON A FEW. THEN I'LL CHEW ON A FEW. THEN I'LL YANK THE REST OUT BY THEIR TENDER ROOTS
DIE, YOU DAISIES!
JIM DAVIS 1-26
BOING! BOING! BOING!
HOW DO YOU LIKE MY PLASTIC FLOWER GARDEN?
CHEATER!

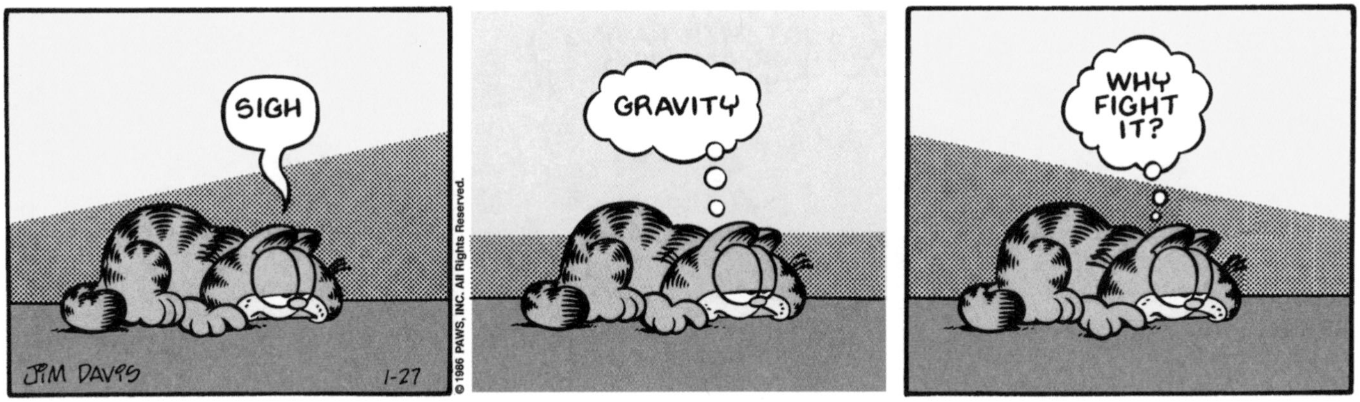
SIGH
GRAVITY
WHY FIGHT IT?
JIM DAVIS
1-27
© 1986 PAWS, INC. All Rights Reserved.

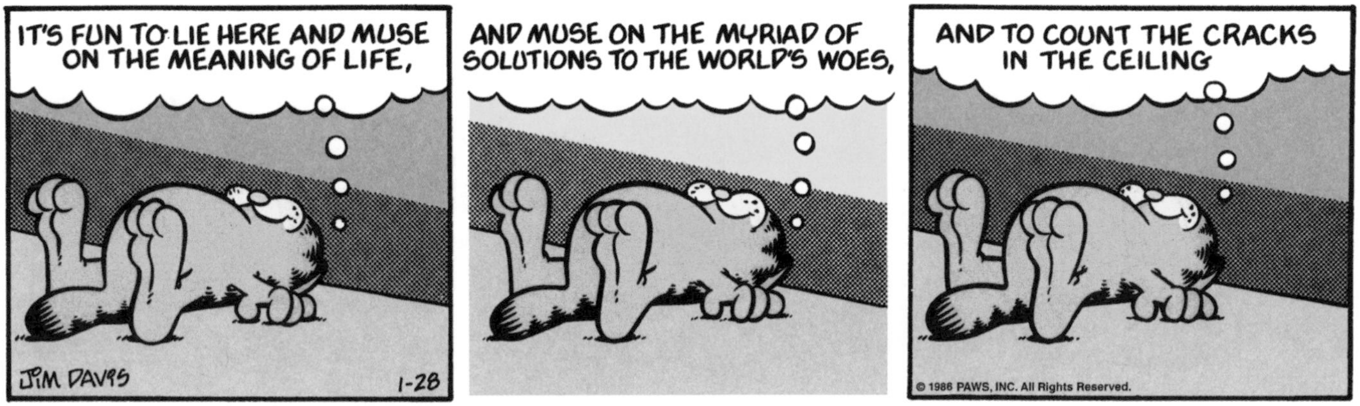
IT'S FUN TO LIE HERE AND MUSE ON THE MEANING OF LIFE,
AND MUSE ON THE MYRIAD OF SOLUTIONS TO THE WORLD'S WOES,
AND TO COUNT THE CRACKS IN THE CEILING
JIM DAVIS
1-28
© 1986 PAWS, INC. All Rights Reserved.

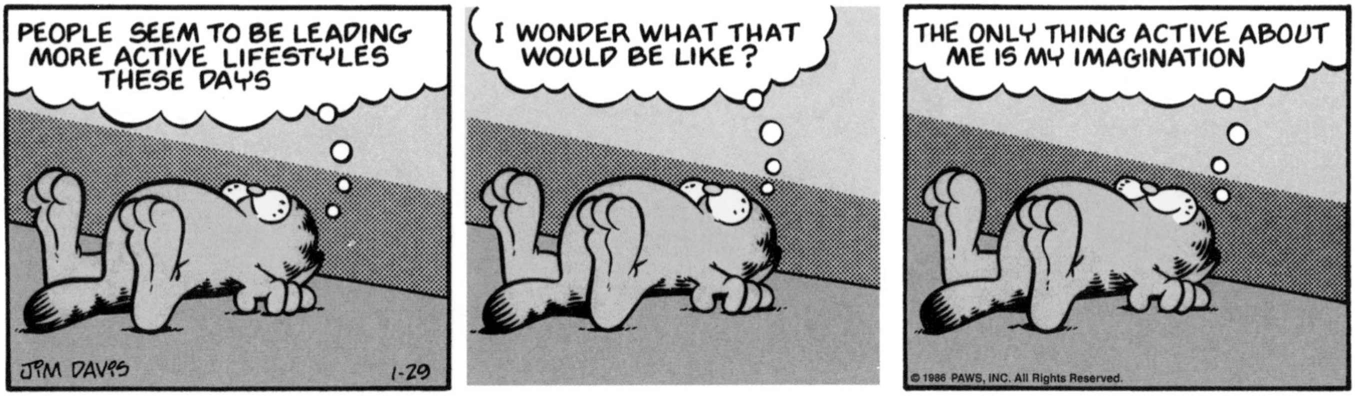
PEOPLE SEEM TO BE LEADING MORE ACTIVE LIFESTYLES THESE DAYS
I WONDER WHAT THAT WOULD BE LIKE?
THE ONLY THING ACTIVE ABOUT ME IS MY IMAGINATION
JIM DAVIS
1-29
© 1986 PAWS, INC. All Rights Reserved.

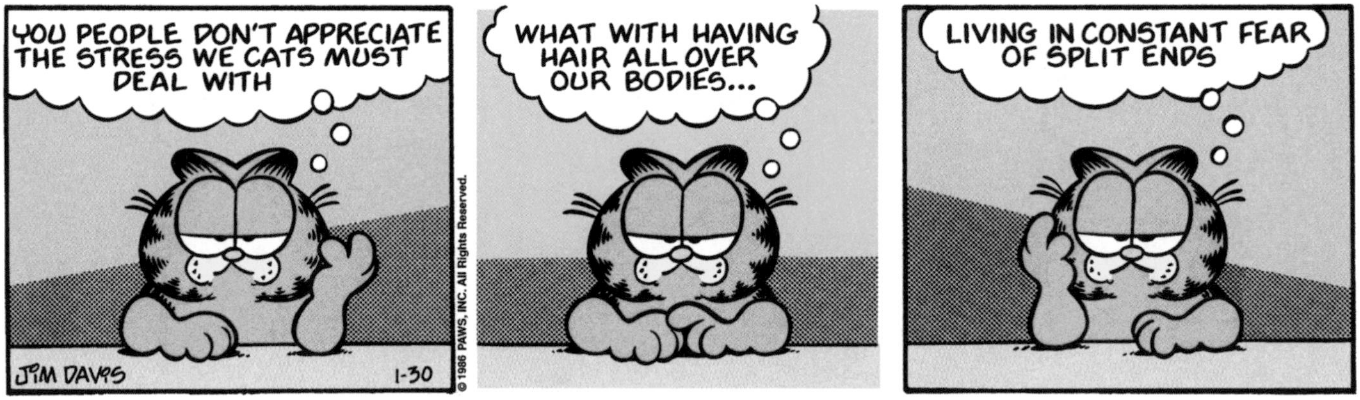
YOU PEOPLE DON'T APPRECIATE THE STRESS WE CATS MUST DEAL WITH
JIM DAVIS 1-30
© 1986 PAWS, INC. All Rights Reserved.
WHAT WITH HAVING HAIR ALL OVER OUR BODIES...
LIVING IN CONSTANT FEAR OF SPLIT ENDS

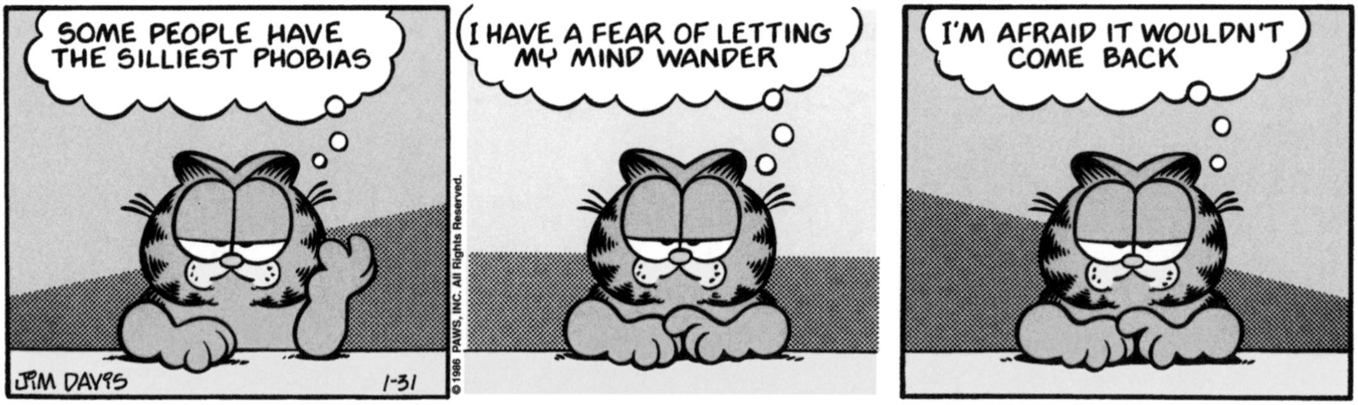
SOME PEOPLE HAVE THE SILLIEST PHOBIAS
JIM DAVIS 1-31
© 1986 PAWS, INC. All Rights Reserved.
I HAVE A FEAR OF LETTING MY MIND WANDER
I'M AFRAID IT WOULDN'T COME BACK

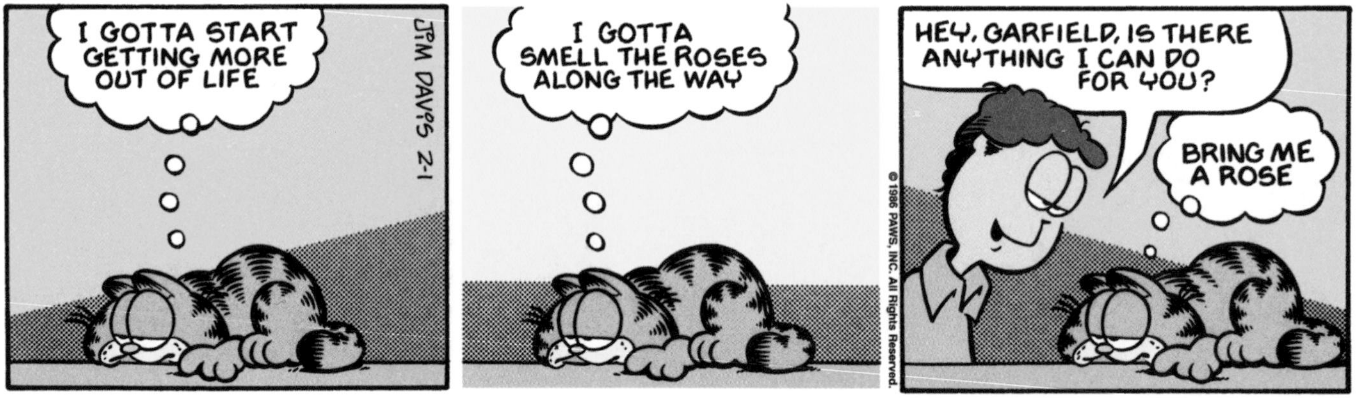
I GOTTA START GETTING MORE OUT OF LIFE
JIM DAVIS 2-1
I GOTTA SMELL THE ROSES ALONG THE WAY
© 1986 PAWS, INC. All Rights Reserved.
HEY, GARFIELD, IS THERE ANYTHING I CAN DO FOR YOU?
BRING ME A ROSE

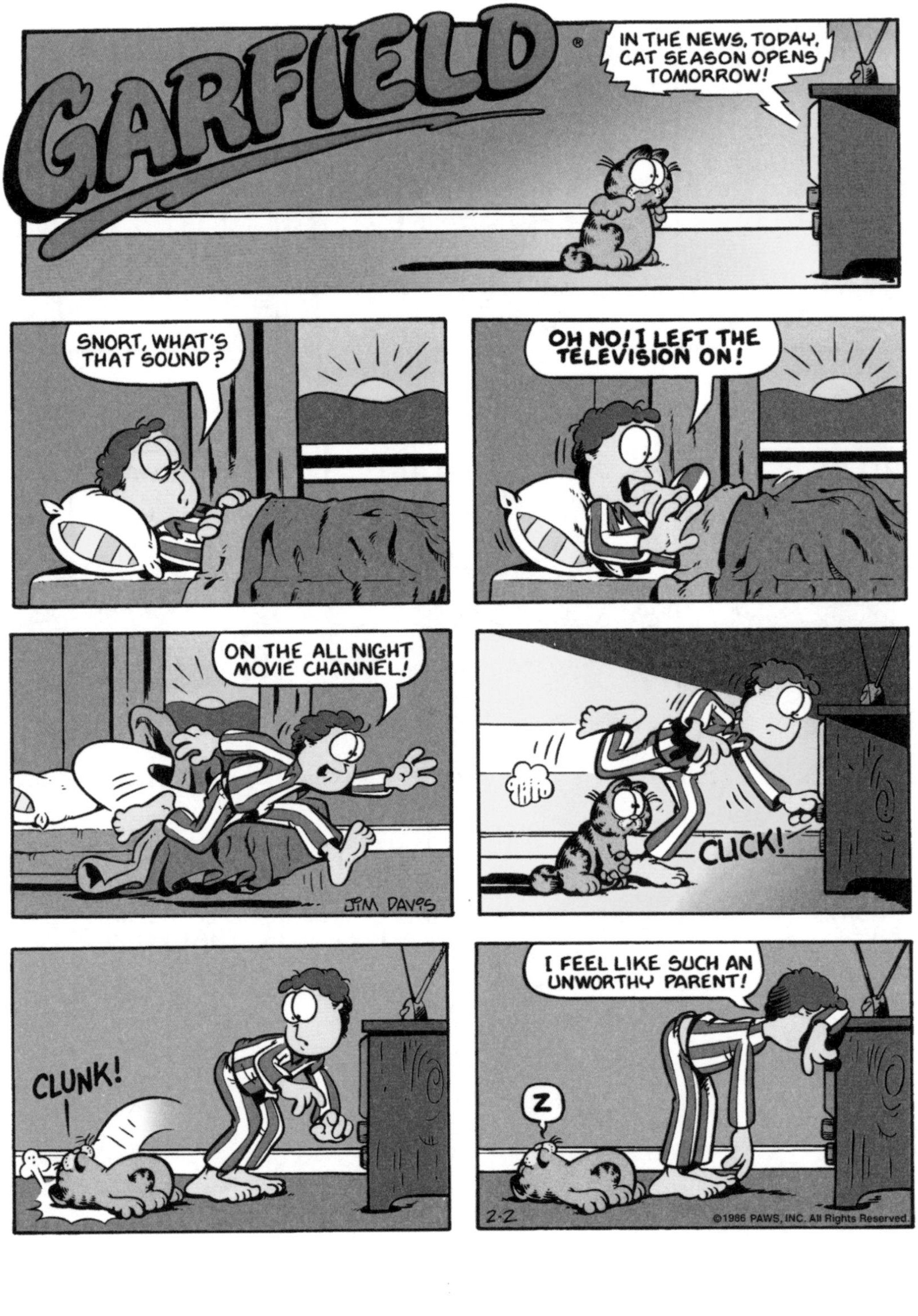
GARFIELD®
IN THE NEWS, TODAY, CAT SEASON OPENS TOMORROW!
SNORT, WHAT'S THAT SOUND?
OH NO! I LEFT THE TELEVISION ON!
ON THE ALL NIGHT MOVIE CHANNEL!
JIM DAVIS
CLICK!
CLUNK!
I FEEL LIKE SUCH AN UNWORTHY PARENT!
Z
2-2
©1986 PAWS, INC. All Rights Reserved.

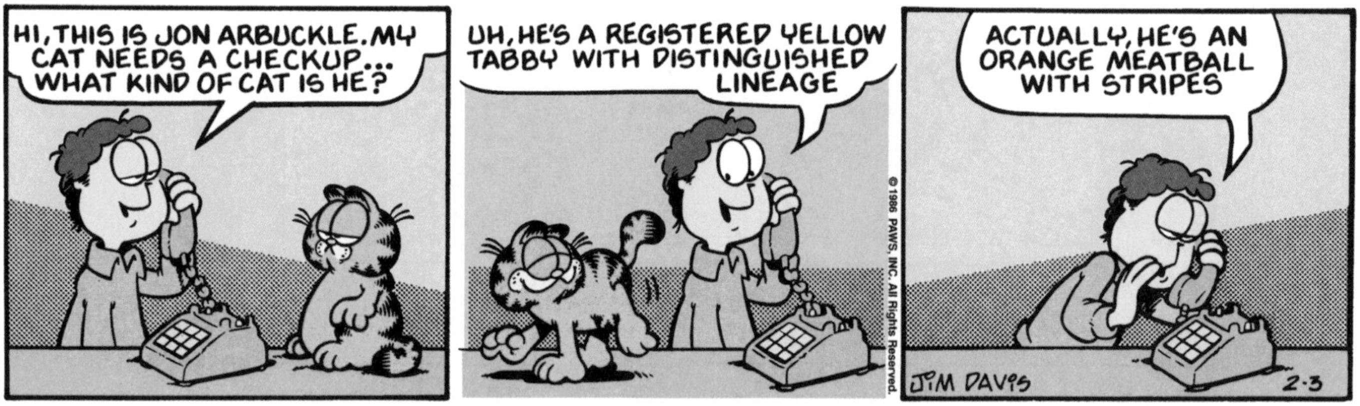
HI, THIS IS JON ARBUCKLE. MY CAT NEEDS A CHECKUP... WHAT KIND OF CAT IS HE?
UH, HE'S A REGISTERED YELLOW TABBY WITH DISTINGUISHED LINEAGE
© 1986 PAWS, INC. All Rights Reserved.
ACTUALLY, HE'S AN ORANGE MEATBALL WITH STRIPES
JIM DAVIS 2-3

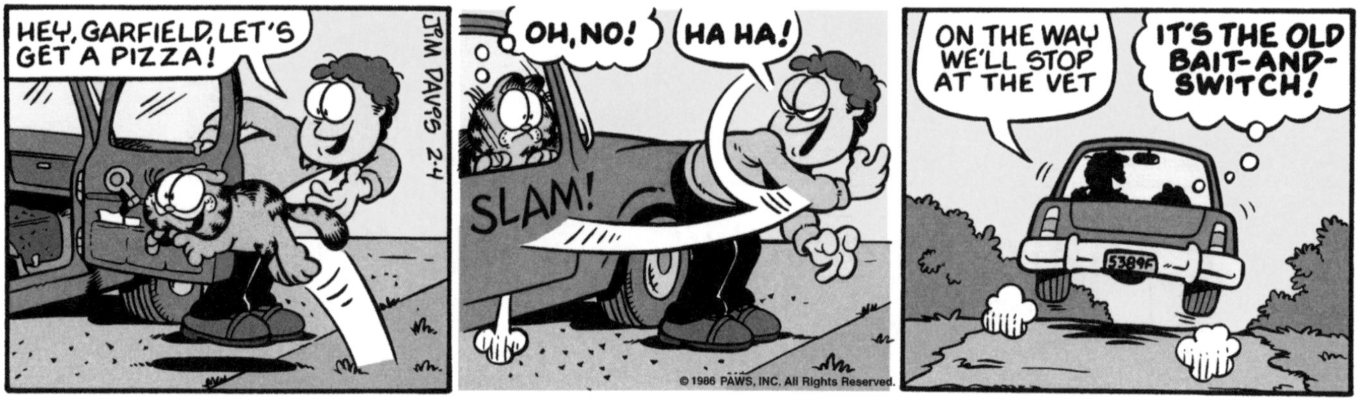
HEY, GARFIELD, LET'S GET A PIZZA!
JIM DAVIS 2-4
OH, NO!
HA HA!
SLAM!
© 1986 PAWS, INC. All Rights Reserved.
ON THE WAY WE'LL STOP AT THE VET
IT'S THE OLD BAIT-AND-SWITCH!
5389F

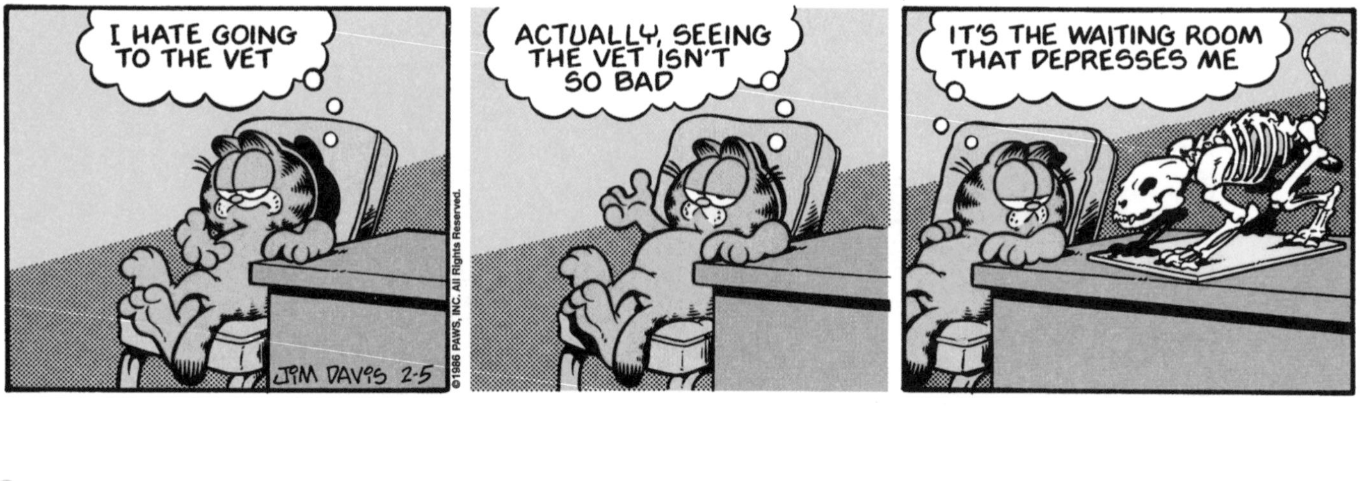
I HATE GOING TO THE VET
© 1986 PAWS, INC. All Rights Reserved.
JIM DAVIS 2-5
ACTUALLY, SEEING THE VET ISN'T SO BAD
IT'S THE WAITING ROOM THAT DEPRESSES ME

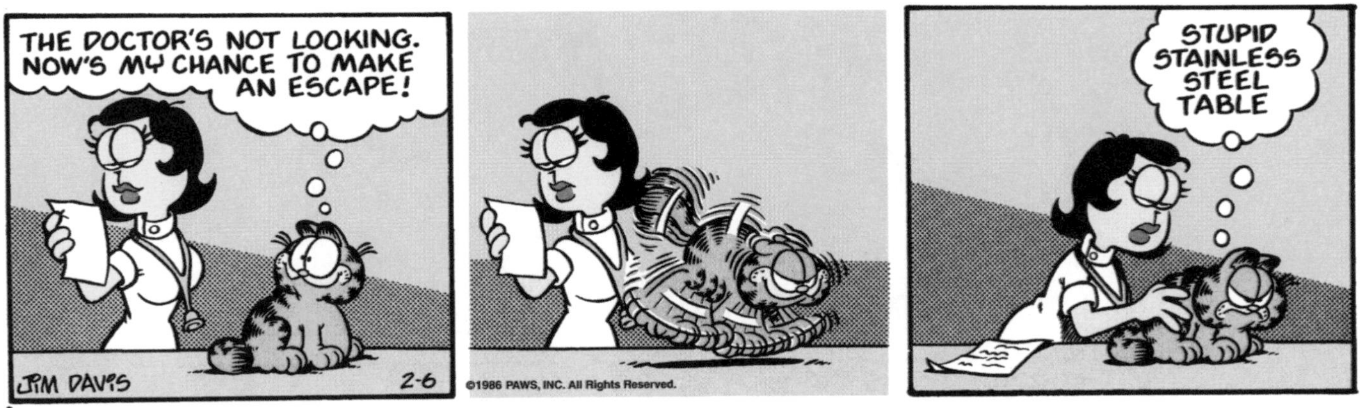
THE DOCTOR'S NOT LOOKING. NOW'S MY CHANCE TO MAKE AN ESCAPE!
JIM DAVIS 2-6
©1986 PAWS, INC. All Rights Reserved.
STUPID STAINLESS STEEL TABLE

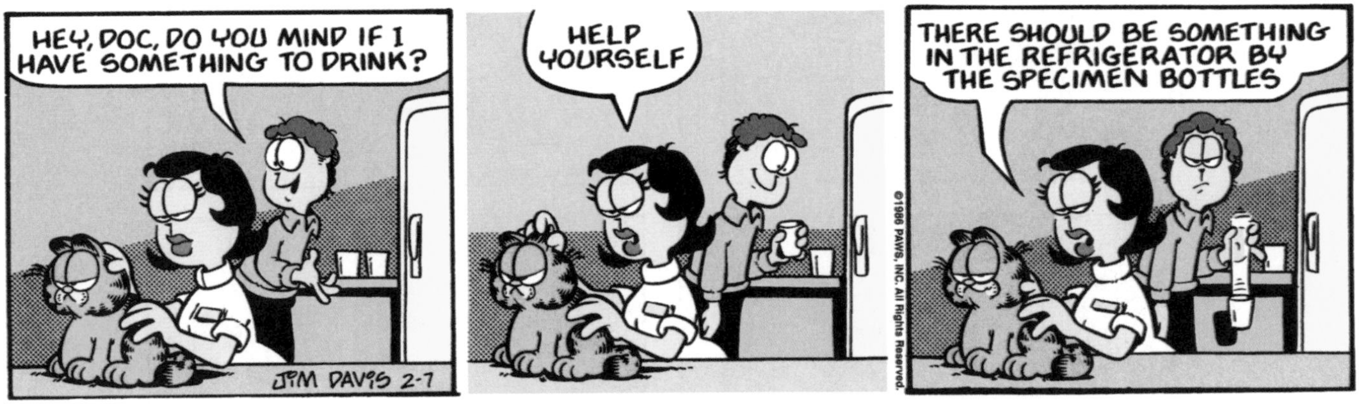
HEY, DOC, DO YOU MIND IF I HAVE SOMETHING TO DRINK?
JIM DAVIS 2-7
HELP YOURSELF
©1986 PAWS, INC. All Rights Reserved.
THERE SHOULD BE SOMETHING IN THE REFRIGERATOR BY THE SPECIMEN BOTTLES

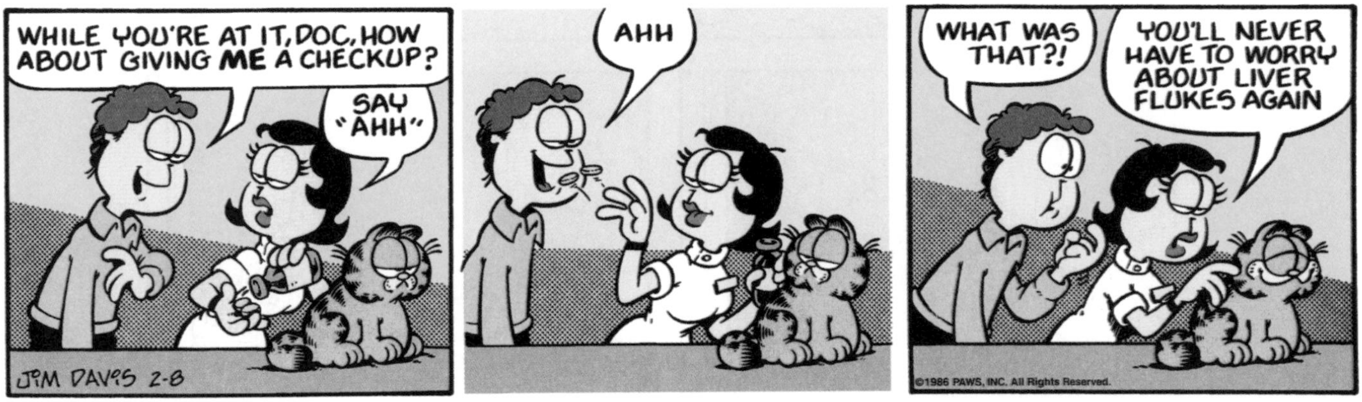
WHILE YOU'RE AT IT, DOC, HOW ABOUT GIVING **ME** A CHECKUP?
SAY "AHH"
JIM DAVIS 2-8
AHH
WHAT WAS THAT?!
YOU'LL NEVER HAVE TO WORRY ABOUT LIVER FLUKES AGAIN
©1986 PAWS, INC. All Rights Reserved.

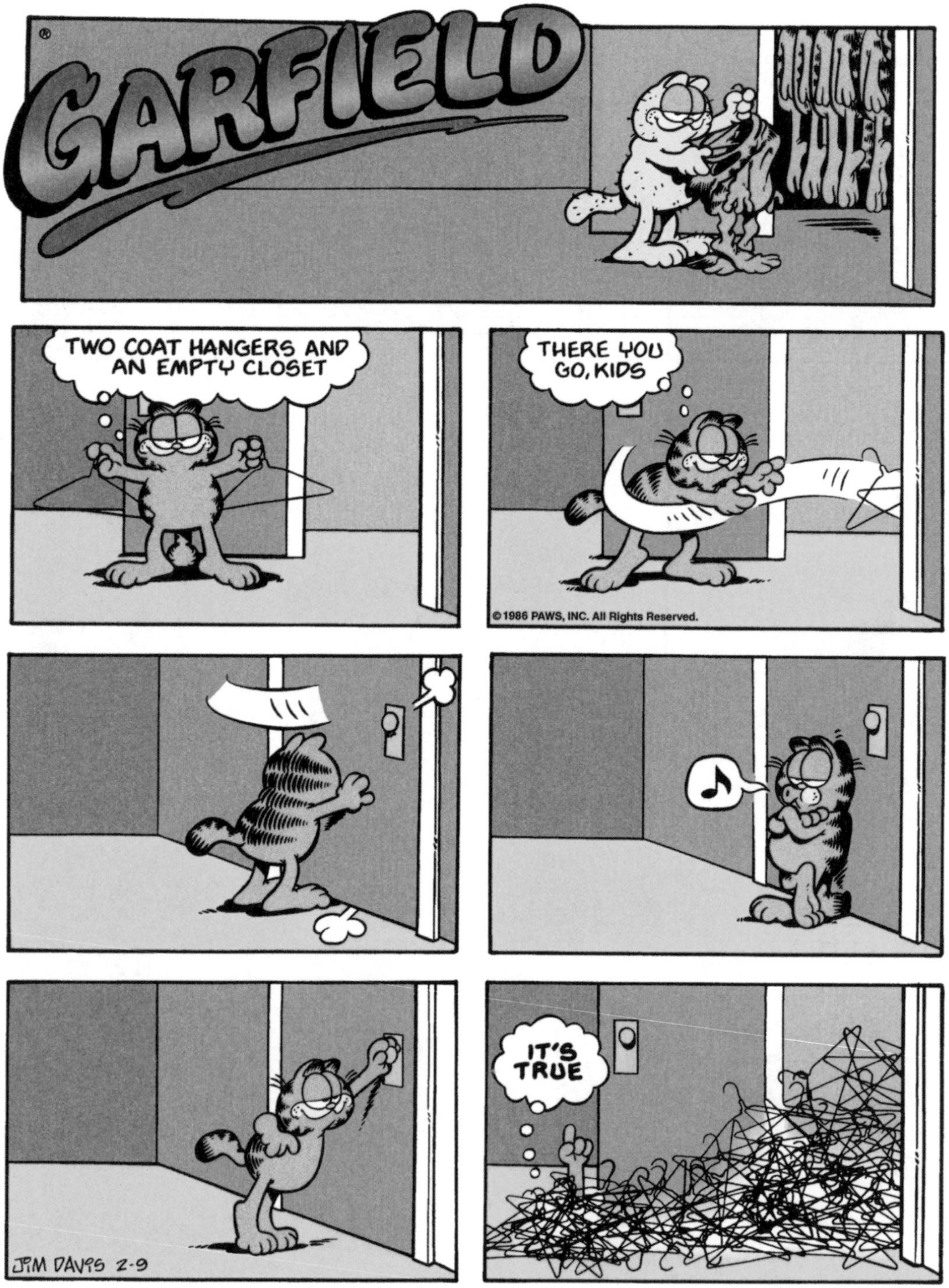
GARFIELD
TWO COAT HANGERS AND AN EMPTY CLOSET
THERE YOU GO, KIDS
©1986 PAWS, INC. All Rights Reserved.
♪
JIM DAVIS 2-9
IT'S TRUE

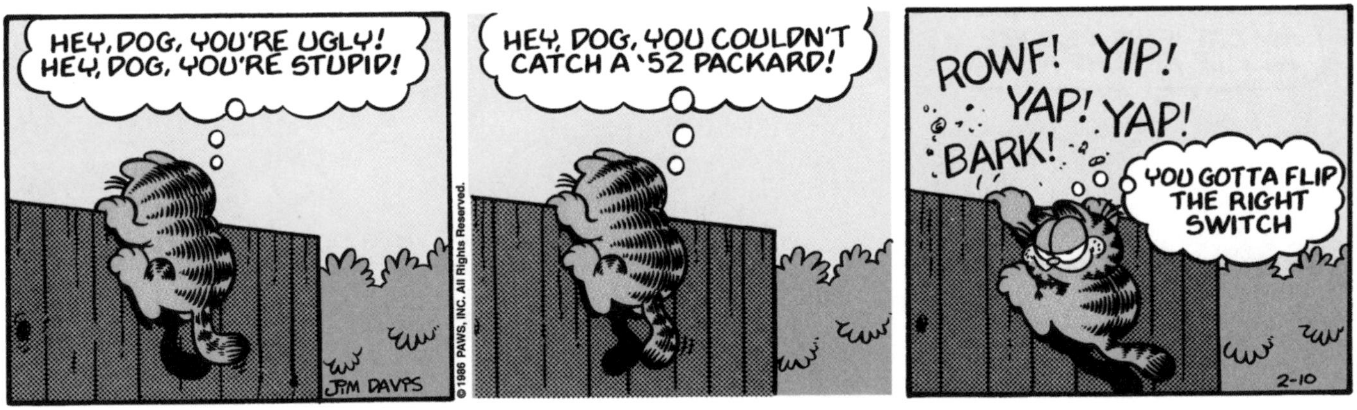
HEY, DOG, YOU'RE UGLY! HEY, DOG, YOU'RE STUPID!
JIM DAVIS
© 1986 PAWS, INC. All Rights Reserved.
HEY, DOG, YOU COULDN'T CATCH A '52 PACKARD!
ROWF! YIP!
YAP! YAP!
BARK!
YOU GOTTA FLIP THE RIGHT SWITCH
2-10

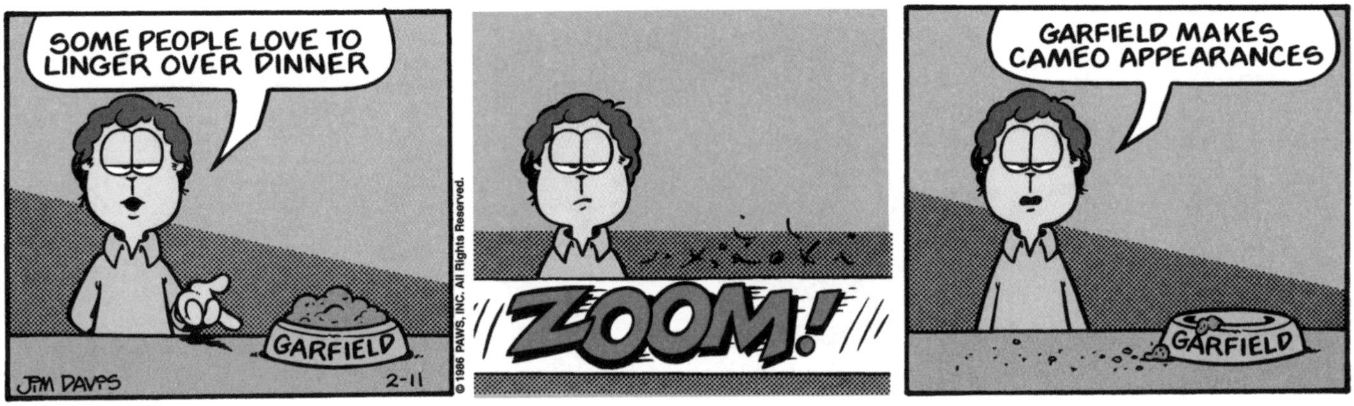
SOME PEOPLE LOVE TO LINGER OVER DINNER
GARFIELD
JIM DAVIS
2-11
© 1986 PAWS, INC. All Rights Reserved.
ZOOM!
GARFIELD MAKES CAMEO APPEARANCES
GARFIELD

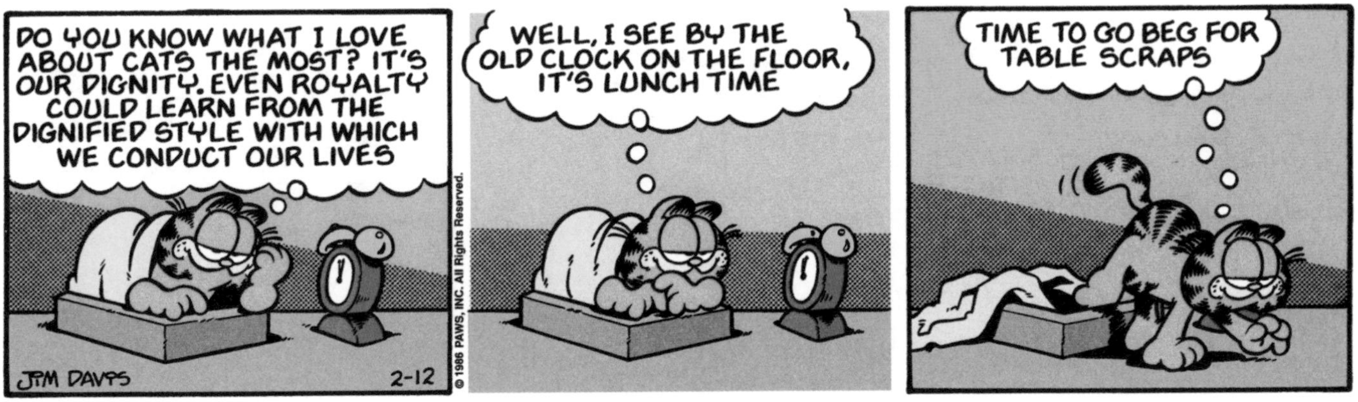
DO YOU KNOW WHAT I LOVE ABOUT CATS THE MOST? IT'S OUR DIGNITY. EVEN ROYALTY COULD LEARN FROM THE DIGNIFIED STYLE WITH WHICH WE CONDUCT OUR LIVES
JIM DAVIS
2-12
© 1986 PAWS, INC. All Rights Reserved.
WELL, I SEE BY THE OLD CLOCK ON THE FLOOR, IT'S LUNCH TIME
TIME TO GO BEG FOR TABLE SCRAPS

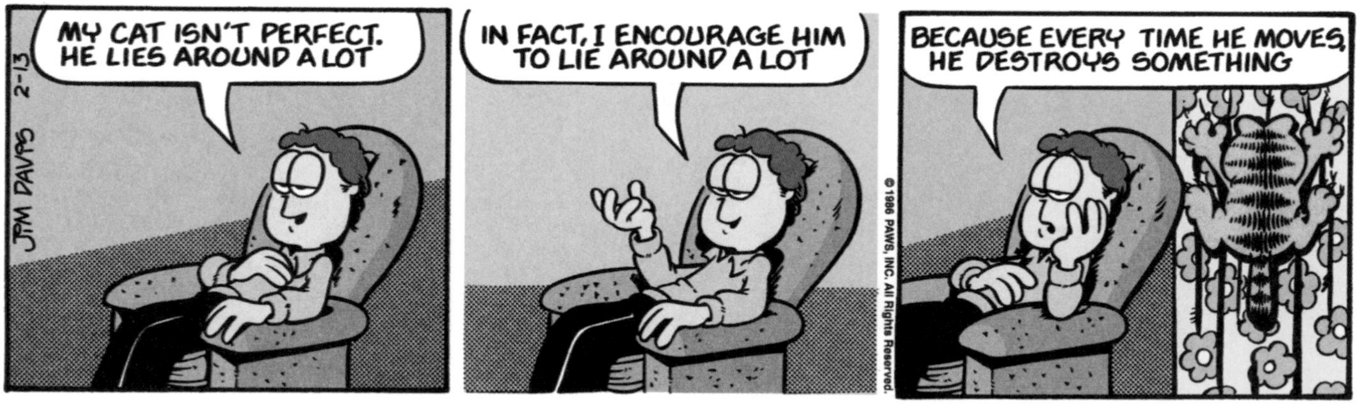
JIM DAVIS 2-13
MY CAT ISN'T PERFECT. HE LIES AROUND A LOT
IN FACT, I ENCOURAGE HIM TO LIE AROUND A LOT
© 1986 PAWS, INC. All Rights Reserved.
BECAUSE EVERY TIME HE MOVES, HE DESTROYS SOMETHING

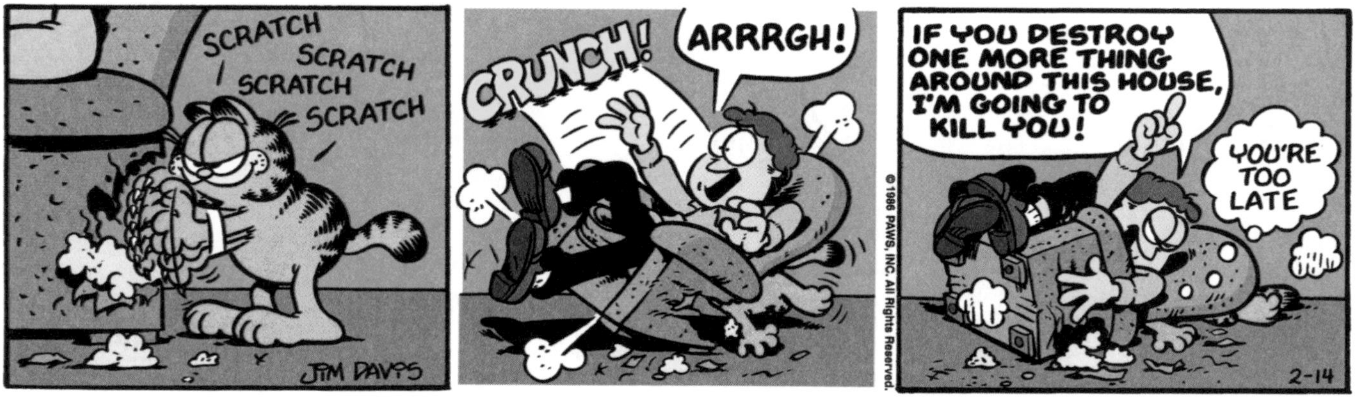
SCRATCH SCRATCH SCRATCH SCRATCH
JIM DAVIS
CRUNCH!
ARRRGH!
© 1986 PAWS, INC. All Rights Reserved.
IF YOU DESTROY ONE MORE THING AROUND THIS HOUSE, I'M GOING TO KILL YOU!
YOU'RE TOO LATE
2-14

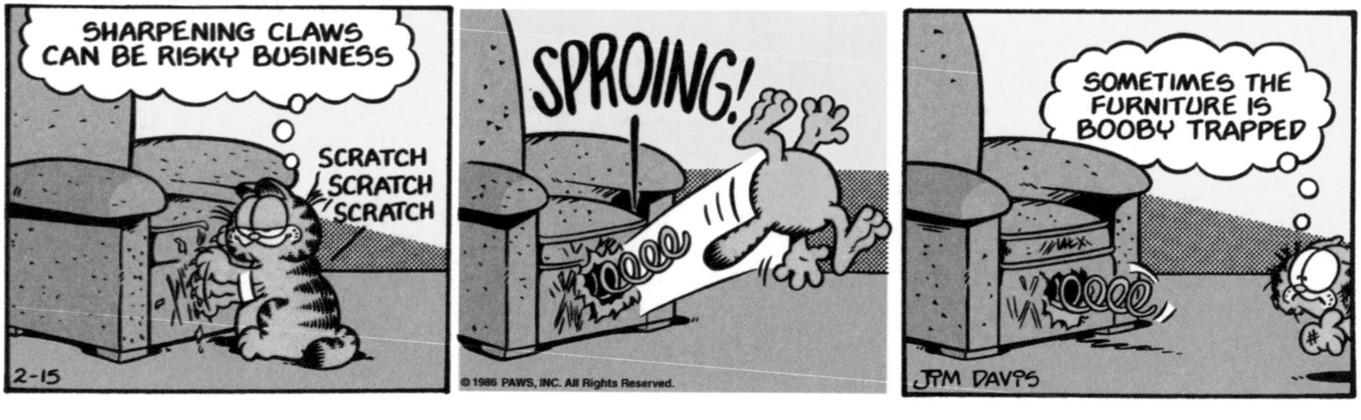
SHARPENING CLAWS CAN BE RISKY BUSINESS
SCRATCH SCRATCH SCRATCH
2-15
SPROING!
© 1986 PAWS, INC. All Rights Reserved.
SOMETIMES THE FURNITURE IS BOOBY TRAPPED
JIM DAVIS

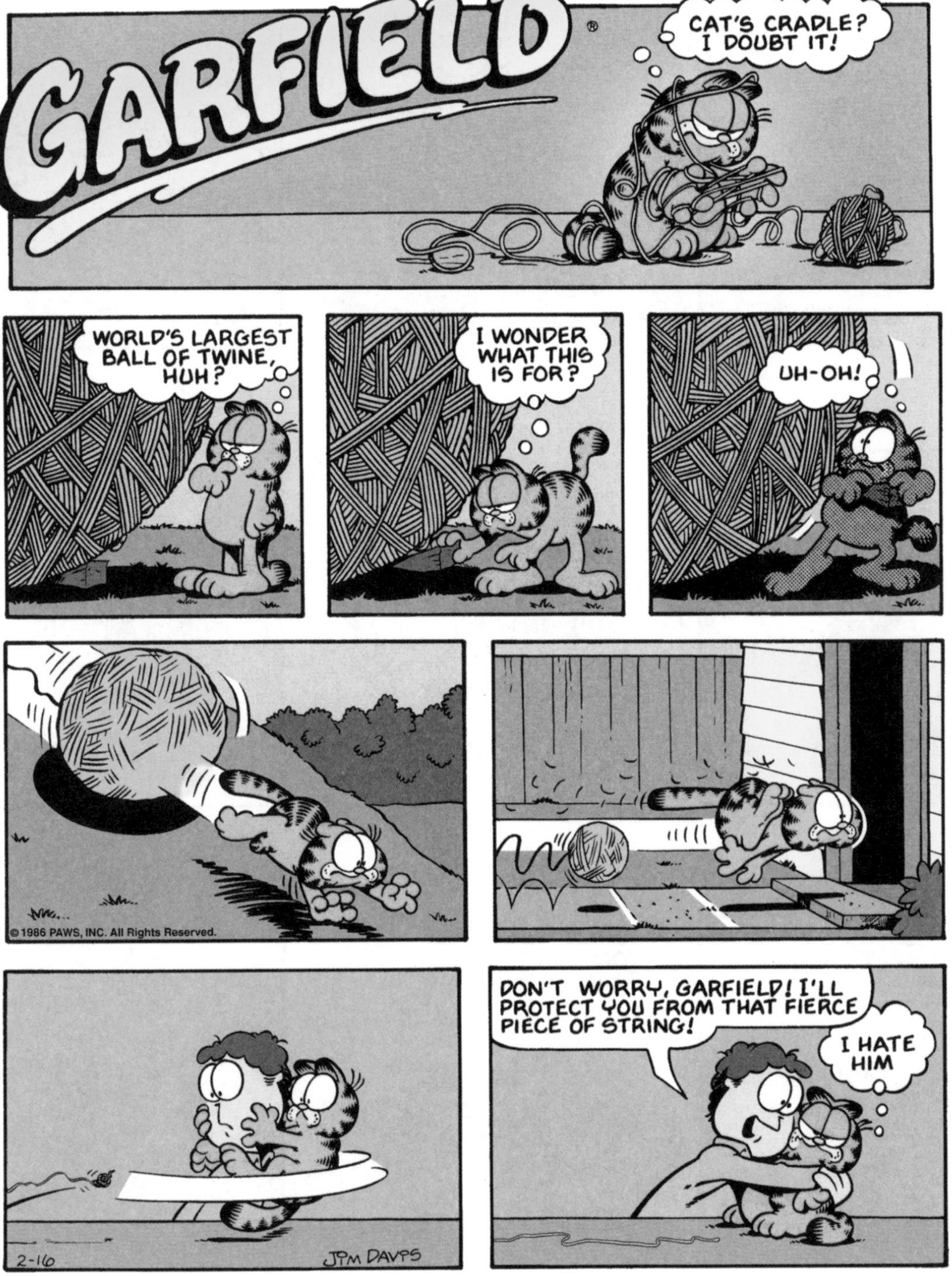
GARFIELD®
CAT'S CRADLE? I DOUBT IT!
WORLD'S LARGEST BALL OF TWINE, HUH?
I WONDER WHAT THIS IS FOR?
UH-OH!
DON'T WORRY, GARFIELD! I'LL PROTECT YOU FROM THAT FIERCE PIECE OF STRING!
I HATE HIM
2-16
JIM DAVIS

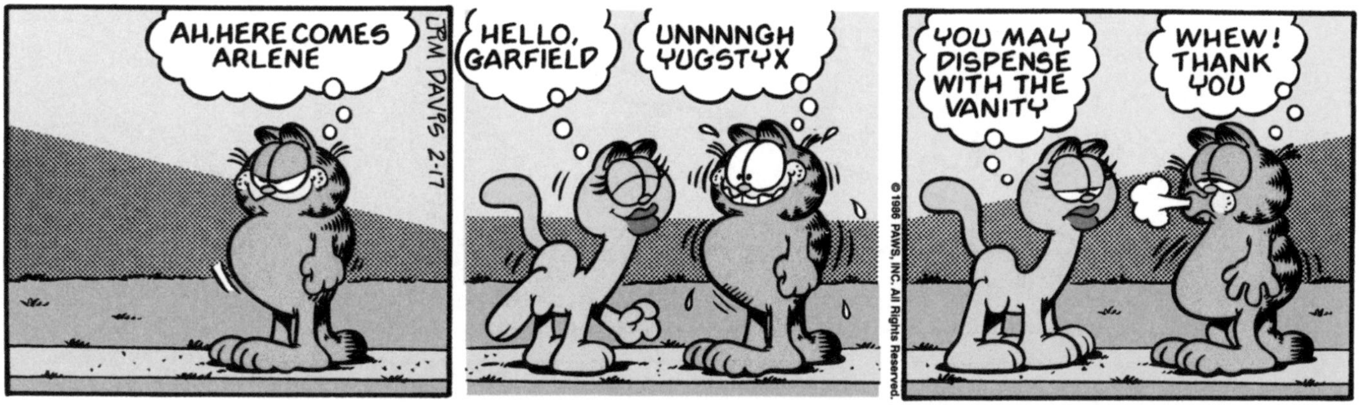
AH, HERE COMES ARLENE
JIM DAVIS 2-17
HELLO, GARFIELD
UNNNNGH YUGSTYX
© 1986 PAWS, INC. All Rights Reserved.
YOU MAY DISPENSE WITH THE VANITY
WHEW! THANK YOU

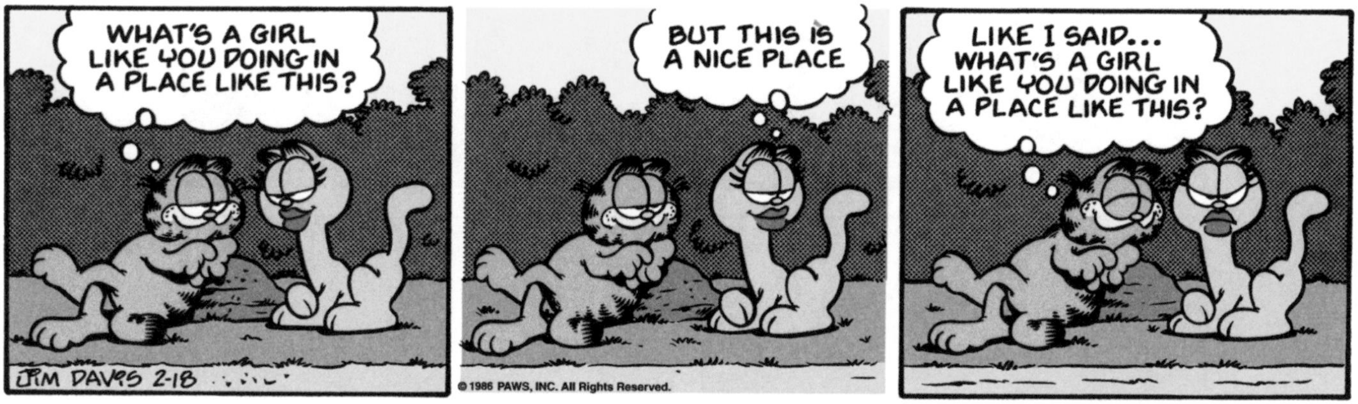
WHAT'S A GIRL LIKE YOU DOING IN A PLACE LIKE THIS?
JIM DAVIS 2-18
BUT THIS IS A NICE PLACE
© 1986 PAWS, INC. All Rights Reserved.
LIKE I SAID... WHAT'S A GIRL LIKE YOU DOING IN A PLACE LIKE THIS?

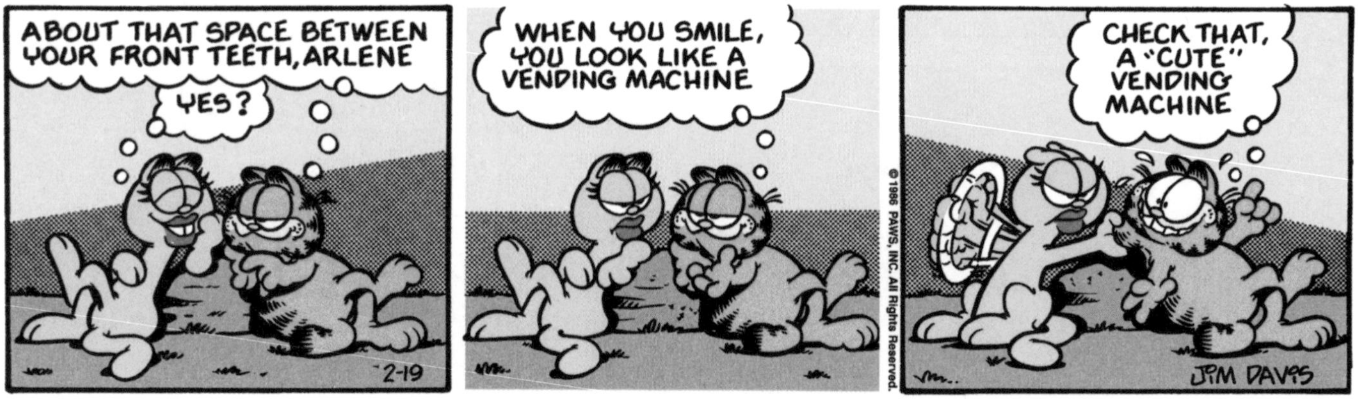
ABOUT THAT SPACE BETWEEN YOUR FRONT TEETH, ARLENE
YES?
2-19
WHEN YOU SMILE, YOU LOOK LIKE A VENDING MACHINE
© 1986 PAWS, INC. All Rights Reserved.
CHECK THAT, A "CUTE" VENDING MACHINE
JIM DAVIS

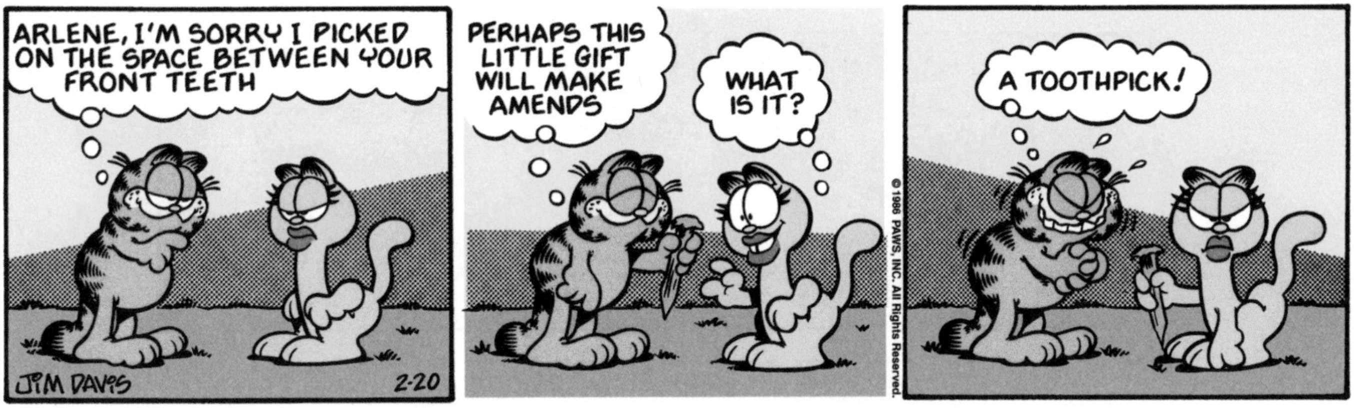
ARLENE, I'M SORRY I PICKED ON THE SPACE BETWEEN YOUR FRONT TEETH
JIM DAVIS
2-20
PERHAPS THIS LITTLE GIFT WILL MAKE AMENDS
WHAT IS IT?
© 1986 PAWS, INC. All Rights Reserved.
A TOOTHPICK!

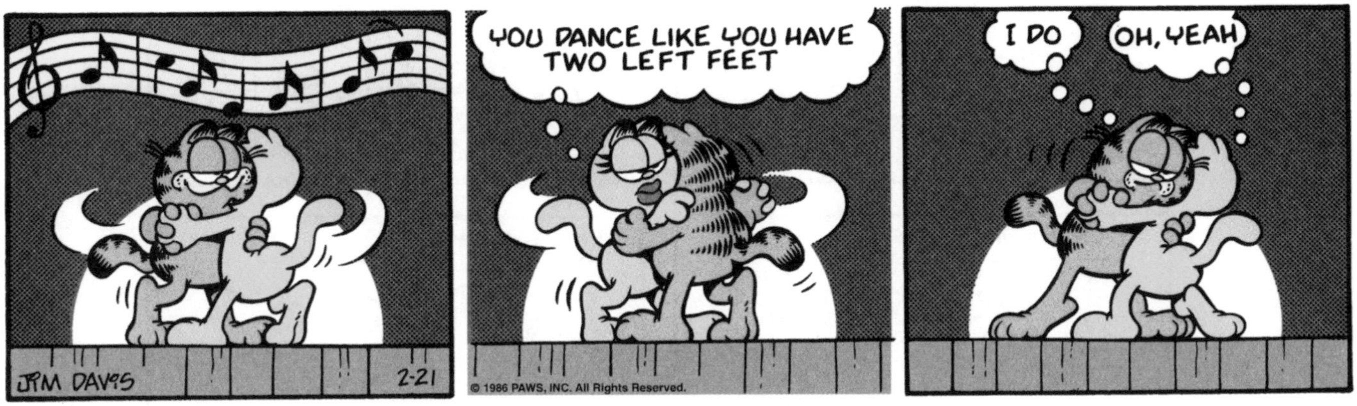
JIM DAVIS
2-21
YOU DANCE LIKE YOU HAVE TWO LEFT FEET
© 1986 PAWS, INC. All Rights Reserved.
I DO
OH, YEAH

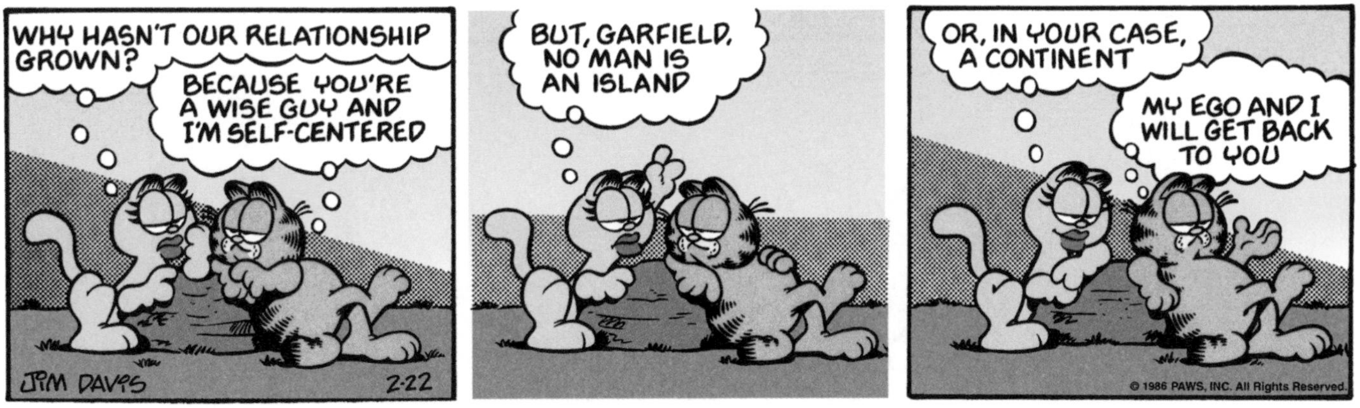
WHY HASN'T OUR RELATIONSHIP GROWN?
BECAUSE YOU'RE A WISE GUY AND I'M SELF-CENTERED
JIM DAVIS
2-22
BUT, GARFIELD, NO MAN IS AN ISLAND
OR, IN YOUR CASE, A CONTINENT
MY EGO AND I WILL GET BACK TO YOU
© 1986 PAWS, INC. All Rights Reserved.

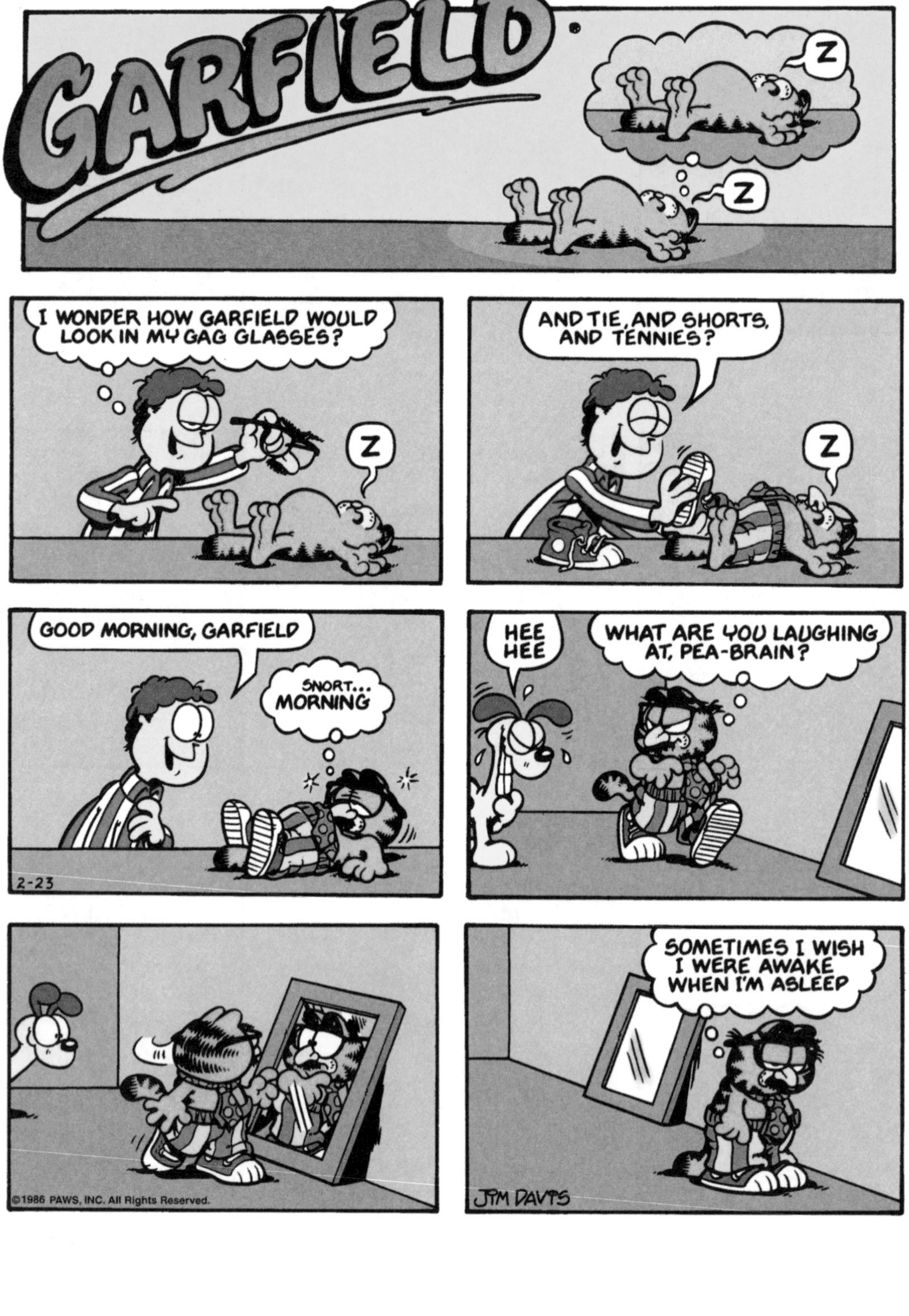
GARFIELD
Z
Z
I WONDER HOW GARFIELD WOULD LOOK IN MY GAG GLASSES?
Z
AND TIE, AND SHORTS, AND TENNIES?
Z
GOOD MORNING, GARFIELD
SNORT... MORNING
2-23
HEE HEE
WHAT ARE YOU LAUGHING AT, PEA-BRAIN?
©1986 PAWS, INC. All Rights Reserved.
SOMETIMES I WISH I WERE AWAKE WHEN I'M ASLEEP
JIM DAVIS

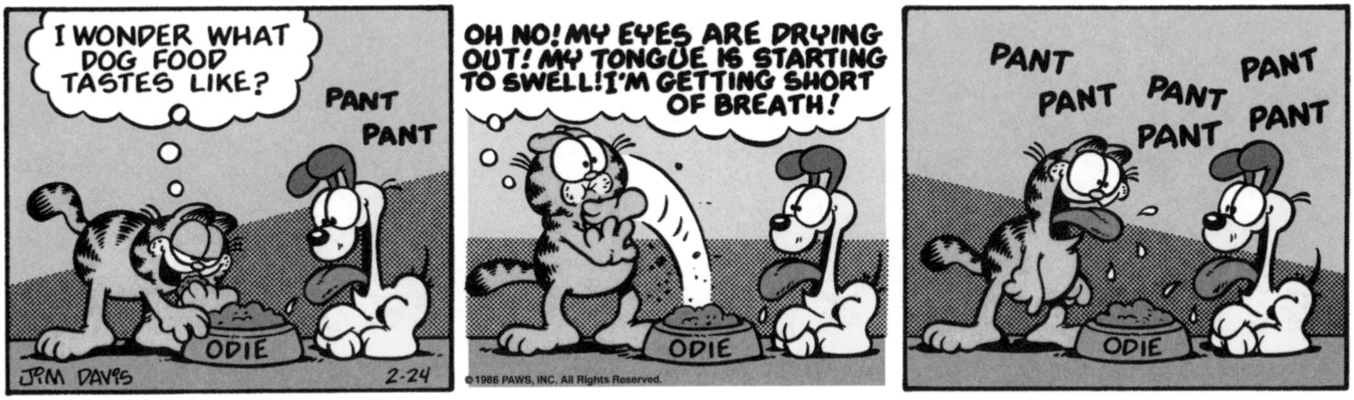
I WONDER WHAT DOG FOOD TASTES LIKE?
PANT
PANT
ODIE
JIM DAVIS
2-24
OH NO! MY EYES ARE DRYING OUT! MY TONGUE IS STARTING TO SWELL! I'M GETTING SHORT OF BREATH!
ODIE
© 1986 PAWS, INC. All Rights Reserved.
PANT
PANT
PANT
PANT
PANT
PANT
ODIE

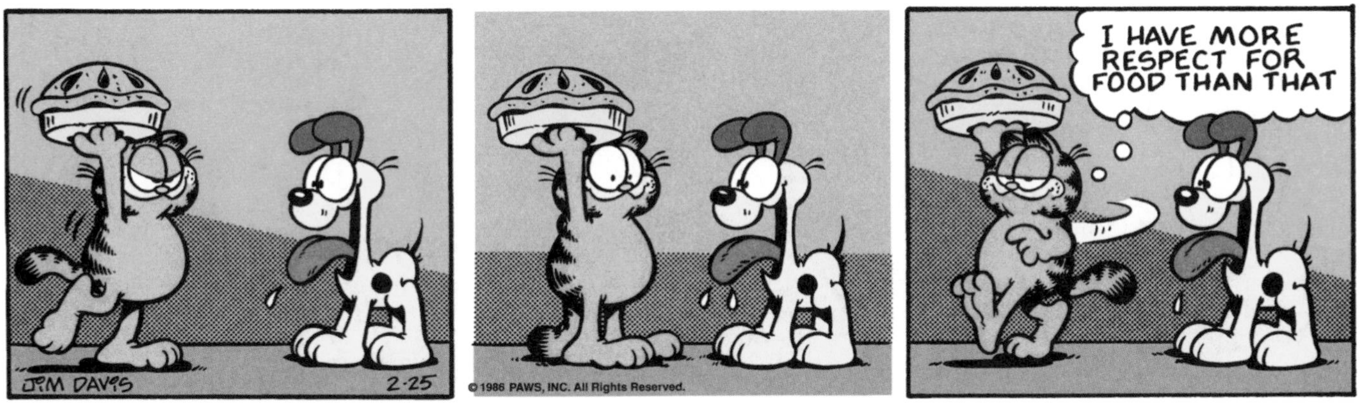
JIM DAVIS
2-25
© 1986 PAWS, INC. All Rights Reserved.
I HAVE MORE RESPECT FOR FOOD THAN THAT

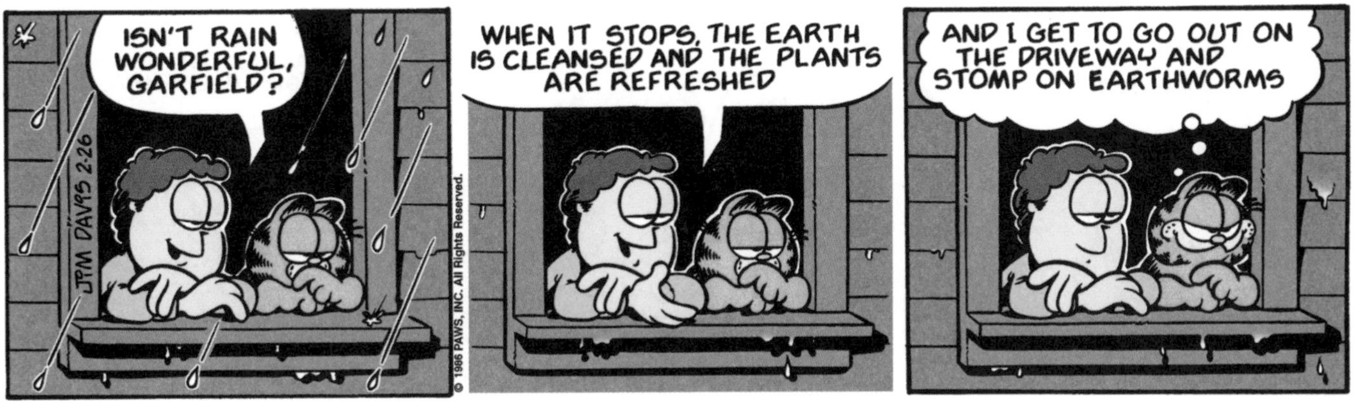
ISN'T RAIN WONDERFUL, GARFIELD?
JIM DAVIS 2-26
© 1986 PAWS, INC. All Rights Reserved.
WHEN IT STOPS, THE EARTH IS CLEANSED AND THE PLANTS ARE REFRESHED
AND I GET TO GO OUT ON THE DRIVEWAY AND STOMP ON EARTHWORMS

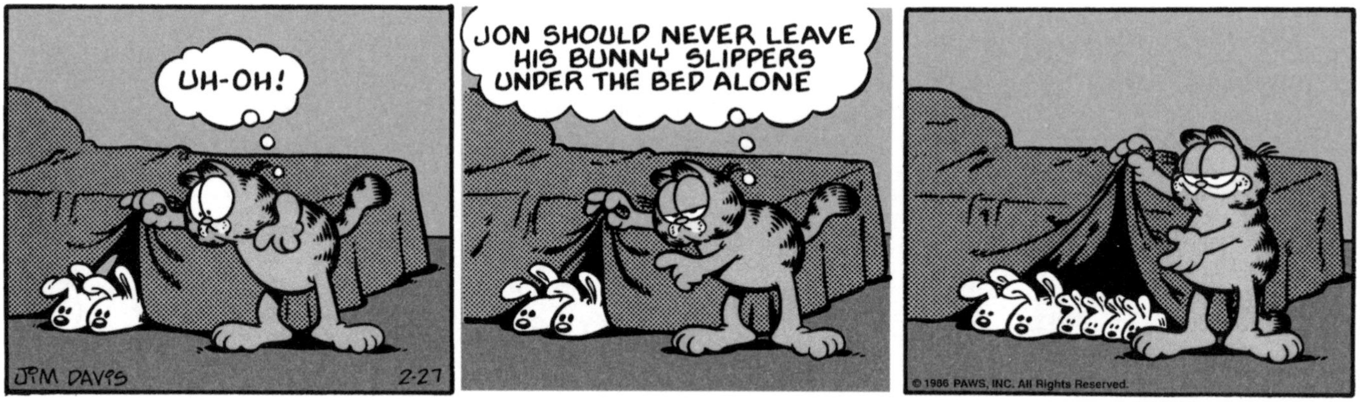
UH-OH!
JIM DAVIS
2-27
JON SHOULD NEVER LEAVE HIS BUNNY SLIPPERS UNDER THE BED ALONE
© 1986 PAWS, INC. All Rights Reserved.

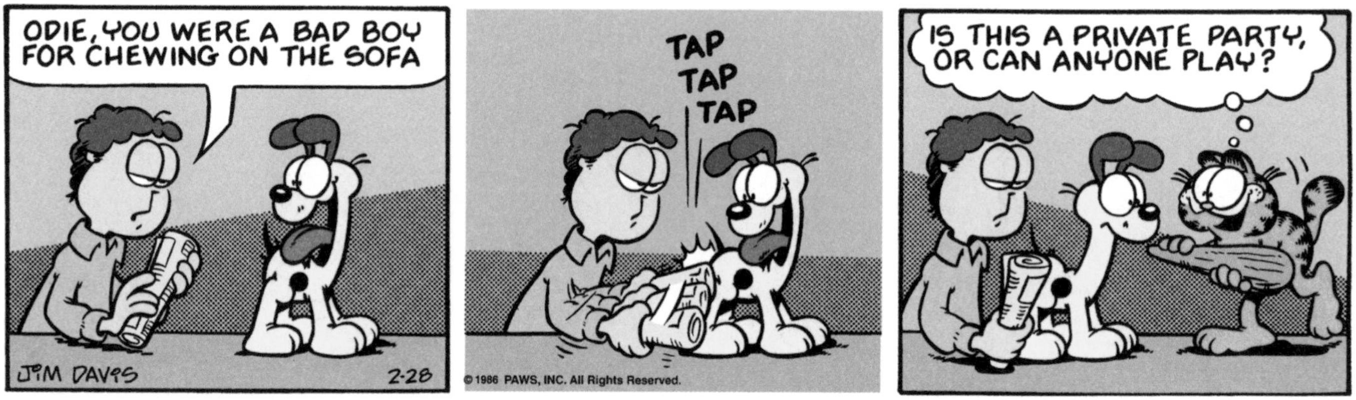
ODIE, YOU WERE A BAD BOY FOR CHEWING ON THE SOFA
JIM DAVIS
2-28
TAP
TAP
TAP
© 1986 PAWS, INC. All Rights Reserved.
IS THIS A PRIVATE PARTY, OR CAN ANYONE PLAY?

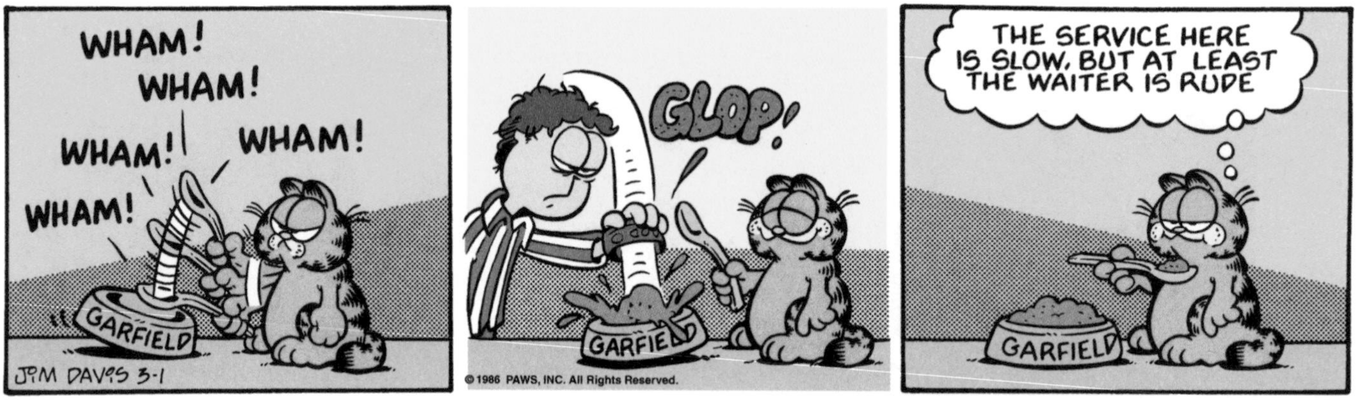
WHAM!
WHAM!
WHAM!
WHAM!
WHAM!
GARFIELD
JIM DAVIS 3-1
GLOP!
GARFIELD
© 1986 PAWS, INC. All Rights Reserved.
THE SERVICE HERE IS SLOW, BUT AT LEAST THE WAITER IS RUDE
GARFIELD

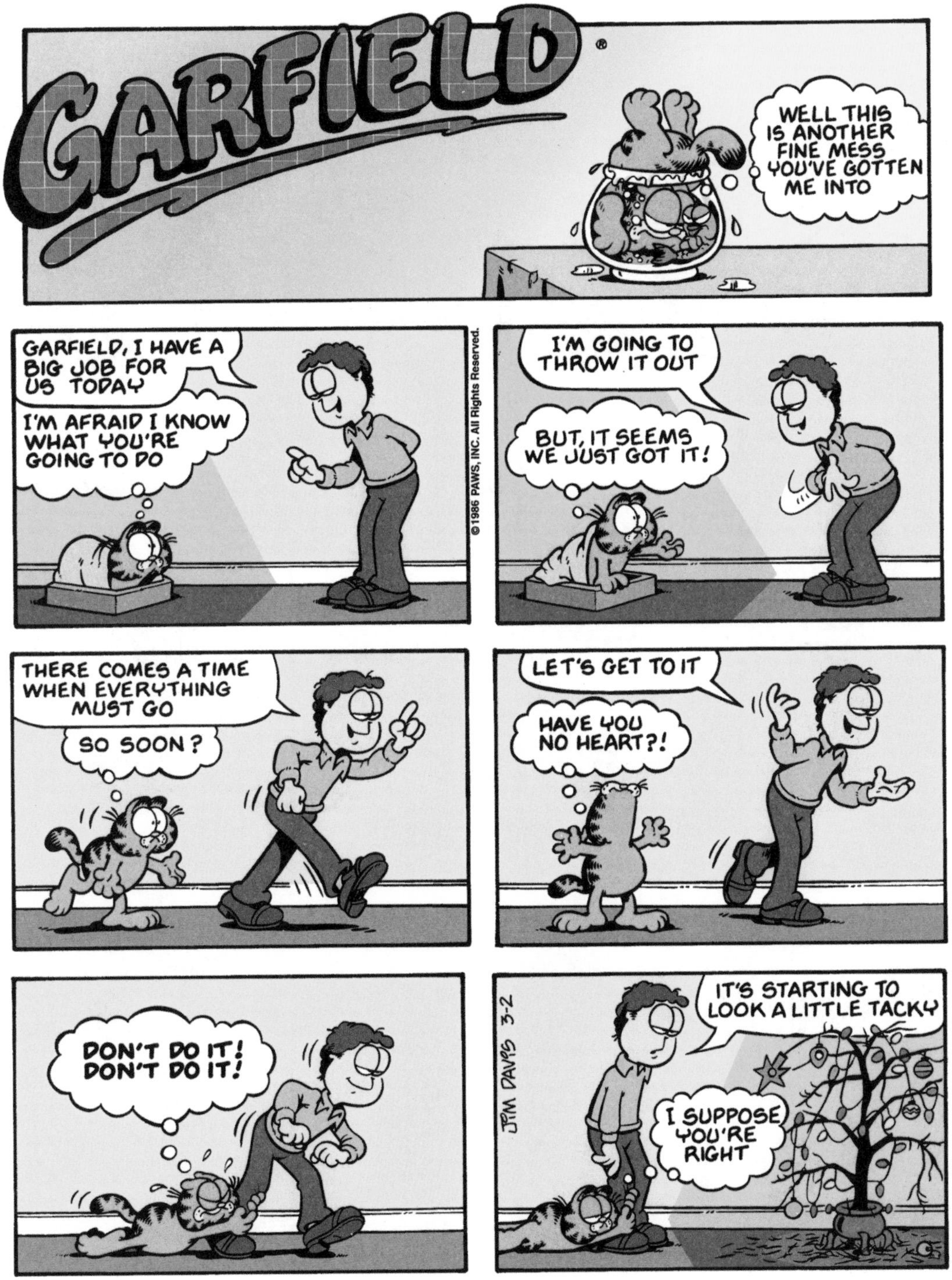

GARFIELD®
WELL THIS IS ANOTHER FINE MESS YOU'VE GOTTEN ME INTO
GARFIELD, I HAVE A BIG JOB FOR US TODAY
I'M AFRAID I KNOW WHAT YOU'RE GOING TO DO
©1986 PAWS, INC. All Rights Reserved.
I'M GOING TO THROW IT OUT
BUT, IT SEEMS WE JUST GOT IT!
THERE COMES A TIME WHEN EVERYTHING MUST GO
SO SOON?
LET'S GET TO IT
HAVE YOU NO HEART?!
DON'T DO IT! DON'T DO IT!
JIM DAVIS 3-2
IT'S STARTING TO LOOK A LITTLE TACKY
I SUPPOSE YOU'RE RIGHT

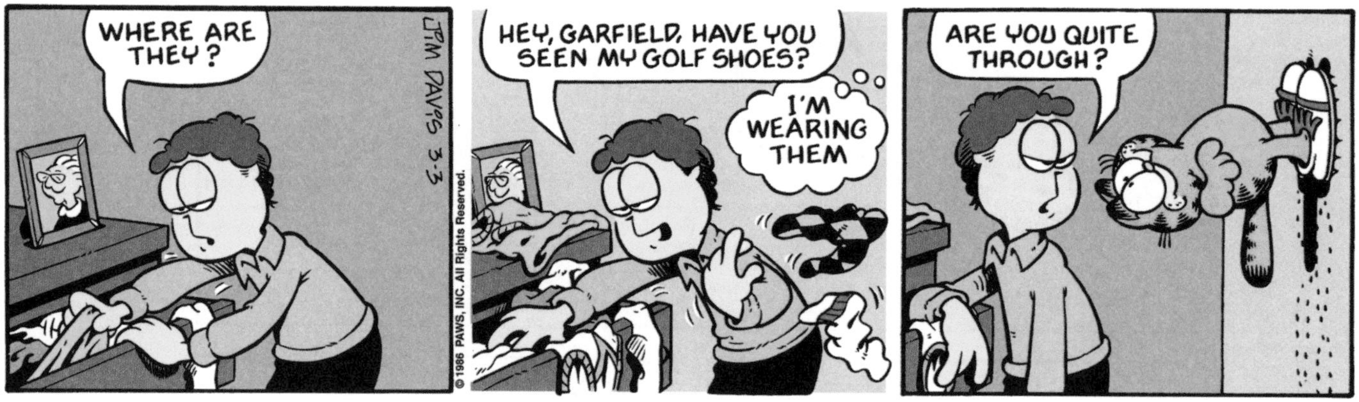
WHERE ARE THEY?
JIM DAVIS 3-3
© 1986 PAWS, INC. All Rights Reserved.
HEY, GARFIELD, HAVE YOU SEEN MY GOLF SHOES?
I'M WEARING THEM
ARE YOU QUITE THROUGH?

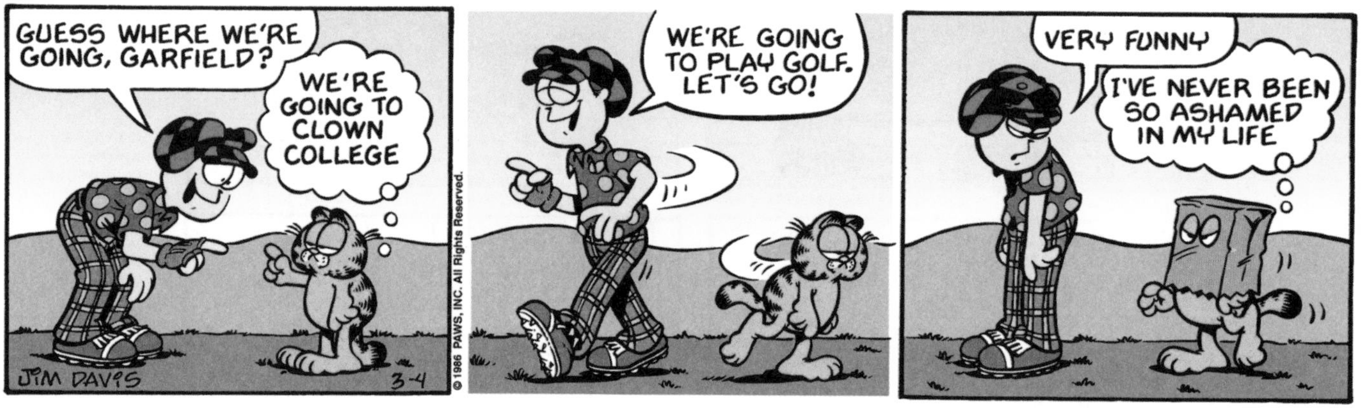
GUESS WHERE WE'RE GOING, GARFIELD?
WE'RE GOING TO CLOWN COLLEGE
JIM DAVIS 3-4
© 1986 PAWS, INC. All Rights Reserved.
WE'RE GOING TO PLAY GOLF. LET'S GO!
VERY FUNNY
I'VE NEVER BEEN SO ASHAMED IN MY LIFE

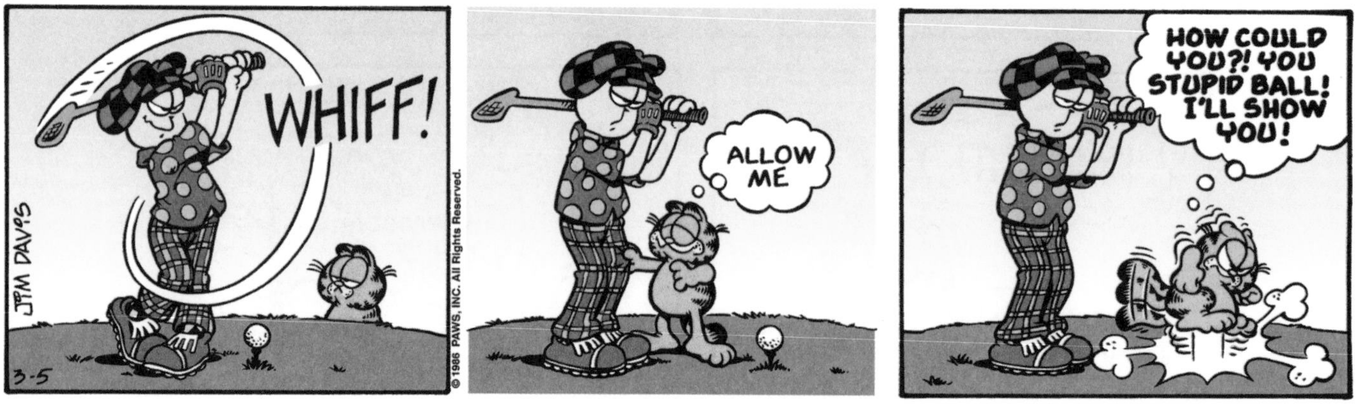
WHIFF!
JIM DAVIS 3-5
© 1986 PAWS, INC. All Rights Reserved.
ALLOW ME
HOW COULD YOU?! YOU STUPID BALL! I'LL SHOW YOU!

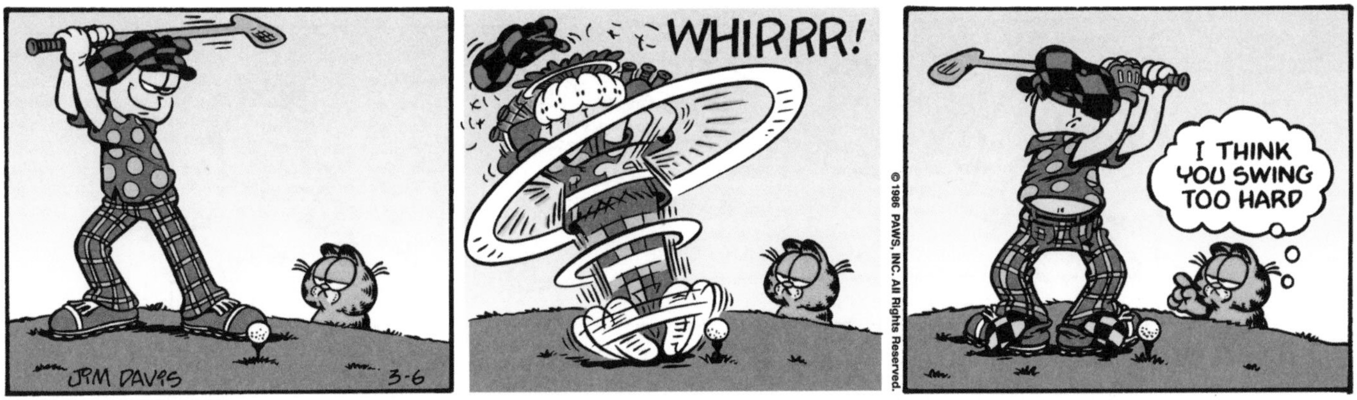
JIM DAVIS 3-6
WHIRRR!
© 1986 PAWS, INC. All Rights Reserved.
I THINK YOU SWING TOO HARD

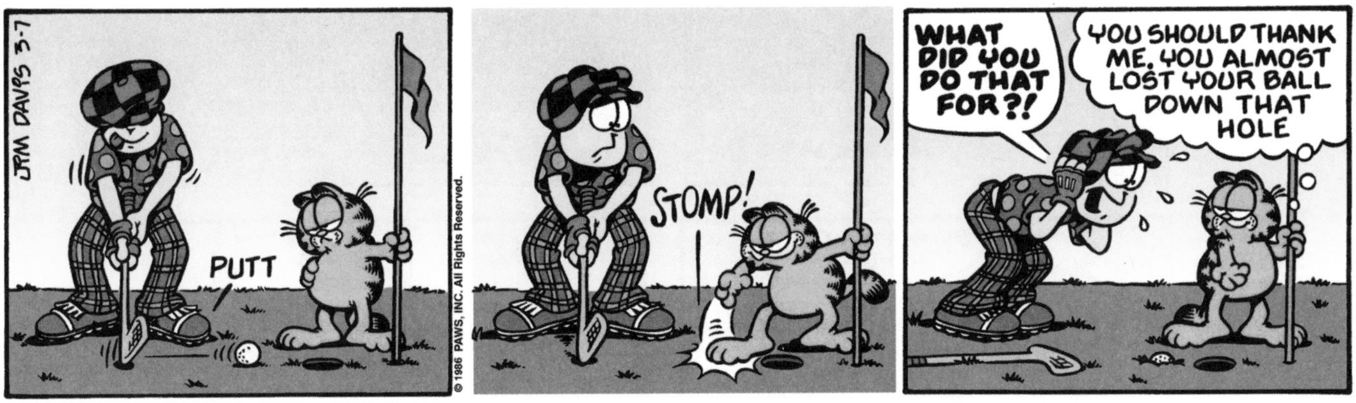
JIM DAVIS 3-7
PUTT
© 1986 PAWS, INC. All Rights Reserved.
STOMP!
WHAT DID YOU DO THAT FOR?!
YOU SHOULD THANK ME. YOU ALMOST LOST YOUR BALL DOWN THAT HOLE

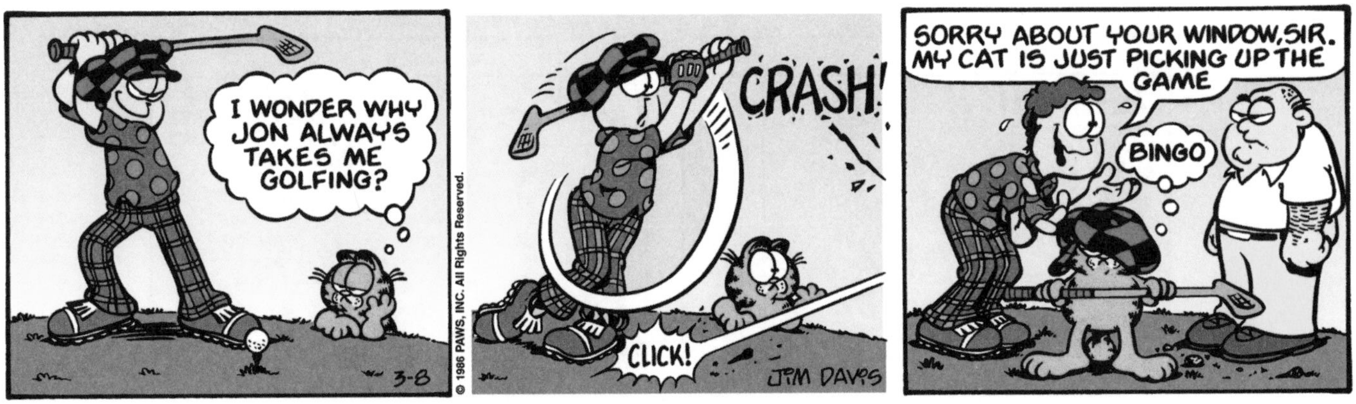
I WONDER WHY JON ALWAYS TAKES ME GOLFING?
3-8
© 1986 PAWS, INC. All Rights Reserved.
CRASH!
CLICK!
JIM DAVIS
SORRY ABOUT YOUR WINDOW, SIR. MY CAT IS JUST PICKING UP THE GAME
BINGO

GARFIELD
I'D BETTER CHECK THIS OUT
© 1986 PAWS, INC. All Rights Reserved.
JPM DAVPS 3-9
ARRRGH!
GOOSH!
WHAT HAPPENED?!
YOU TURNED MY WATER COLLECTION LOOSE! THAT'S WHAT HAPPENED!

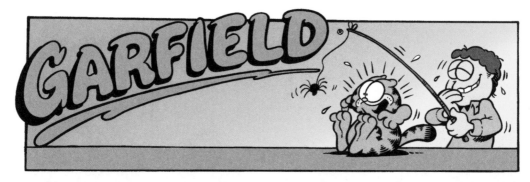

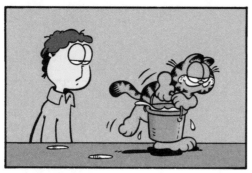

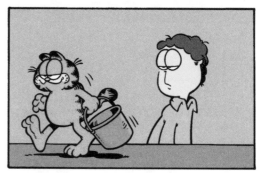

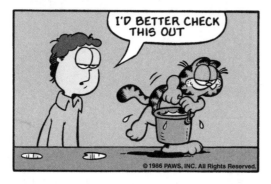

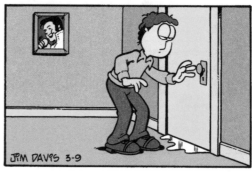

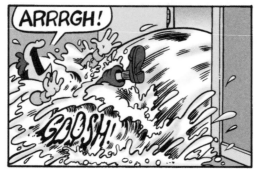

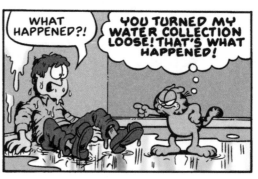